PRECIOUS BLOOD

Jerome Boggs drew his father's .22-caliber pistol from its holster, stuck the muzzle against the back of Blister's head, so he couldn't miss, and pulled the trigger.

Blister slipped off the front of the couch onto the floor, still alive, but apparently unconscious, since Jerome did not feel the need to shoot him a second time. The main threat, Blister Cook, had been eliminated. No one else could stop the robbery, but someone else had seen the murder and could pinpoint Jerome as the killer. As T.J. jerked to look at his father, Jerome fired again, the bullet striking the boy in the chest. T.J. fell on his back on the floor, but didn't die immediately. Instead, he began crying.

There were still six bullets in the revolver. Jerome Boggs stepped around the couch, pressed the gun barrel against T.J.'s tiny chest, and fired again.

PRECIOUS BLOOD

SAM ADAMS

PINNACLE BOOKS
Kensington Publishing Corp.
http://www.kensingtonbooks.com

PINNACLE BOOKS are published by

Kensington Publishing Corp.
850 Third Avenue
New York, NY 10022

All Kensington Titles, Imprints, and Distributed Lines are available at special quantity discounts for bulk purchases for sales promotions, premiums, fund-raising, and educational or institutional use. Special book excerpts or customized printings can also be created to fit specific needs. For details, write or phone the office of the Kensington special sales manager: Kensington Publishing Corp., 850 Third Avenue, New York, NY 10022, attn: Special Sales Department, Phone: 1-800-221-2647.

Pinnacle and the P logo Reg. U.S. Pat. & TM Off.

ISBN-13: 978-0-7860-1849-9
ISBN-10: 0-7860-1849-6

First Printing: April 2007

10 9 8 7 6 5 4 3 2 1

Printed in the United States of America

Prologue

Whitesburg, Kentucky, is a friendly little town cuddled up against the northwestern slope of Pine Mountain. According to the welcome sign, it is home to 1,534 friendly people and only two grouches.

It is the business and government center where all 25,000 Letcher County residents must eventually go to pay their taxes, renew a driver's license, see a doctor, or go shopping. The courthouse and the banks have kept Main Street alive long after Wal-Mart moved into the shopping center on the edge of town, and most of the small merchants downtown closed their doors for the last time.

Most of the eighty-year-old brick storefronts are either empty or occupied by lawyers' offices or struggling specialty shops. Even the drugstores and the liar's benches, where idle locals would swap gossip and spit tobacco, have fled to the edges of town. Now old men gather at the local Dairy Queen or McDonald's to talk about glory days and politics over biscuits and gravy.

Kids skateboard unmolested along sidewalks that were last repaired sixty-five years ago, the fastest-moving living things in sight in a city where the few businessmen left still stop to chat on their way to the bank with a bag of cash, and anglers drop their lines off the Main Street Bridge.

There are no bars in Whitesburg and the restaurants don't serve beer or wine. Like fifty-four other of Kentucky's 120 counties, Letcher is "dry," meaning all sales of alcoholic beverages are outlawed. The town opened up after Prohibition ended, but when the young men went off to fight World War II, the temperance crowd took over again.

By the time the soldiers returned home, Letcher County was as dry as the North African desert where many of them had served.

Since then, determined drinkers have had to find their libations at the local veterans' clubs or climb in the car and drive fourteen miles to Virginia, or forty miles to Hazard or Pikeville. If the drive is too far, there are always the occasional bootleg joints in the hollows outside town.

Whitesburg is the kind of place where people keep their front doors unlocked while they sleep or work, and leave the car windows down on hot summer days. The biggest crimes police have to investigate are the increasingly frequent cases of prescription fraud and drug trafficking or an occasional convenience store robbery out on the four-lane.

No one remembers the last time a bank was robbed in town and the county coroner rarely makes house calls inside the city limits unless someone dies in his sleep.

Except for a few car accidents, Whitesburg people tend to die of natural causes—cancer, heart attack, black lung disease from the coal mines. The advent of drug overdoses is a recent phenomenon, and one still largely spoken of only in whispered gossip, as though to talk of it aloud would ruin the town's reputation.

Until February 17, 2002, there had not been a

murder in the city limits of Whitesburg in nearly twenty years.

That changed before two-thirty that Sunday afternoon. By then, two of the mythical 1,534 friendly people would be dead—shot in their own home—and the rest would feel a little less safe and a lot less friendly.

Chapter 1

February 17, 2002, was a painful day in Whitesburg. The groundhog had predicted six more weeks of winter, and it was looking as though he had been right.

The temperature hovered in the mid-30s and a cold, damp breeze blew in from the north, following the ridge of Pine Mountain and bringing the wind chill into the 20s. There was no snow, but the wind cut through clothing like a ripsaw and made cheeks and ears sting as though they had been slapped. The sun never broke through the clouds to counter the stiff breeze and the air was sharp with the smells of dry leaves and coal smoke from chimneys.

Though the temperature was far from a record low, police officers remember it as the coldest day they have ever seen. Maybe it was that chill north wind, or the 14-degree drop in temperature that occurred in the past twenty-four hours. Or maybe it was the task that brought them outside that Sunday afternoon.

Whatever the reason, February 17, 2002, was a day when most people preferred to stay indoors. Kentucky State Police Detective Chuck Bledsoe was doing paperwork in a lounge/squad room in the

Whitesburg Police Department (WPD). It had been a quiet day and the fourteen-year veteran police officer was looking forward to clocking out at three o'clock and driving back across Pine Mountain to his wife and daughters, at home near the Harlan County line.

He had spent his shift sitting at a tiny table shoved up against the plaster wall, finishing reports and making phone calls while the nineteen-inch color television on the counter under the sliding window into the hallway blared out background noise from *COPS* and *The Andy Griffith Show*. He had not received a single complaint that sleepy Sunday.

In retrospect, Bledsoe summed up his day until that time with a single cliché: "It was like they say—'the calm before the storm.'"

The first call of any significance wasn't for him. In fact, it didn't even go to the 911 call center, forty miles away at Kentucky State Police (KSP) Post 13 in Hazard. A resident in West Whitesburg called the Whitesburg City Police Station directly to report shots fired. The weekend dispatcher upstairs in the fire department got on the UHF radio and called Sergeant Randy Slone, the lone officer on duty that day, to drive to the neighborhood to check it out.

Though Bledsoe was bored stiff, Slone had not had enough time to get bored that day. Slone was a former Democratic political operative who had left his job as constituent services director for the governor when his boss left office.

He had joined the newly formed police department in the tiny college hamlet of Pippa Passes in neighboring Knott County, and then moved to Whitesburg when a job opened up there. He had recently been promoted to sergeant, though he still filled most of the same mundane duties that he did as a patrolman. Tall and lanky with a deceptively naive smile, Slone was rarely seen in the department's heather blue Class A uniform, instead preferring the dark blue utilities, the tail of the shirt invariably hanging out in back. But despite his rumpled appearance, Slone was the department's resident computer whiz—the first man in the department to be blessed with a laptop in his cruiser by virtue of being the first fully trained to use it.

Slone recalled that February 17 was a very busy day for him from the time he came in at dawn to the time when he left late that night.

He had reported to the emergency room at Whitesburg Appalachian Regional Hospital immediately after he came on duty at 6:00 A.M. A woman from central Kentucky traveling with a small-time music group had reported that some of the band's entourage had passed through Whitesburg during the predawn hours. She told police that the member of the band with whom she had been riding stopped the car in a restaurant parking lot in Whitesburg and raped her.

The woman went to the hospital, less than a mile away along the bypass around town, and the hospital reported the incident to the 911 center. Slone had gone to the emergency room to deliver a rape kit and help a Kentucky State Police trooper with the investigation.

He had barely cleared that call and eaten lunch, when he and Letcher County deputy sheriff Breman Slone had been called to quell a domestic dispute.

The Slones, who were not related, had gone their separate ways less than a minute before the "shots fired" call came in, and Sergeant Slone radioed the deputy to come back and give him a hand again.

Though it was only prudent to ask for backup when investigating a report of shots fired, no one took the call very seriously.

Letcher County was a very rural part of a very rural state, and shots were fired every day. Virtually, everyone in the area owned at least one gun, and on any given day, someone within hearing might be target shooting or hunting in the woods. And though much of the area was wooded, it could hardly be called wilderness.

Communities butted up against the forest wall, and many homes stood on isolated hillsides, sheltered by the trees. Residents had but to step out the back door to fire their guns in a safe direction.

To police officers in southeastern Kentucky, a report of shots fired meant beer cans on a fallen log or children taking aim for the first time with a .22 rifle. It was just as likely to be firecrackers. Any fireworks that exploded were illegal in Kentucky, but the law was generally enforced with a wink and a nod. It was only six weeks past New Year's, when fireworks tents sprout like springtime daisies, and someone surely had a few leftovers to shoot. Or maybe someone had been to Tennessee, where fireworks were available year-round. Either way, there was little cause to worry.

But this time the shots were not fireworks or target practice. Randy Slone said it seemed like only a few seconds until another call came in.

At 2:38 P.M., less than five minutes after Whitesburg City Police received the "shots fired" complaint, alphanumeric pagers carried by all police officers in the area began to buzz. This time it was a call from the 911 center in Hazard for all officers in the area. This call reported that someone had been shot.

"When the first 'shots fired' call came across . . . we didn't think much about it at the time, but when the second call came in that someone was down, that stepped it up a whole lot," Randy Slone said.

Belinda Hall Cook was calling to report that her husband, Timothy Louis "Blister" Cook, had shot himself in the head at his trailer and was dead. Bledsoe, the only detective in the area on duty that day, climbed into his unmarked green Ford and drove toward Kentucky Highway (KY) 15 and the scene of the reported suicide.

Bledsoe was no rookie. Police officers see death almost every day, and Bledsoe had been a police officer for a long time. He had seen people killed with handguns, shotguns, and even a circular saw. He had been the officer on duty when a man missing for a whole summer was found inside his pickup truck, parked in the woods. He was prepared for anything, he thought. He was not prepared to find another veteran trooper walking off the hill from the Cook trailer, clearly distraught.

Like Bledsoe, Trooper Rick Watts had worked the roads for a long time, but this crime scene had clearly affected him.

It had been fourteen minutes since the first report went in to the 911 center in Hazard, forty miles away, and an ambulance was already sitting at the trailer, along with a city cruiser and a sheriff's car. The trooper had already been in the trailer and was going back to his car for equipment he needed to secure the scene and begin the investigation.

"I remember him coming down, all to pieces— Rick was tore up—telling me about this child that had been shot," Bledsoe said.

Like Bledsoe, the trooper had children of his own. They were boys, both about the same age as the smaller of the two victims up the hill.

Randy Slone was shaken up, too. He and the deputy had gone into the trailer to clear it and make sure a shooter was not still inside. When the police sergeant pushed open a bedroom door, he found a tiny figure lying on his back on the carpet, his chest covered with blood. Slone knelt down beside the little boy to check his pulse. It was obvious that he was dead, and obvious that he had been dead for much longer than the one minute it had taken the officers to get to the scene. There was no pulse and his skin was cold to the touch.

Slone also had two children, his oldest the same age as the tiny victim on the floor beside him.

"It's not like you feel any less for an adult, but you kind of expect that," he said. "You don't expect it to happen to a four-year-old kid."

City police Chief Paul Miles was getting ready for a family outing with his wife, Ronna, their five-year-old daughter, and their nine-year-old son. The Miles family lived outside town, where the slope of Pine Mountain falls sharply into Cowan Creek, but they had come to town that Sunday afternoon before leaving on their day trip.

"We saw all that [police activity] as we were leaving town, and then they paged me that something had happened," Miles recalled. Miles had his wife drop him off at the convenience store at the foot of the hill and take the kids home while he walked up the hill to the crime scene.

Only in his midthirties, Miles had spent eleven years behind a badge and had helped investigate suicides and even a shotgun murder when he was a Letcher County deputy sheriff, before joining the city police department. None of that prepared him for the murders inside the little single-wide mobile home. He said it affected him as nothing had before.

Miles, a stocky, swarthy man, with salt-and-pepper hair and a bulldog face, whose thundercloud brows belie an affable, humorous personality, couldn't muster a smile about anything having to do with February 17. He acknowledged that he sometimes wished he had gone on with his family, "but wherever I went, I would have just been called back to it. There wasn't any getting away from it.

"Death scenes bother you to a point, but you get immune to them," Miles said. "You try to work them with respect for the families, but you've got no emotion about them usually. But seeing that child really affected everybody."

Police officers and others who spend their lives close to death often develop a kind of gallows humor as a defense against emotions. But Miles said jokes were absent that Sunday afternoon.

"A lot of people look down on you for joking, but I guess it's just our way of dealing with things," he said, drawing his bushy eyebrows together in a scowl. "There wasn't any of that this time. Nobody ever wants to be on a death scene, but definitely nobody wanted to be on this one."

An eerie silence came over the scene as officers spoke only when they had to in order to do their jobs.

In the case of Miles and his city police officers, that job was to secure the scene and assist Detective Bledsoe, who was assigned the duty of lead investigator.

Miles, who often compared Whitesburg to Andy Griffith's Mayberry, and joked about maybe coming to work without his gun, said the death of little Timothy James "T.J." Cook had a profound effect not only on officers, but on Whitesburg.

"The innocence was shattered or something," he said sadly.

Oddly enough, though the trailer where police had been called was within fifty to seventy-five yards of the victims' family members' homes, most of them had been unaware of the murders until police began arriving. One brother, Donald "Keetsie" Cook, his wife, and his son had gone to the trailer before police; so had a niece and her husband.

A 911 tape of the call from Belinda Cook recorded the screams and crying the moment family members walked in and found the bodies.

A Cook family member, speaking for the rest of the clan, said it still hurt too much to talk about the events of February 17, but victims impact statements filed with the Letcher Circuit Court show how devastating the murders were.

Pam Collins, a sister of Timothy "Blister" Cook, found out about the deaths purely by chance, and on a day when she was already emotionally taxed. The natural mother of Collins's stepdaughter had died the day before and visitation had been set for that day at one of the funeral homes in town. She and her family were on their way to Whitesburg to attend those services.

Collins, her husband, and her stepdaughter were driving down the steep hill that descends into the west end of Whitesburg when they saw the police cars at the foot of her brother's driveway. Then they saw the ambulance parked at the trailer.

Already upset because of the other death, the family pulled into Susan Cook Drive, named for her grandmother, and learned that Collins's brother and nephew had been killed.

Now, in addition to comforting her stepdaughter and being with her and her father during the other funeral, Collins found herself planning a double funeral.

Letcher County deputy coroner Robbie Campbell was directing a funeral a few miles out of town when

911 dispatchers paged the Whitesburg Fire Department (WFD) to a double shooting. Campbell, a robust, middle-aged man, with the jovial manner to match his appearance, was an embalmer, funeral director, and the owner of Letcher Funeral Home. He also served as a volunteer fireman and rescue worker, and got his first job as an ambulance driver when he was just seventeen years old.

He had been a certified coroner for sixteen years when the murders took place and had served as a deputy coroner in Letcher County through the terms of six elected coroners. He still wasn't prepared for finding T.J.

Campbell left the funeral after receiving a page for the fire department at 2:50 P.M., telling firefighters that two people had been shot. He expected to help with a rescue or with crowd control, but when he arrived, police were putting Blister Cook's estranged wife in the back of a cruiser for questioning. It was then he learned police needed his services as a coroner, not a fireman.

"When I walked in, that boy (Blister) was sitting on the floor with his back up against the couch, and he'd been shot behind the ear," Campbell remembered.

Police told him there were two victims, so he went into the bedroom to find the other one.

"There he was in the middle of his little toys and him laying on his back like a doll, shot for no reason except he saw who did it," Campbell said bitterly. "It was heartrending."

He left the room as soon as he pronounced T.J. dead, and went outside into the cold, fresh air. The victims' family—Timothy Cook's parents, brothers, sister, nieces, nephews, in-laws—stood outside the police line asking him why it was taking so long and who did it, questions Campbell couldn't answer.

Then Pam Collins asked him to take Timmy and

T.J. to his funeral home for burial and made a request he had never had before: bury them together in the same casket.

"We had a great big ol' casket and we just put the little boy in his arms," Campbell said. "That's the first time I'd ever done that."

Now, with a grandson of his own, Campbell said he sometimes imagined what it would be like to have to live through something like that.

"That was so sad. I've seen people shot, and people who have shot themselves, but this is really the first time I'd seen a little child shot," he said.

"It's the first time I'd ever seen anything like that, and I don't care to see it again."

Though police wished they hadn't seen what had happened at the Cook trailer, plenty of others wanted a good, long look. Police noted that the curtains were drawn back in a number of motel rooms on the other side of the river as people tried to get a glimpse of the horrible happenings a stone's throw away.

Slone recalled pointing out the rubbernecking bystanders to one of the detectives.

"There were several people over there watching and it dawned on me that they (the killer or killers) might be over there watching," he said.

Police had no way of knowing at the time whether Slone was right, but if they had looked hard enough, they might have seen the face of the murderer behind the glass, his jaws crammed with pizza, a cold beer in his hand, gloating about what he had gotten away with.

As police were beginning their investigation, the killer and his wife were several miles on the opposite side of Whitesburg. They were in Wise County, Virginia, the nearest legal beer store. Soon they would be on their way back across Pound Gap and driving the fourteen miles from the state line back to Whitesburg.

The man who had just dropped the hammer on a four-year-old child had a special night in mind—a real celebration. He had a case of beer and two gallon-size plastic bags of pot for a party, and he would soon have a new engagement ring from Wal-Mart to give to his wife of two months. Super 8 Motel had rooms that featured Jacuzzi tubs and he had more than $1,000 in his pocket—enough to pay for ten nights if he wanted.

But police said later that a romantic night with his new bride wasn't what he had in mind. Otherwise, why would he invite friends over after first cajoling them to go to the American Legion club and buy bootleg liquor?

The killer, they said, was returning as close to the scene of the crime as he could. He had stayed at the motel before, but in a Jacuzzi room that faced the parking lot at the front of the building.

This time he asked the clerk for a Jacuzzi room with a view of the river. And on the steep hillside overlooking the river from the other side was the Cook trailer, swarming with police. The killer paid cash, went to his room, and ordered dinner. Then he sat on the couch, carried on a casual conversation, ate his pizza, and watched.

He watched as police held back the crowd. He watched as the coroner talked with the family.

He watched as paramedics carried two green vinyl body bags out of the trailer and placed them carefully in the back of a hearse.

* * *

It was a painful day in Whitesburg. The wind cut
to the bone, but the loss of a four-year-old child hurt
clear into the soul. T.J. Cook was an innocent,
beloved little boy. People who knew him still get
misty-eyed when they talk about him and his death.
He was smart and cute and funny. And he was loved,
not just by his family, but by everyone who had met
him. T.J. Cook would not soon be forgotten, and
neither would the creature who had murdered him.

People at the Cook trailer on February 17, 2002,
agreed: this was not a normal murder. It wasn't
normal that it was in Whitesburg, and it wasn't
normal that someone would do that to a child. It
wasn't normal that seasoned police officers, cal-
loused by years of death and gore, would be so affected by a murder scene.

"The feel at that death scene was different from all
the others," Miles said. "It was surreal."

"In eastern Kentucky, it seems like it (murder) is
always over alcohol or property," Bledsoe said. "This
one, what really stunned the community and the
county, was there was a baby who had no part of
what his parents or anybody else was involved in
whatsoever, and had only been in the world four
years, and he wound up being a victim just over
greed . . . and heartless people."

"It was an eerie day, just a strange feeling standing
out there on that porch," Campbell said. "Maybe it
was where he was watching us; you know you get this
little subconscious thing goin' on."

Chapter 2

Chuck Bledsoe was a thirty-seven-year-old newly minted detective with thinning brown hair, and a perpetually sunny disposition, even in the face of horrific crimes. He was often the one to break up the tension in serious conversations with wisecracks delivered in nasal, staccato bursts vaguely reminiscent of Sergeant Joe Friday, only with a sarcastic sense of humor. Something of a health nut, Bledsoe finished off his meals of lean chicken with fat-free candies and spent his off-hours lifting weights. In 2002, he was bench-pressing nearly five hundred pounds and sometimes entered bodybuilding competitions when he wasn't policing.

When not lifting, he channeled his energy into constant movement. He tapped his feet, drummed his fingers, and in general presented the very picture of raw energy trapped inside a tightly capped bottle, apt to explode in a thousand directions at any moment.

He had fifteen years on the Kentucky State Police, first as a trooper, then a detective. He made his bones in narcotics, going undercover to bust dealers even before he was officially made a detective. But like all KSP detectives, he had investigated everything from burglary to murder, and everyone from drunk drivers to strong-arm thugs.

He now specialized in white-collar crime for the KSP's Division of Drug Enforcement and Special Investigations, known by troopers as DESI East, but in 2002, he was the coat-and-tie cop who got called to investigate many of the murders, suicides, and decaying bodies in the eastern reaches of the five-county Post 13 area. He was the only detective assigned primarily to Letcher County and he was naturally the detective called to the Cook trailer on February 17, 2002.

The Cook's single-wide mobile home was perched on the side of a mountain in the west end of Whitesburg. Being just off Kentucky Highway 15, the main road through town, it was nearly surrounded by fast-food restaurants, shopping centers, and assorted other businesses, many of the same sort of uninspired architecture as the trailer.

A fieldstone-faced convenience store sat next to the road, its pump islands a hive of activity twenty-four hours a day, seven days a week. The edge of the parking lot was packed with U-Haul trailers and moving vans from the rental store next door. The opposite side of the Kentucky River bristled with restaurants, a motel, a bank, a gas station, a supermarket, a medical clinic, and assorted other businesses. On weekdays, that part of Whitesburg was teeming with traffic. Drivers fumed as they waited to pull out onto the highway, edging their way closer and closer to the road and unbroken strings of cars that stretched out between red lights along the bottlenecked section of two-lane asphalt. It was quieter on Sundays, but it still saw its share of after-church diners at the restaurants and shoppers at the grocery stores.

That community of businesses was part of what impressed Bledsoe as he arrived at the scene.

The area around the murder scene was a busy place. Cars were constantly coming and going to get gas, pick up a soft drink, or perform some other daily routine. To get to the Cook trailer, cars have to drive between closely packed homes and businesses or through the parking lot of the convenience store.

When one entered Susan Cook Drive, the first building was the Pentecostal Faith Tabernacle. Blister's driveway turned up the hill just to the right of the church and its gravel parking lot. The killer would have had to go past that church, and it was Sunday. Surely, someone in church or someone buying gas at the foot of the hill had seen something. If not, then maybe someone at the Wendy's restaurant drive-through window across the Kentucky River had seen the killer.

Those would be avenues to explore later, but Detective Bledsoe had other things to do first. Sergeant Slone, Deputy Slone, and an ambulance were already at the Cook trailer, so Bledsoe took a few minutes to talk to his fellow trooper about what had happened at the trailer and to give him an opportunity to collect himself before hiking up the steep driveway to the murder scene.

When Bledsoe walked up on the porch and through the front door, forty-one-year-old Timothy Louis "Blister" Cook was reclining on the floor of the living room, his back propped up against the front of a sectional couch and his right elbow resting on the couch cushions. He was dressed in Red Kap uniform pants and uniform shirt with his name, Tim, on a patch over the pocket, and a gray pocket T-shirt. His legs were folded back and his feet, clad in socks, were under the coffee table in the middle of the floor.

His head was limp on the crook of his arm, as though he were sleeping, but a trail of blood down his face led back to the small-caliber bullet hole among the long brown hair on the top, back side of his head. The bullet had entered near the crown, slightly behind the left ear. Because of the blood, police could not tell if the bullet had exited. A paper bag lay in the victim's lap containing sixty-one cents

in change, an unopened pack of Winston brand cigarettes, an empty cigarette pack, and three loose, un-
smoked cigarettes.

Police would take a closer look in a little while.
They could not move the body or anything else in
the trailer to get a closer look until after a coroner
arrived. Though police investigate crimes, Kentucky
law placed the scene of death under the control and
supervision of the county coroner. Police could only
secure the scene until the coroner gave them permission to do otherwise.

Other than the dead body, there was little awry in
the trailer. Blister had been the only adult in the
home for some time before he married his second
wife and he had been separated from her for three
days, but this was not a bachelor's home. Timothy
Cook ran a tight ship. The floors were swept and
mopped, the dishes were done, and the rooms were
as neat as anyone could expect in any household
that included a four-year-old boy. A Yoo-Hoo soda
bottle sat on the counter, and there was an unemp-
tied ashtray, but overall the home was neat and unremarkable. There were toy cars on the floor in
front of the coffee table, and there was blood, but
the boy's body was not in the room.

Like most single-wide mobile homes, the front
door opened into a combined living room/dining
room/kitchen. There was a hallway to the left that led
to a bathroom and one bedroom. A door in the right-
hand living-room wall opened to a second bedroom.
Four-year-old T.J. Cook was in that room—his room—
lying on his back on the rug just to the left of the
door. He was rolled very slightly to his left side; his
feet were together, his hands and arms at his sides as
though they had been placed there. He was wearing
white socks, blue jeans, and a dark gray sweatshirt,
which was now soaked in blood. He had been shot
twice in the chest. Police later noted that he had bled

profusely, thrown up, and there were tears in his eyes, all indications that he had not died immediately.

From all the evidence, it appeared as though he had been moved from the living room, where he had been shot, to the bedroom. Police believed that the murderer had moved T.J., possibly so he would not have to listen to him cry or look at him lying on the floor while he completed the robbery. Tests would show more later, but all of the questions would never be answered.

Even today, a murder investigation in Whitesburg, Kentucky, bears little resemblance to television's *CSI* series. There are no crime scene technicians in disposable jumpsuits, no model-pretty women in high heels and gun harnesses. Crime scenes here are handled by cops, who in the Kentucky State Police happen to be 98 percent male.

In 2002, in Letcher County, there was only one female officer in all of the local departments combined—and she was a plainclothes deputy sheriff who worked only on child sex abuse and rape cases.

Current murder cases in the rural parts of Kentucky are almost exclusively the purview of the state police. There are more than four hundred cities in Kentucky, but only four with more than fifty-thousand residents. City police departments are too undermanned to take on such major crimes. Sheriff's departments are in even worse shape. Until after the Cook murders, deputies were not even required to have academy training and most in rural Kentucky did not. Sheriffs' primary duties are the collection of taxes and the delivery of warrants, summonses, and subpoenas. Though all sheriffs put up at least a pretext of everyday law enforcement, murder cases are beyond the expertise of all but a few of the most professional departments.

What was to be done at the Cook trailer had to

be done by the officers at the scene, and this was more than one detective could handle, even with the assistance of the local departments. If only one person was there, the killer could be getting farther and farther away while the detective processed the crime scene. If the detective immediately went looking for the killer, evidence essential to a conviction could be removed or damaged while he was gone. Troopers have the same training as detectives, but it is their responsibility to assess and secure the scene until the detectives arrive, not run the investigation.

To make matters worse, the scene outside was deteriorating rapidly as distraught family members and friends gathered on the lawn.

The family wanted in, and they wanted to know why police had allowed something like this to happen.

Belinda Cook was there, too, just back from three days of separation from her husband. A tall, skinny woman with long jet-black hair and a vaguely owlish look, due to her thick, oversize glasses, Belinda Cook was obviously not welcome at the home, and police believed she was in danger there.

Blister Cook's family didn't like her in the best of times. Now she had been the first person to the scene of the murders and her jacket was covered in blood. The family was deeply suspicious of her. Blister had been the one who had forced her into drug rehab. They had been separated for three days and she had been staying first with her ex-husband, then with a male friend. Blister had been planning to divorce her and now he was dead.

Sergeant Randy Slone, Deputy Breman Slone, and Trooper Rick Watts were alone with crowd control for twenty to thirty minutes and there were so many people they were having trouble keeping order. The mood was tense, and Randy Slone said he had to keep reminding himself to try and put himself in the victims' family's place.

"When we were controlling that scene for the first twenty minutes, it was just about to the point of 'guns drawn and everybody clear the area,'" Randy Slone said. "It was chaotic."

They were the only three uniformed officers working in the entire 339-square-mile county, except for maybe one officer in the city of Jenkins fifteen miles away. They began calling for backup from anyone who could come out and Bledsoe still needed more help as well. Luckily, the shift was about to change at the Kentucky State Police Post and more officers would soon be coming to work.

More troopers and several off-duty local police officers arrived to help, taking pressure off the four who had been there alone. Officers were able to take more control of the scene.

Belinda Cook had already been in a physical fight with Donald "Keetsie" Cook, Blister's brother, inside the trailer just before police arrived. Trouble was brewing and for the woman's own safety, police put her in the back of Trooper Ben McCray's cruiser. But as they put her in the car, her son by an earlier marriage showed up and dived on top of the cruiser. Police arrested him. Things were falling apart.

Deputy Bert Slone, the brother of the first deputy to arrive, told Belinda that it would be safer for her to leave and escorted her to Whitesburg fire chief Truman Thompson's car for a ride to the sheriff's department. Thompson let the two of them out at the courthouse and Slone took her inside.

Bert Slone, a short, wide-shouldered redhead, with an outgoing, friendly manner, was the circuit court bailiff at the time. He said in a statement to state police that while he was waiting with Belinda for Bledsoe to arrive, she began to talk about drug dealers and their telephone numbers, and about reasons some people might want to kill Blister Cook.

Bert Slone said he read a Miranda warning to her at

that point, but informed her that she was not under arrest when she asked. She had then asked for medical treatment for injuries she had received in the fight with Blister's brother. Slone called an ambulance.

Since it was a Sunday, Bledsoe was one of only two state police detectives working in the five-county Post 13 area. Bledsoe asked the dispatcher to send Detective Ken Duff to assist him. It would take valuable time for Duff to arrive from Perry County, thirty miles away, but Bledsoe got lucky that day.

Detective John Pratt, another veteran of the KSP, worked in his spare time as a high-school basketball referee. It was the middle of basketball season and he was on his way to a regional meeting of referees in Whitesburg when he received the page from the 911 center and saw the police cars and ambulances just off the highway. Though he was on his day off, he parked his car and went up the hill to help.

While Bledsoe was a bear of a man, Pratt was more like one of the mountains that surround Whitesburg. He towered over those around him, blocking out the sun. And while Bledsoe's face was plastered with a permanent grin, Pratt's craggy countenance had the serious air of a man looking for the right piece to fit into a thousand-piece puzzle.

When Pratt arrived, Bledsoe turned the crime scene over to him for photographs and processing. When Duff arrived from Perry County, he and Bledsoe split up the possible witnesses. Bledsoe went to the sheriff's department to talk to Belinda Cook, who by this time was being treated by a paramedic. Duff began canvassing the neighborhood. This was a bad case and things could turn even uglier if something didn't break soon.

Blister Cook's brother lived only fifty to seventy-five yards away, but he was inside his trailer and heard nothing. He had glanced out the window once and seen a pickup truck parked there, but thought nothing of it. The same thing was true of Cook's parents, who lived on the hill above their sons, and other neighbors.

Blister Cook, Timmy to most of his family, had a lot of company, and no one paid much attention to who visited him that day. Bledsoe had heard rumors about Blister Cook's company long before the murders occurred, and he knew why no one paid much attention. There were a lot of cars at the trailer. It was normal.

"The victim was alleged in the past to have trafficked in marijuana, so it wasn't unusual for people to pull up, get out, and stay a few minutes, or whatever, and go back off the hill," Bledsoe said. "That's one reason why nobody was paying any attention to who came and went."

Family members steadfastly told reporters and the court that they didn't know about that aspect of Cook's life. After the killings, some people said the community had known for years and blamed police for letting it go on. Some even claimed that the trailer had been under surveillance and that some police officers were Cook's customers. Police readily acknowledged that they had information that Blister Cook sold marijuana, but said that if other officers frequented the home, they knew nothing about it. They had many reports that Blister sold marijuana, and Bledsoe had even busted Blister's wife for trafficking in the prescription drugs OxyContin, Lortab, and Tylox, but he had never had proof Blister was involved.

And there had been no surveillance. If so, Bledsoe said, the on-duty officers would have seen the killer leave. And if there had been surveillance, the officers on that duty would have been the first to arrive at the scene.

Still, the rumors of pot sales had been strong enough that police believed there was no doubt of their truth. If Blister Cook had really been selling pot, then something was missing—the drugs. When Pratt searched the trailer, he found no marijuana or other drugs of any kind and no money. He also found no wallet in Blister's pockets.

The missing wallet indicated that robbery may have been the motive for the killing, and witness statements later showed that Cook indeed had had substantial quantities of marijuana in the trailer shortly before the killings.

Police already suspected that the trailer had been used to deal in marijuana, and it didn't take long to learn there should have been pot still there. But finding out specifics was not going to be easy.

Instead, Bledsoe spent three days and three sleepless nights talking to neighbors and following dead-end leads. No one saw, no one heard, no one suspected anything. The murders were committed on a Sunday and there was a church at the corner. But the shootings didn't occur until sometime between one o'clock and 2:30 P.M. Church services were over; most people were already gone by the time the murders occurred. There were a few left for choir practice, but they were busy with their own activities. It wasn't that they had seen nothing, but what they had seen seemed of limited usefulness to police.

A woman had been sitting at the piano in the church and had seen a car drop off T.J. and his father, at least a half hour before the murders. Two other women told Detective Duff that they had seen a man running off the hill around 1:00 P.M., but their descriptions were vague. The only thing either of them remembered was that the man was wearing a shirt that appeared to be blue denim with brown trim. Neither was able to identify anyone in a photo lineup used by police four days later.

The U-Haul dealer and two-way radio store at the end of Blister Cook's driveway was closed. The waiters and waitresses at the Wendy's drive-through window were too busy taking and handing out orders to notice anything on the other side of the river, until police started to arrive. One waitress, however, remembered seeing someone come up the riverbank into the parking lot. When police investigated, they found the incident was unrelated to the murders.

With neighbors' interviews turning up zilch, Bledsoe turned to the next possibility. There were security cameras at the Shell Oil station near Susan Cook Drive, and with luck they would show exactly who the killer was. Cameras don't blink. They don't become busy or bored or jaded and then stop paying attention to their surroundings. If there was one camera pointing in the right direction, police should have a photograph of the last person up the driveway—irrefutable evidence that the person on the tape had the opportunity to kill.

The Shell station, popularly known as Sugar Shack because of an earlier incarnation as a doughnut shop and restaurant, was part of a chain of Double Kwik convenience stores based in Whitesburg. Other stores in the chain had been frequent targets of armed robbers in the past, and Childers Oil, the parent company, had a penchant for surveillance and security. Video cameras were trained on the checkout counter, the gas pumps, and the parking lot—everywhere that one might expect. In fact, the cameras at another Childers store had led police directly to a robber who had taken off his mask after taking money from the clerk at gunpoint.

And sure enough, when Bledsoe checked, he found that one of the cameras at the Sugar Shack was pointed straight toward Susan Cook Drive, which runs just behind the station's kerosene pump. If police were lucky, it would show not only the vehicle used in the crimes, but also the license number. It might also have a clear picture of the man witnesses said they saw running off the hill.

But when Bledsoe watched the security tapes, they showed nothing but the police cars that had arrived after Belinda Cook called 911. The earlier tape showed nothing unusual at all.

The first tape had ended shortly before the time police determined that the murders had to have occurred. Store employees hadn't replaced it for one critical hour—the hour during which a killer had gone up the hill and back again, leaving two dead bodies in his wake. The murderer had escaped notice again.

A search of the neighborhood turned up two other video cameras pointing in the general direction of the Cook trailer. A security camera in the automatic teller machine at Whitaker Bank, just across the river, was a little too far away to be reliable, and it might be blocked by the U-Haul dealership, but Bledsoe thought it was worth checking. Unfortunately, it had burned out the week before the murders and the technician had not arrived to repair it.

A camera at Frazier's Farmers' Supply, located catty-cornered across the bridge from the Sugar Shack, pointed in the right direction to see anyone entering the street where the murders were committed. But when police asked at the store, they learned that the security system was new and the camera that police needed had not yet been connected to the system.

Three surveillance cameras, all pointed in the direction of the murder scene, and all were either inoperable or out of tape. It was an almost unbelievable coincidence. Three chances to see the killer, all lost.

The cameras had blinked after all. It seemed as though the killer was the luckiest man alive. There were witnesses within one hundred yards of the crime, there were video cameras pointed directly at him, yet he had gotten away without a single neighbor or a single camera seeing him—at least not clearly. The only person police knew without a doubt had seen Timothy "Blister" Cook's killer had been his own son, T.J. And the killer had made dead sure T.J. would take that secret to his grave.

Chapter 3

Mountain Montessori School, an ugly hodge-podge of building styles wrapped into one freshly painted, ribbed-steel skin, started off as a 1920s-era bungalow; the dormered roof of the house still projects out of the top of the structure. A metal pole building was built around the old house sometime in the 1970s, when it was converted into an auto parts store. The Montessori board bought the building around 2000, gave it a fresh coat of paint and some colorful stickers in the plate glass windows, and built a playground on top of the old parking lot.

It served children from preschool through kindergarten.

When visitors walk up the treated wood ramp and into the little alcove at the entryway to the school, the first thing they see is a framed paper certificate from the Whitesburg Fire Department. It says: "In Memory of T.J. Cook," and is dated June 12, 2002, not quite four months after T.J. was murdered.

Though the children there now are too young to have known T.J., there are reminders of him here and there around the school, particularly in the office of teacher Ann Leslie Hissom, who is also director of the school. One cabinet is for T.J.'s belongings. Among other things, a zippered plastic bag bulges with toy cars left behind when T.J. died.

A big-shouldered woman, with prematurely graying hair, Hissom got teary-eyed when discussing T.J., and was fiercely defensive of Blister Cook and his family.

T.J., she said, was special. He started preschool at 2½ years old, he was gone for a brief period, and then started back again after his father remarried. T.J. was eager to come to school and "carried himself like a little man," she said.

His biggest fear, she said, was getting hurt.

"He was scared of falling, he really didn't want to be around the dog that might jump on him," she said.

Even so, he rarely cried. And he was smart and witty, with a face that adults couldn't resist.

T.J.'s fortunes had not always seemed so bright. He was born while his mother was in prison. She was so skinny during the pregnancy that friends worried she would never carry the baby to term. When she did, T.J. went to live with his father, who, with the help of family, began the job of raising the child. When a sister was born a couple of years later, two babies were more than Blister could handle alone. T.J. continued to live with his father, but the sister was moved in with an aunt.

The family wasn't split up entirely, however. T.J. and Blister would visit with the girl and she would visit with them. She was always T.J.'s sister, even though she didn't live with him, and he loved to go visit her and play with her.

But in many ways, T.J. Cook was not a typical four-year-old. He was precocious, he played with toy cars, but he was different. T.J. Cook had spent his short life around adults and his conversation skills were far beyond those of most preschool-aged kids.

Want to know who that guy was cutting weeds downtown? T.J. could tell you. What about the car parked over there? T.J. knew the make and model. Looking for a new weed trimmer or power saw? T.J. would give his recommendations on brand and size as readily as most kids could tell you their favorite flavor of ice cream.

He especially knew about weed trimmers. He could draw a WeedEater or make the noise of one starting perfectly, and he loved to take them apart and play with them. His dad and his uncle had a home garage, where they worked on cars constantly, and T.J. was learning early about carburetors and spark plugs. He had a working model of an engine complete with a video about how it worked, and he could change the oil in a lawn mower as readily as most kids could build a sand castle.

But while he loved machines and brought tool brochures to preschool, T.J.'s real love was people. He liked to talk and he knew everyone he talked to. If he didn't know someone, he'd ask who they were, and when he saw them again, he would remember their name and any little tidbit of information he had heard about them. T.J. was a people person— a born politician with a quick smile, a quick wit, and a willingness to glad-hand everyone he met.

And not only did T.J. love people; people loved T.J. His inquisitive nature and outgoing ways were infectious. Everyone who met him had to talk to him. They had to spend time with him.

"The other parents would step over their own child to see T.J.," Hissom said. "He was so cute."

It was T.J.'s knack for knowing people that investigators felt sure led to his death. The killer wasn't someone who randomly picked out someone to shoot. It was someone Tim and T.J. knew. It was a friend or a customer. It was someone who knew them both; this explained how he could get behind Blister so readily, someone who was known for being observant. Most of all, why would he kill a four-year-old child? A stranger might worry that the child could identify him, but not if he never saw him again.

Hissom recalled the fear she felt knowing also that the killer was someone who knew T.J. and Blister. She and her husband, "Bear," left town when they heard about the murders and drove to his parents' home one hundred miles away. They returned for the funeral and it was, she said, "the blackest funeral I've ever been to."

During the service, Hissom said, she could not help but look from person to person and wonder if one of them had killed Blister and T.J. There were people there, certainly, that Blister would not have wanted. It was uncomfortable to sit in the midst of them.

Timothy L. "Blister" Cook, dressed in jeans and a black leather motorcycle jacket, lay in the oversize casket at the front of the room. T.J., dressed identically, lay on the left side of his chest, cradled in the crook of his father's arm.

"The only comfort I could find, when I looked in that casket, was he looked like a baby again," Hissom said. "He was not a little man anymore."

The "little man" and his father were buried in a hillside cemetery outside Whitesburg. The single black-granite gravestone featured an elaborate, photo-realistic engraving of the two, along with Blister's beloved Ford Mustang and a weed trimmer, over the words "Enjoying heaven together."

While police were obviously concerned that there had been two murders, and were shocked that one of the victims was a four-year-old child, they were not very surprised that Blister Cook was the other one.

It's not that anyone hated him or that anyone expected him to be murdered, but after the fact, his background seemed to include several telltale signs that Blister Cook was living on the edge.

Cook wasn't a bad man—he was well-liked by most of the people who knew him and had never been in any serious trouble with the law—but police knew who he was. He liked fast cars and he liked to drink beer and smoke pot. He had a minor police record with several arrests including charges of public intoxication, driving under the influence, and driving on a suspended license. Bledsoe had arrested him once on a possession of marijuana charge, and he had been arrested again in March of 2000 for public intoxication involving controlled substances. He had been fined $25 and court costs that time.

Though they had never gathered enough evidence to arrest Cook for drug trafficking, police said it was "common knowledge" that he sold marijuana. In addition to that, his wife was under indictment at the time for "doctor shopping," the practice of visiting numerous doctors in order to obtain prescription painkillers. Police alleged that she obtained many more than she could use herself, then sold the surplus.

But while Blister Cook had a wild side, friends say he was much more complex. He was streetwise and wily, but also a leader. He demanded respect, Ann Leslie Hissom said, and he got it.

Like the work uniform he was wearing when he was murdered, the man his family knew as Timmy was blue-collar through and through. He wore work clothes, usually with the shirt unbuttoned, but showed no qualms about mixing with people in suits and ties. A veteran of the U.S. Army, Cook had worked as a coal miner before he lost his job. He was working as a carpenter when he was killed, and he doted on his young son.

He had paid the tuition for the private Montessori School when he was working. When he was out of work, he had lent his skills as a carpenter to help the school and T.J. attended classes on a scholarship. Blister gave the school lumber that he had at home, and brought a whole crew to help with the construction of the playground.

Hissom said Cook was "a leader, and people looked up to him.

"He was some of my best help down here," she said.

Hissom said Cook put his son before everything else, and an incident at the school a few days before the murders had led to his trouble with his wife. Belinda Cook had arrived to drive T.J. home from school and Hissom had refused to let her take him. She had not driven him home from school before; she was smoking in the classroom and, in Hissom's opinion, appeared to be intoxicated.

When Hissom told Blister Cook, he had immediately reacted by sending his wife to a drug rehab program. A few days later, Hissom said, he told friends he planned to divorce Belinda Cook. His reason was that he could not let anything happen to his son.

But something did happen to his son only a few days later, and while Blister's family members blamed Belinda Cook, many in the community blamed Blister and his family for allowing T.J. to live in that environment.

Hissom rejected that argument, angrily defending Blister as a good father who did everything he could for his son and everything he could with his son.

Burying Blister and T.J. in the same casket was fitting for a father and son who seemed to go everywhere together, Hissom said.

"I never knew any two that were any closer."

Chapter 4

As the day and night of February 17 wore on, calls began pouring into the Kentucky State Police dispatch room at Post 13 in Hazard. There were reports that someone had seen something, someone had heard something, someone had said something. Unfortunately, all those somethings added up to exactly nothing.

Police continued to look for a killer that no one, seemingly, had seen—or if they had seen him, they could not identify him.

Clues were few and far between. A woman still at the church below the Cook home had seen a burgundy car stop at the foot of the hill about 12:30 P.M. and drop off Blister and T.J. Blister had carried his son, who was in socks but no shoes, up the hill to the trailer.

A neighbor claimed to have heard several "pops," then saw two women run out of the trailer and sit down. Moments later, a state police trooper pulled up. Police determined the noises the woman heard and reported to city police as shots fired could not have been gunshots because of the time frame between the sounds and the arrival of the police.

Only a few clues seemed fruitful. Two women said

they had seen a man running off the hill wearing a blue-and-tan shirt, but that conflicted with a statement by one of Blister's brothers that he had seen a blue pickup at the trailer about the time of the murders. If the killer had been driving a pickup truck, why would he have run off the hill, and how could he have returned unseen to get his vehicle? Could the person running away have been a witness? Or perhaps the person in the truck had been the witness.

A friend of Blister's reported on February 18 that he had been talking to Blister on the phone shortly before the murders and heard him speak to someone named Donnie, who, he assumed, was Donnie Baker, another friend.

Bledsoe contacted the Kentucky State Police Intelligence Division to run a DMV search of all trucks matching the description given by the women in the church at the foot of the hill. He was looking for a blue, standard cab, four-wheel-drive Ford F-150 pickup. Its model year would probably be between 1980 and 1990. Rather than wade through all of the trucks in the region, Bledsoe specified that it be limited to such trucks registered in Letcher County. The search showed that Donnie Baker indeed owned such a truck.

That triggered an intense, two-day search for Baker, who was at the moment the closest thing police had to a suspect.

Detective Pratt knew Baker from a case in Perry County and knew where he lived, so he and Bledsoe drove out to find him. Baker was not to be found at his home, and police soon found what they thought was the reason. Belinda Cook had called his wife and told her that police were looking for him. Police did not believe she was attempting to tip him off, instead marking down the call to a misguided attempt to help police. The wife was scared by the call, saying that Belinda Cook had been telling her that Donnie was a suspect in the murders and had better turn himself in. It was the kind of help police didn't need.

"Everything we would do or try to find out, she was out blabbing to anybody who would listen," Bledsoe said.

Police arrested Belinda Cook and charged her with hindering apprehension. But while she was charged with a crime, police said they wanted to apprehend Baker, not so much because he was a suspect, but because he was a witness. Bledsoe had become convinced that even if Baker was not the killer, he at least knew something of value and it was imperative that police locate him and talk to him. Police issued a bulletin for officers to look for the Ford pickup truck. Everyone was a suspect at that point, and Baker was a person of special interest.

Police left word with Baker's wife: if he had not committed the crime, he had nothing to fear from them. If he continued to stay out of reach, their suspicions would only become more intense, and so would their search. He needed to call them and come in so they could talk.

While police searched for Baker, the trail of the real killer was getting colder and colder, and investigators still had few concrete clues.

Commonwealth's Attorney Edison Banks had issued grand jury subpoenas for phone records for Blister's home and his brother's home, a nearby auto parts store from which Belinda Cook said she had tried to call her husband, the home where she had been staying for the past three days, and the home of her first husband.

BellSouth, the provider of local phone service in Whitesburg and much of Letcher County, had not yet proffered those records, but the request seemed to be little more than an exercise in thoroughness anyway. Danny Webb, a retired state police captain who was campaigning for the office of sheriff, had already provided an alibi for Belinda Cook. He had seen her walking along the main highway toward the trailer as he was leaving the Food City supermarket. The cash register receipt he had received at the store confirmed the time that he left and made it highly unlikely that Belinda Cook could have been at the trailer when the murders were committed.

On top of Webb's statement, a security camera at the auto parts store from which Belinda Cook told police she tried to call home showed that she was indeed at the store when she said she was.

A sweep of the trailer had uncovered no fingerprints of value, and little else. The most significant finding was a bloody, mushroomed bullet tangled in the pile carpet of the living room. It was a brass-washed .22-caliber hollow-point slug, as common as dirt in the area, but perhaps ballistics could do something with it.

Police dutifully bagged the bullet and passed it to technicians at the state crime lab, but when the lab completed its report, it seemed to be of little use.

Except for shotguns, gun barrels contain "rifling," a series of grooves and lands that spiral up the inside of the barrel. That rifling causes the bullet to spin in the same way a quarterback spins a football. The spin makes a bullet stabilize and fly straight to the target.

Since the diameter of a gun barrel between lands of rifling is slightly less than the diameter of the bullet, the rifling leaves telltale markings along any bullet that passes through the barrel. Since each gun is fired a different number of times and subjected to different environmental circumstances, the rifling of different barrels develop different anomalies—

scratches, nicks, and rough spots—as unique as human fingerprints. The markings left on a bullet by those individual features can, in some cases, be used to identify the gun from which the bullet was fired.

The examination of the bullet sent in by police advanced the investigation very little.

State crime lab examiners found the bullet to have been fired from a gun with six grooves and lands, and a right-hand twist. That narrowed the field only marginally. The crime lab gave police a list of 109 models of rifles, revolvers, and semiautomatic pistols that matched that kind of rifling. With 109 models on the market, hundreds of thousands of guns surely would have been sold. Hundreds might be found in Letcher County alone, since many of the guns on the list were common, inexpensive, and popular models.

The information seemed unhelpful at the time, but police knew that could change if the murder weapon could be located. The ballistics report was stored in the case file for later use.

The other bullet police had recovered was even less helpful. The slugs used to kill the Cooks were hollow-points, bullets designed for one purpose—killing. Hollow-points have a hole molded into the tip of the bullet, which causes the bullet to expand into a broad, flat mushroom shape when it strikes the soft tissue of a person or animal, or fragment on impact when it hits something hard, like bone. The design is intended to cause the maximum damage and transfer the maximum energy while reducing the danger of the bullet traveling through its intended target and striking something else.

The state medical examiner's office reported that Timothy "Blister" Cook had been shot once and the bullet had broken up into eight pieces inside his skull, making that slug of virtually no use to investigators. T.J. Cook had been shot twice and both bullets had exited his body. But so far, police had found only one—the bullet that had been lying on top of the pile carpeting in the living room. Its energy had been so depleted that it had not even penetrated the carpet backing. With that information in mind, police began tearing apart the trailer, looking for the second bullet. There were no bullet holes in the walls, no slugs found in vacuuming the floor. Bledsoe and Pratt even peeled the carpet and padding from the floor, but they found nothing.

Bledsoe later surmised that the second bullet might also have been lying on top of the carpet in the living room and someone—perhaps a police officer or a paramedic—had unknowingly carried it away in the tread of a heavy winter boot. Another possibility was that the front door was open when the bullet was fired and the bullet traveled outside the trailer. Either scenario would make it highly improbable that the bullet would ever be located.

But while the bullets so far had produced nothing extraordinary, the Kentucky State Medical Examiner's Office had other information that was much more helpful to police. While it shed little light on who did the killing, it shed a lot of light on how the killings were carried out. It also gave police some insight into the mind of the killer.

Blister Cook had been a relatively healthy man of forty-one. He had been shot one time. The bullet had entered a couple of inches behind and slightly above his left ear, in the area known medically as the left posterior supra-auricular parietal region. It had been fired from behind and slightly to the left, and had come from extremely close range, probably direct contact. The evidence was a pattern of gunpowder and soot particles imbedded in the skin immediately around the entrance wound.

T.J. Cook had been shot once in the upper chest

from an undetermined range. The other bullet hole, an inch lower than the first, was a contact wound, again characterized by the soot and other particulate material around the wound.

To police, this built a picture of the murder and of the murderer. The killer had been standing behind the couch where his first victim was seated. That told police that the killer was someone known to the victims—someone Blister Cook would not have considered to be a threat. Cook was a careful man, and from everything police could learn, he would never have let someone behind him unless it was someone he knew and, to some extent, trusted. The killer must have kept the gun hidden until he was ready to fire, then he drew it from a concealed holster, a pocket or the waistband of his pants, and fired a single shot into Blister Cook's head. After that first shot, he turned the gun on the four-year-old child on the other side of the coffee table and fired again.

According to the medical examiner, Blister Cook died within minutes of being shot. The autopsy report for T.J. Cook does not specify how long he lived, but results of the examination make it clear that his death was not instantaneous. From the evidence uncovered by the medical examiner, police believe the killer saw that T.J. was still alive after the first shot. He walked around the couch, placed the muzzle of his gun against the chest of the thirty-two-pound youngster, and pulled the trigger again.

When the child still didn't die immediately, police say, the killer dragged T.J. into the bedroom and placed him on the floor beside the door, where he would not have to look at him and listen to him as he robbed the trailer.

Police were dealing with someone who had no feeling at all for what he had done. If he would do this to a child, he was likely to kill again. They had to find him, and find him soon. They had to find him before he ran out of money and drugs, and went looking for another victim. The last thing police needed was another murder to panic an already edgy community.

After three exhausting days and nights, Bledsoe fell into bed at 3:00 A.M. on February 20. He thought about the case before he went to sleep, he dreamed about it when he was asleep, and he was awakened at 7:00 A.M. with news about it.

The Letcher County Sheriff's Department was calling to tell him that Donnie Baker had heard police were looking for him and had turned himself in at the sheriff's department. He wanted to talk.

Bledsoe traveled back across Pine Mountain to the courthouse in Whitesburg, where he picked up Baker and interviewed him about what had happened on February 17. He quickly came to believe that Baker was not the monster that had killed Blister and T.J. Cook. But Bledsoe believed he had seen the killer and he could lead them to him.

Unable and unwilling to take anyone's testimony at face value, Bledsoe loaded Baker into the front seat of his "S.P." and drove to the home of Paul Williams Jr., whom Baker had named as a witness to confirm his account.

Williams and Baker told the same story, and it was a believable story. Police finally had a solid suspect.

Chapter 5

It had been three days since Blister and T.J. Cook had been shot, and it had not been an easy three days. Nearly everyone in the county was speculating about who the killer was. Surely, it was someone who knew the victims. Surely, it wasn't a random killing. Random killings were unusual in Kentucky, and they were almost unheard of in eastern Kentucky. Most of the killings were among family members or friends, and as Bledsoe had observed, these usually involved alcohol or property disputes.

Everyone who had had any contact with T.J. knew his gift for finding out about people and remembering what he learned. He would have known the killer. He would have been able to identify the man who had shot his daddy. If the killer knew these things, then he was someone local—someone who was still nearby.

Even if the murders weren't random, the shooting of a child still had a chilling effect on the community. If the killer could go into one person's home and do this, he could get into someone else's home and do the same thing again. Doors that had been left unlocked at night were suddenly bolted in broad daylight. Guns were loaded. Parents kept their children home from school.

On February 18, the day after the murders, attendance at West Whitesburg Elementary School was 91 percent, down 2 percent from the Friday before. Attendance continued to fall for the next two weeks, until finally 11 percent of the children were not attending classes.

Many in the community feared their homes could be next, but police said that unlike burglaries, home invasions were rare occurrences and most people had nothing to fear. Police said, in most cases, the victims of home invasions were either criminals themselves or elderly people who couldn't defend themselves. Rarely do people pick occupied homes to rob at random. While a nice house, an expensive car, or other trappings of luxury might attract thieves, most of those thieves would pass up occupied homes.

Still, the brazenness of the Cook murders was frightening. They happened in broad daylight in a busy part of town and relatively nice community. Blister Cook might have lived in a trailer, but so did a lot of other people in Letcher County, where there is little flat land and it is easy to level a small lot for a mobile home on the side of a mountain. The murderer had picked a home that seemingly could have belonged to anyone. In a tight-knit community like Whitesburg, it was easy to imagine the same thing happening to a friend, to a neighbor, or to oneself.

The community was outraged and to police, the anger was palpable. Rumors were circulating about who had done the killings and what could have been done to prevent them. Tips, mostly useless ones, were phoned into the 911 center. Death threats aimed at anyone who might be associated with the killer, or anyone who might prevent the killer from being dealt with properly, were being lobbed around

freely in public places, including "Speak Your Piece,"
the anonymous reader comment section in *The
Mountain Eagle* newspaper.

Detectives and patrolmen alike were under pressure to find the murderer, and their break finally
came when Chuck Bledsoe's ringing telephone
jarred him awake at 7:00 A.M. on February 20.

The Letcher County Sheriff's Department was in
the front corner of the modern, three-story courthouse on Main Street in Whitesburg, just behind the
wall that bore the names of scores of Letcher County
men killed in the twentieth century's four major wars.

The fourth courthouse in the history of the 160-
year-old county, the blocky stucco building still occupied the same space as the last two courthouses
before it. Each one became progressively larger until
the latest, a complete remodel of the building that
was erected in 1964 during Lyndon Johnson's War
on Poverty, took up the entirety of what was once the
town square.

Bledsoe parked his shiny police model Crown Victoria among the line of mismatched sheriff's vehicles, went through a side door and up a half flight of
stairs to the first floor.

Though the remodel had been completed only
two years before, and it was officially a smoke-free
building, the new paint and Pine-Sol could not over-
ride the smell of stale cigarettes from the sheriff's
office.

Donnie Baker was sitting inside the office. Since
he was not under arrest, he was not handcuffed and
had not been read his rights. Bledsoe took neither
action, instead asking him if he would mind accom-
panying him to the commonwealth's attorney's
office, three blocks away on East Main.

Baker agreed and rode to the office in the passenger
seat of Bledsoe's car.

There could not be a greater contrast between the county courthouse and Whitesburg City Hall, which also housed the 47th District Commonwealth's Attorney's Office.

While the courthouse was sleek and modern, with a fiberglass stucco exterior and brick trim, the city hall was solid red-orange brick, fired on site in 1914, and laid in decorative arches over the windows. Sandstone cut by the Italian stone masons who built the railroad bridges and tunnels highlighted the brick and massive blocks of the ashlar stone made up the foundations.

The building was built for a grocery wholesale company and the commonwealth's attorney's office occupied the front quarter of the ground floor in the 1921 warehouse addition.

Bledsoe let himself in through the police entrance that led to a hallway between the commonwealth's attorney's office and the Whitesburg Police Station, then ushered Baker in the back door of the prosecutor's office to a conference room. Seated at the long table surrounded by shelves of law books, Baker began to tell his story.

He was reluctant to talk about why he went to Blister's at first, but Bledsoe assured him that he was not interested in marijuana, and had no plans to arrest Baker for admitting to smoking marijuana. He was interested in murder, and he wanted to know what Baker knew.

Slowly the events of February 17 began to take shape and Bledsoe came to believe that Baker was not the shooter. Still, he had to be sure.

Would Baker sign a sworn statement? Yes, he would. Would he go to his friend's house and show the detective where it was? Again the answer was yes. Bledsoe wrote out the statement Baker had given him in a notebook and handed it over. When Baker had signed, Bledsoe again asked him to take a ride.

The two got back into the unmarked cruiser and drove to the Kodak community in Perry County, where the man who had been with Baker, Paul Williams Jr., lived. He told basically the same story as Baker, only from a different point of view.

According to the two signed statements given to the state police, Baker had picked up his friend Williams about 12:30 or 1:00 P.M. on February 17, and the two had driven to Whitesburg in Baker's Ford pickup truck. Baker parked in front of Blister Cook's trailer and went inside while Williams waited outside in the truck. The admission meshed with what police had already been told about a blue Ford pickup sitting in the driveway.

When Baker walked in, he kicked his shoes off at the door and took a seat on the couch next to Blister. T.J. was playing on the floor in front of the coffee table. Baker and Blister talked for a few minutes. Blister was planning to take a retraining class so he could get his mining certification renewed and he could go back to work. He had been a miner before and the pay was the best he could expect anywhere.

Coal was king all over eastern Kentucky, but since the coming of the railroad in 1912, coal has been the *only* industry in Letcher County. Everything is dependent on the mines—the stores, the restaurants, even the schools. Tax money from coal paves and gravels the roads, and the paychecks of the miners fuel the local economy. In the boom and bust cycles of the coal industry, everyone suffers together when coal prices drop and the mines close.

The jobs underground are dangerous, dirty, and backbreaking, but they pay more than anything else available for someone without a law degree, a medical license, or a nurse's certificate. For someone willing to work long hours in an environment where they often can't stand up straight for an entire ten-hour shift, even a grade-school dropout can earn more money than a college professor. Never mind the fact that they end their lives prematurely, unable to breathe because of the accumulated coal dust in their lungs. Miners universally have an "it won't happen to me" attitude, without which they could not venture under thousands of tons of rock every day. For most people, money—not safety—is the only issue.

People who don't work in the mines live on sub-standard pay and substandard benefits. Retail stores mostly pay minimum wage. The fast-food places often pay less, a practice allowed in Kentucky be-cause restaurant workers are expected to make up the difference in tips. Even more recent industries brought in by zealous economic developers in an at-tempt to diversify the economy pay as little as possi-ble, knowing that some people will work for pennies just to have a job that doesn't require crawling all day long in the dark.

A third of the population lives on SSI, often known locally as "crazy checks," welfare, or Social Security disability payments. Often fraudulently obtained, the benefits are still an honest living for many unable to stand either the physical or mental stresses of the mines. In an area where coal mining is the primary industry, disability payments are a big deal.

As Blister and Donnie Baker discussed mining, the phone rang, interrupting their conversation, and Blister talked to the caller for a few minutes while Baker waited. Again the information matched what police had already been told.

Another friend of Blister's, James "Porky" York, had already told police he was talking to Blister on the phone about the time the murders occurred. York remembered the day because of the murders, but also because it was the day of a big NASCAR race and he and Blister were planning to watch it together. York told police he heard his friend ask someone named Donnie to get a soft drink out of the refrigerator for T.J. So far, Baker's story matched what police already knew.

Paul Williams told police that Baker was still inside and he had been waiting in the truck about five minutes when a man walked around the driver's side and went into the trailer. Williams didn't know him, but said he had wavy brown hair sticking out from under a baseball cap.

Baker noted the man when he came inside, because he did know him, at least in passing. They had gone to elementary school together, but Baker couldn't quite place him. He was a stocky man about six feet tall with a big belly. He was wearing blue jeans and a T-shirt, with a baseball cap covering most of his curly brown hair.

The man just hung around the stereo and he gazed out the window while Blister talked on the phone. Baker, sitting on the couch beside Blister, was a little curious about why the newcomer was acting so strange. He kept his face turned away, as though purposefully hiding it from Baker's view. Blister hung up the phone and handed Baker two small packages of marijuana. As Baker left the trailer, he took another glance at the man who had come in after him, but again the man turned his head as Baker left, leaving only a fleeting impression of his profile. It was a profile he knew, but Baker thought the man obviously didn't want to be recognized, so he didn't force a conversation.

Baker gave the pot to Williams, who hid it inside a cigarette pack for safekeeping before they left the driveway. Both Baker and Williams agreed that there was no other car in sight outside. Baker said he discounted the oddities of the man inside as the normal strangeness seen around the home of a pot dealer.

A lot of people were nervous about buying drugs, even such a benign and widely used drug as marijuana. It could have been someone with some sort of standing in the community—someone who, for whatever personal reason, didn't want anyone, even other customers, to know he was buying pot. Maybe he was a regular in one of the scores of churches and didn't want other members of the congregation to think bad of him. Maybe his wife disapproved of his drug use and he didn't want someone to inadvertently mention it to her. Baker didn't know why the man didn't want to be recognized and it really wasn't any of his business.

As for the fact that there was no vehicle, maybe the guy saw Baker's truck and didn't want to block him in. Maybe he didn't want anyone passing by on the highway or picking up lunch at Wendy's to see the vehicle in front of Blister Cook's house. Whatever the reason for the man's strange behavior, Baker attached no sinister significance to it.

Baker turned the truck and left Blister Cook's trailer, but neither he nor Williams ever saw a vehicle that they thought the man they had seen would be in. That didn't seem unusual to Baker, since the man he saw regularly walked around Whitesburg. Maybe he didn't even own a car.

Again the information Baker had given them made sense to police officers. The two women at the church had seen a man run off the hill from the Cook trailer. Now it was clear that he had run away because he didn't have a vehicle—at least not with him when the murders were committed.

Finally police had a solid description of the man who killed Timothy and T.J. Cook. He was about six feet tall, stocky, with a big belly, and curly brown hair. He was wearing a baseball cap and a T-shirt when Baker saw him; a baseball cap and a blue-and-tan shirt when the women saw him. Now if police could only attach a name and address to the description, they could at least pick him up for questioning. If he thought police had enough evidence to arrest him, he might confess.

Baker was sure he knew the man, but he just couldn't think of a name. It was on the tip of his tongue. He knew this guy. He had a brother and Baker knew him, too. He had gone to high school with him, he thought.

Boggs. That was it, Boggs. But what was his first name?

Again Baker couldn't think of it. By this time, Bledsoe had a good idea of who it was, but he didn't want to poison the well by giving Baker a name. Edison Banks, the commonwealth's attorney, had a good idea, too. For anyone in law enforcement in Letcher County, a violent crime, a man named Boggs, and the description Baker had given brought one person to mind.

Baker kept telling them it was a funny name, Banks said. "G-something" or "Ji." Finally a name came to him without prompting: "Ji-rome."

Jerome? Banks asked.

Jerome, Baker finally said. Jerome Boggs.

The name clicked in Bledsoe's head, and it was the name he had been thinking of since he first heard the name Boggs.

Banks sent for yearbooks from Cowan Elementary School, a few miles outside town, and from Whitesburg High School on the hill right behind city hall, and set up a "six-pack" photo lineup for Baker, with the photos visible, but the names hidden.

"He picked 'Ji-rome' out of the lineup," Banks said.

Banks and Bledsoe knew Jerome Boggs, as did

most of the police and officers of the court in the area. If they hadn't arrested him or prosecuted him personally, they well knew what he had done.

Burglary. Robbery. Assault. Almost murder.

But was he capable of placing the muzzle of a gun against a four-year-old child and pulling the trigger?

Yes, Bledsoe thought. *Yes, he was.*

Chapter 6

Jerome Boggs had been a small-time crook for years. A criminal-records check showed that he had been charged with dozens of counts ranging from traffic offenses to felonies in three Kentucky counties over the nine years preceding the murders. Many of those had been either dismissed outright, or the sentences had been suspended when he pleaded guilty to other charges.

The earliest, in 1993, were nonviolent crimes, but Jerome had shown a much higher aptitude for crime than for school. He dropped out of school after the seventh grade, but he graduated from one level of crime to another, starting with traffic violations and misdemeanors and ending with violent felonies.

He was charged in 1993 with two misdemeanors and two traffic offenses, both dismissed. He had also pleaded guilty to two counts of third-degree burglary, and felony theft for stealing from the home, car, and outbuilding of his aunt and uncle.

For his guilty plea, Boggs got a three-year suspended sentence on the condition that he obtain a high-school equivalency certificate and attend Narcotics Anonymous twice a month.

From 1994 to 1996, he was charged with numerous traffic citations, again all dismissed. The only charges during those years that brought any punishments were charges of public intoxication (controlled substances) and possession of marijuana. Both charges were brought in neighboring Perry County and resulted in total fines of $100, plus court costs.

The next year, he was back in court in Letcher County on a misdemeanor theft charge. Once again, he paid $62 court costs and had his ten-day jail sentence suspended on the condition that he stay out of trouble for a year.

Police arrested him less than two weeks later in Harlan County for driving under the influence. But traffic tickets that police gave him in Letcher County a week later were dismissed when he pleaded guilty to a first offense of driving under the influence in that county and paid a fine of $200, plus costs.

Boggs continued to play games with the courts and the police, appearing here, failing to appear there, and getting off with minor fines for multiple offenses.

His Harlan County charge of first offense DUI came to trial two months after he pleaded guilty to the same charge in Letcher County. He pleaded guilty to a first offense again. And again paid a $200 fine, plus court costs, his guilty plea in Letcher County apparently having had no effect on his sentence in Harlan County.

In the meantime, he had already been charged twice more with driving on a license that had been suspended for DUI. Harlan County charged him with failure to appear at a hearing to answer one of those charges, but records were not clear about whether he was ever punished for that offense.

Letcher County gave him five days in jail and required him to pay $57 in court costs.

Charges continued to pile up. Fraudulent use of a credit card was added to his rap sheet in Perry County and Harlan County, and criminal possession of a forged instrument was added in Letcher County. The credit card charges all tied into the theft of a purse belonging to the music director at First Baptist Church of Whitesburg.

The church, probably the largest in Letcher County, was located in the middle of a residential neighborhood on Madison Avenue. The purse was stolen right out of the church while the music director was inside practicing with the choir. Boggs was never charged with stealing it, but he was charged with using the credit cards that were inside.

Despite the seriousness of the new charges, none of them was causing Jerome Boggs a real problem. His luck couldn't last forever.

Figuratively speaking, Jerome Boggs was getting away with murder and his crimes were getting bolder and bolder. He started off stealing from relatives and committing relatively minor traffic offenses. He then graduated to stealing from total strangers and committing drug crimes. He was playing the system and building confidence as he continued to commit crime after crime without paying any serious consequences.

About 11:45 A.M., on October 6, 1997, Whitesburg police chief Paul Miles, Patrolman Sean Blair, and Mayor Nathan Baker, himself a former police chief and director of public safety, were eating lunch at a Long John Silver's seafood restaurant in West Whitesburg when dispatch paged the officers to the Paschal Fields Service Station on Bentley Avenue.

Fields, who was eighty-eight years old, had owned and operated the little white block service station on the corner of Bentley Avenue and Church Street since 1941, and had lived in the white clapboard house next door the whole time. By 1997, he had been pumping gas either for himself or for someone else for seventy years.

Fields was a short man, far less than six feet tall, small-framed and frail. When police arrived at the station, Fields had gone home. He was at the kitchen table, bleeding profusely from a wound on his scalp. Passersby had seen him standing in front of the gas station with a wound to his head and they helped him next door to his house, where they could try to stop the bleeding and call police.

Fields was conscious and able to talk to police. What he didn't tell them then, he would fill in later. Fields had been working in his station that morning when a young man had driven up in front of the doors and asked him to check the oil in his car. Fields obliged and told him the oil level was fine. The man then asked for change for a $1 bill and followed Fields inside the service station to get it.

When Fields opened the old-fashioned cash register, the man grabbed a hammer that Fields had been using around the station and hit him on the head with it.

Police said Fields was struck at least three times— once on the side of the head and twice on the back of the head—probably with the wooden handle of the hammer rather than the steel hammer head. The man then grabbed $180 in cash out of the register drawer and ran. He drove away in a dark maroon sedan.

Police did not know it at the time, but the man who had wielded the claw hammer was Jerome Boggs.

Police took Fields to the hospital, but he refused to stay the night, worried that someone would break into his house or gas station if he was gone. Doctors stitched him up and sent him home. Though Fields stayed home, he never fully recovered from the attack. His gas station closed when he was robbed, and it never reopened. He moved to the nursing home at the other end of town not long after that. Fields died six days after police arrested Boggs for the murder of Timothy and T.J. Cook.

All during the time that police were investigating the Fields robbery, they were also keeping pressure on Jerome Boggs. Charges continued to pile up, but despite the arrests and the credit card charges against Boggs, Blair said, authorities could not seem to keep him in jail.

"We'd go arrest him on one warrant and he'd be right back home in ten minutes," Blair said.

Blair, now a bearded, burly sergeant with the Whitesburg Police Department, who is attached to a regional drug-enforcement task force, blamed the court system for the Cook murders, citing the litany of dismissed charges against Boggs. He said he believed someone was pulling strings to keep Boggs out of trouble, but said he had no idea who was involved or why.

"I hope whoever pulled the strings and got him out has to live with that every night, knowing if they had done the right thing, maybe he wouldn't have killed that little boy," he said.

Blair said it took months to take the Paschal Fields case before the grand jury, but when it finally got there, he had testified less than five minutes when a grand juror interrupted him.

"He said 'I know that bastard. He broke into my uncle's house,'" Blair said.

Police caught up with Boggs for the Fields robbery in July 1998, the same month that he was arrested again in Harlan County for possession of cocaine.

The Letcher County grand jury indicted Boggs on charges of first-degree robbery—which carried up to twenty years in prison—second-degree criminal possession of a forged instrument, being a persistent felony offender in the second degree (PFO second), PFO first, and fraudulent use of a credit card.

The PFO charges should have enhanced Boggs's sentence, forcing him to spend more time in prison. Instead, he pleaded guilty in November 1998 to a reduced charge of theft by unlawfully taking over $300 and fraudulent use of a credit card. He was sentenced to four years in the state penitentiary. He subsequently pleaded guilty to the cocaine possession charge in Harlan County and that sentence was added to be served concurrent to the theft and fraud charges in Letcher County. All that kept him from facing the more serious charges was that Paschal Fields didn't want to testify at the trial.

Up until then, Jerome Boggs was like a greased pig in a pen full of little boys. No matter how many times police grabbed him, he would always slide away. Even many of the charges related to beating Paschal Fields wouldn't stick to him. The four-year prison sentence in that case was a fifth of what police wanted him to serve, and with good behavior and time already served taken into account, he spent even less time behind bars.

He served out his sentence in its entirety on June 29, 2001, two years and seven months after pleading guilty. He served out the Harlan County drug sentence at the same time. When he left the prison, he went straight back to Letcher County.

The community was outraged, but there was little that could be done legally. There was a misconception that the governor had freed Boggs early, but in fact there was just no more time that he could legally be forced to serve. As far as the state was concerned, Jerome had fully served his debt to society.

Boggs had come up for parole once, but his application was denied, largely because of letters written to the parole board by Mayor Baker, Chief Miles, and then Commonwealth's Attorney William Lewis Collins. Instead, he had served out all of the time for which he was eligible under his sentence. Ironically, he would have been much more closely watched if he had received parole when he asked for it. Since there is no provision in Kentucky law for supervision of former prisoners who have served out their sentences, Boggs was under no obligation to report to a Probation and Parole officer. He did not have to stay in the county or state. He did not have to register his address with anyone. His civil rights had been restored by the governor, allowing him to vote if he wanted or even run for public office if he wanted.

Jerome Boggs was a free man.

Some homeowners near Jerome's home on Little Cowan took to keeping a gun handy, and one reported picking up a pistol and sending Boggs packing when he stopped to ask for gas for a four-wheeler.

Even though police and neighbors had other suspicions, as far as the courts were concerned, Jerome Boggs was rehabilitated and keeping his nose clean. There was nothing they could do to keep tabs on him without risking a lawsuit.

But now police had a reason. He was a suspect in two murders and police could hound him all they wanted. Eight months after returning to a decidedly unwelcoming community, Jerome Boggs was a hunted man. This time police were determined that he would not slip out of their grasp.

They began asking questions and looking in the obvious places for Boggs immediately. That's when they learned that he was no longer an isolated loner.

He had married only a couple of months earlier and had been living with his new wife, April, in his parents' home.

He wasn't working at all and his wife was doing odd jobs, mostly for Jerome's parents and brother. Boggs had a seventh-grade education and a prison record. No one was going to hire him. His wife was more hirable, but she had only a high-school diploma and little work experience. To make matters worse, she was married to Jerome and that stigma alone was a huge weight to bear. They had no money, no jobs, no prospects for anything better.

But suddenly Jerome's luck had changed and he had come into some money, and that was a tantalizing fact to police. After Boggs's name surfaced in connection with the murders, police began speculating on other robberies that had been occurring around Letcher County. An auto parts store in Whitesburg had been robbed one morning; a gas station owner another. A convenience store was robbed on the main highway, and another gas station had been hit at Jenkins. Police had no evidence to link Boggs to any of them except their suspicions, but there were some curious parallels.

One crime in particular stood out. Convenience store owner and oil distributor David Larkey had picked up the weekend receipts from one of his Chevron Jiffy Marts about six o'clock on the morning of Monday, January 14. He was leaving the store with a brown paper bag full of cash when a man wearing a ski mask and brandishing a revolver forced him into his own pickup truck. The man shoved Larkey into the passenger seat and took the wheel, telling the gas station owner they were going for a drive up Pine Mountain.

More than one homicide victim had been found on that mountain over the years, and police speculated that the robber might have intended to kill Larkey and dump him along a remote section of Little Shepherd Trail, a fire road that ran along the ridgetop. There were several old limestone quarries dotting the mountainside as well, and they too could be a prime location to dispose of a body. Larkey knew of the dangers as well and didn't want to find out what the robber had planned for him. He jumped out of the moving truck as it started to pull out of the parking lot, receiving a cut on his head, but no major injuries.

Police found the pickup truck abandoned, the motor still running, on a back road in Whitesburg near the Letcher Manor nursing home, about a mile from the convenience store. Neighbors reported seeing a car parked nearby there earlier that morning.

At least two people were involved in the crime because of the distance from the station where the robber's getaway car was parked. Someone would have had to drop the robber off at the station, and then wait to pick him up after he dumped the truck and Larkey. There were no weapons, no fingerprints, and no other evidence to connect Boggs to the crime, but it was an intriguing coincidence. It made it more intriguing that there had been another robbery in Jenkins, believed to be by the same person.

In the Jenkins robbery, the robber had pointed a revolver at the gas station clerk and got away in a small car with a "bushy-headed woman" driving. Again there was nothing tying Boggs to the crime other than the location and the fact that the target was a gas station, but police again found the similarities very peculiar.

Two people were involved in all of the crimes— twice police deduced that someone had dropped off the perpetrator and the third time a witness had seen a getaway driver. All of the crimes were committed with a handgun. The murders were the priority, but if other crimes could be cleared up at the same time, all the better. Police decided they would look into the other crimes more, once they had arrested Jerome Boggs.

Jerome and April Boggs had rented a low-income apartment in a housing project in Jenkins and were in the process of moving into it.

If police had anything to say about it, they would never get to live there.

Chapter 7

Police had no proof that Jerome Boggs had killed Blister and T.J. Cook. All they had was the word of two men who had equal opportunity to commit the crime. But while the other two had the opportunity, they didn't have the background. Baker had a police record and would later be charged in a homicide himself, but that death was caused by drunk driving. It wasn't a cold-blooded murder. Also, neither Williams nor Baker suddenly appeared to be flush with money.

Jerome Boggs, however, was a different story. He had the means, the opportunity, and the motive. He had a history of violence, and he had money in his pocket when he had no visible means of support.

Jerome was more than just a person of interest, he was a full-fledged suspect. The escalating nature of his crimes indicated to Bledsoe that he might well be capable of committing murder. The fact that his last victim was an eighty-eight-year-old man who was too old and frail to protect himself was another indicator. Paschal Fields could easily have been killed by the hammer blows to the head.

Bledsoe and the other investigators knew they were getting close to the killer, but they could not have known how close.

The KSP was still the lead agency in the case, with Whitesburg City Police and the Letcher County Sheriff's Department providing support wherever and whenever they could. By February 21, the KSP Post had formed a mini task force to work on the case, and that morning the group met to begin dividing up duties for the day. The top priority was to find Jerome Boggs, question him, and hopefully sniff out enough to decide whether he was really the murderer.

Detective Ken Duff, Detective John Pratt, and Detective Lieutenant Vic Brown took on the preliminary search for Jerome. A starting point wasn't difficult. He had been in trouble for years and his address of record was his parents' house at Grizzly Hollow, on Little Cowan.

A hollow, pronounced locally "holler," is a narrow, steep-sided valley that follows a small stream out from between the mountains. The road follows the creek along the valley floor, and homes sit in "the bottoms," the precious slivers of level ground in the floodplain, or perch on the sides of the hills, their porches jutting out over the slopes below. Little Cowan is a medium-size hollow, just outside Whitesburg. It follows Little Cowan Creek from its headwaters at the junction of Pine Mountain and Cowan Mountain to its mouth at Big Cowan Creek. It is rare because both ends of the hollow met with a main highway.

Most hollows dead-end when they become too narrow or too steep for a car to travel, or they meet a mine road that leads to one of the many strip mines that have leveled the mountaintops and connected formerly isolated communities to one another.

Little Cowan was home to only a few extended families, and a few recent arrivals drawn by the quiet, the cool shade of the mountains, and the inexpen-

sive land. In addition to Jerome Boggs's family, the
hollow was home to prosecutor Edison Banks and his
family.

Lieutenant Brown and Detective Bledsoe took the
address for Jerome Boggs and drove up Little Cowan
to the home of Lee and Mary Lou Boggs, but they
were too late to find Jerome. His father told police
that Jerome and his new wife, April, had just rented
an apartment at Mountain Breeze Apartments in
Jenkins, and had left to take a load of their belongings there.

Out of luck for the moment, Brown and Bledsoe
left the Boggs home and met with Duff, Pratt, and
Sergeant Claude Little at the commonwealth's attorney's office in Whitesburg. Again duties were divided up. Jerome Boggs was somewhere on the road
between Little Cowan and Jenkins, or he was at the
new apartment in the far end of Jenkins. Little and
Trooper Derek Hall, a Jenkins native, left for Hall's
hometown to check the apartment complex and
start asking questions, while Brown and Bledsoe
went back to Little Cowan and staked out the road
leading up the hollow from Highway 931 at Cowan.
Pratt and Duff parked along U.S. 119 on Pine Mountain to watch the road down the creek.

At 2:30 P.M., eight minutes shy of four days from the
time the murders were reported, Little radioed Bledsoe. They had found Jerome and April Boggs at the
apartment complex, and Hall had arrested Jerome
for driving on a suspended license.

It was a nothing charge—the kind of thing
Jerome Boggs had been slipping out of for years.
But this time police weren't going to make him
available to the court system just yet. They wanted
time to question him—time to gather evidence
for a charge of murder. A traffic charge was pretty
thin—especially since he was not on parole or

probation—but it would allow them to hold him
for a little while at least.

   Jenkins is the largest city by population in Letcher
County, with one thousand more people than the
county seat of Whitesburg. But Jenkins is largely a
bedroom community with few businesses. Its main
promise now is a reclaimed strip mine at the edge of
town that is being offered as an industrial site.
   Once a model city built for Consolidation Coal
Company in 1912, Jenkins had lost its former
grandeur. The historic old buildings along Old U.S.
23, the main street, had mostly been torn down, replaced by drab boxes and a single fast-food restaurant.
The county library district was in the process of building a new branch on the street, and a nonprofit corporation remodeled the old railroad depot as a coal and
railroad museum.
   Outside downtown, there was even less activity.
Streets and neighborhoods named for obscure
mining company officials, financiers, or mine portals
dot the hills around the center of town. Some of the
old "camp houses" built to house miners and their
families before 1920 had been remodeled, but many
had fallen into disrepair, their porch roofs hanging at
crazy angles from the rest of the structure. The city
had been pursuing the demolition of some of the
worst properties for twenty years, but pockets of decay
still existed all over the town.
   Nestled into a couple of tiny coves high up on the
hill, Mountain Breeze Apartments looks like a
breath of new life. Built in the early 1980s as a low-
income housing development on Ben's Branch
Road, it is in the Burdine section of Jenkins. To get
there, visitors have to drive past wildly contrasting
sections of the city before turning into Number 2

Bottom, a ninety-year-old residential area named for Consolidation Coal's Number 2 mine.

Mountain Breeze lies up the hollow beyond the well-maintained row houses. The apartments sit in the middle of a loop of asphalt, surrounded by modest mobile homes. The apartment complex itself is a planned community with underground utility lines, playgrounds, and laundry facilities.

But while the apartments are neat and clean on the exterior, the appearance belies the reputation. It was intended as a development to allow poor families and the disabled a measure of dignity, but it is also a hub of drug activity and other crime in Jenkins.

In 1986, the Jenkins Police Department (JPD), under the leadership of newly appointed chief Bill Tackett, began pressing public intoxication arrests and were hauling away six carloads of prisoners at a time, usually in private cars because the city couldn't afford enough police cruisers. After a month, the number of cars required dropped to two, but the area continued to be plagued with dealers, users, and petty criminals who tended to move in and out of apartments rented by spouses or lovers with more respectable court records.

Given the sixteen-year history of strict enforcement in the neighborhood, the two state police cruisers and two JPD cars were not unusual, but were still conspicuous at the two-story brick apartment buildings. For other residents, it was not a question *if* someone was being arrested, but *why*.

When Bledsoe and Pratt arrived, Jerome Boggs was already handcuffed in the back of Hall's gray Ford, but April Boggs had not been arrested. She waited outside apartment 327 with her mother, a pickup truck full of furniture and other belongings, and a white compact car belonging to her in-laws.

April Boggs was twenty years old, much younger

than Jerome Boggs, but like Jerome, she was overweight and at the moment she appeared as though she
hadn't had a shower in several days.

Since the apartment was rented in her name, Bledsoe asked for permission to search it without a warrant. She refused, and since there was not enough
evidence to get a warrant yet, the search would have
to wait.

Bledsoe didn't arrest her, but instead asked if she
would mind going to the Whitesburg Police Department to answer a few questions. April Boggs agreed
to do that and got in the back of Chief Tackett's
cruiser.

Tackett, a retired soldier who wore a neatly clipped
gray mustache and a carefully creased police baseball
cap, with his black uniform, put April in the back of
his unmarked white Crown Victoria and started for
Whitesburg. He had barely left the parking lot and
turned left down the mountain when Whitesburg
chief Paul Miles contacted Bledsoe.

Miles had been on the street in Whitesburg with
Mayor Baker when someone had stopped them and
informed them that Jerome and April Boggs had
spent the night of the murders in the Super 8 Motel,
just across the river from the crime scene.

Detectives Duff and Pratt immediately went to the
motel and spoke with Lisa Reed, the desk clerk, who
confirmed that the couple had stayed there on the
night of February 17. Jerome had come into the
motel at 3:00 P.M., twenty-two minutes after the 911
call to police reporting the murders.

They were not a hard couple to remember. Jerome
and April had come in together, and when Reed requested identification, April gave her a driver's license. She was under twenty-one, so Reed said she
couldn't rent the room to her and asked Jerome if he

had a license. He told her he did not because he had just gotten out of prison.

April, apparently nervous, contradicted him, telling Reed that he had been out for quite a while and they had stayed there before. The clerk then got Jerome's Social Security number and looked up his past stay.

The clerk told police that Boggs had stayed there before in a room at the front of the motel.

This time he had specifically asked for a room overlooking the river and asked if room 101, which featured a Jacuzzi tub in the bedroom, was available. Reed informed him that it was and Jerome Boggs handed over two $50 dollar bills. The room was at the back of the building, on the opposite side from the parking lot. When Pratt and Duff entered the room, they saw what they were now convinced had attracted Jerome Boggs to the room.

The Cook trailer sat just across the river, its front door in plain view of the motel room window.

It seemed almost a cliché—the criminal returning to the scene of the crime. But had it really happened? Had Jerome Boggs watched police investigate the murders he himself had committed?

Reed confirmed that it was even more perverse than that. Boggs had called her to the room complaining that the heat didn't work. When she and the housekeeper arrived to check it, Jerome and April Boggs were sitting on the couch staring out the window and eating pizza, which had been delivered to the room. Police cars sat all over the yard and driveway of Blister Cook's trailer and officers moved in and out of the trailer.

Jerome Boggs asked Reed if she knew what happened. A murder, she replied. Someone killed that man and his baby. Reed recalled that she didn't mention the name. She didn't have to. Jerome

Boggs knew the name immediately, and April Boggs quickly added "and his baby."

Pratt and Duff searched the room, lifting couch cushions and checking the carpets for blood. The search turned up little of known value, but it did garner several items of interest to police. The room had not been rented since Jerome and April had checked out three days earlier and police were able to collect what appeared to be marijuana residue from the carpet near the couch. They also confiscated a telephone book, its plastic cover scribbled with flowery script spelling out Jerome and April Boggs's names, and a cushion cover with a stain that could have been blood. They also took the contents of the trash can.

While Duff and Pratt were visiting the Super 8 Motel, April Boggs was on her way to Whitesburg City Hall, where she would wait for two hours until the detectives could arrive. She was quiet during the ride down U.S. 119 to Whitesburg, and remained quiet at city hall, until police arrived around four-thirty, and read her rights to her.

April Boggs began talking right away, telling Detectives Pratt and Duff that she knew about the murders that had occurred on Sunday because Jerome had told her he had committed them.

While she insisted that she did not know what Jerome had in mind when she dropped him off near Blister Cook's home that Sunday afternoon, she said he readily told her he had killed two people when she picked him up again. She also told police she had seen Jerome throw a leather holster out the car window as the two drove to Virginia to a beer store after she picked him up on a bridge near the scene of the murders. She assumed he had already gotten rid of the gun, because she had never seen him with it, either before or after the killings. When she asked him about it later, he told her he had gotten rid of it before she picked him up.

Bledsoe was collecting evidence in Jenkins, and troopers were about to split into two different teams to check out April's story and look for the evidence she claimed existed.

Police desperately wanted to wrap up the case and put the killer behind bars. With luck, they would soon know whether Jerome would stay in jail for murder or wiggle once again out of a minor traffic charge.

If Jerome Boggs's newlywed wife was telling the truth, police would soon have the evidence they needed to put the career criminal in the death chamber. They still weren't sure whether April deserved to be there as well.

Much of her story would be easy to check out. It was already late afternoon, but if police hurried, they might find some of the evidence she had told them about before it got dark. The area's straight stretch of road where the holster was supposedly thrown was about a mile long, but maybe she could narrow down the area some if officers took her with them. The gun was a bigger problem, given the size of the area where Jerome Boggs could have gotten rid of it, but they had no choice but to look. They would have to find something if they intended to keep him behind bars. What they had so far was much too thin to charge Jerome Boggs with murder. If they took only an uncorroborated story from April Boggs to a judge, the case would be thrown out of court almost as fast as it got there.

But if she was telling the truth, there would be plenty of physical evidence to back up her story. There would be a gun, a holster—maybe even clothing with bloodstains. With that evidence in hand, police would be able to make the charge stick—at least long enough to find more proof. They could put Jerome Boggs in jail and the prosecutor could ask the judge to hold him there without bond or with a bond so high that he would never be able to pay it and walk free. After all, he was a convicted felon with a pending murder charge. At the very least there was a risk that he would flee the state and hide out. More worrisome was the possibility that he would try to eliminate more witnesses or steal money to make an escape. Surely the judge wouldn't let someone like him walk away from jail.

It had taken them four days to find the man they were sure had killed two people. They weren't about to let him back out on the street again.

Chapter 8

February 21 had been a day of big breaks in the Cook murder case. Police had found their number one suspect, his wife had implicated him in the killings, and now there was a chance that the murder weapon was within their reach.

April Boggs claimed she dropped her husband off on February 17 at the old Sugar Shack convenience store on Hazard Road and drove away with strict orders to return in twenty minutes. But she swore she had not known what he intended to do. He had a little money in his pocket, and she assumed that he intended to buy marijuana from Blister.

She didn't go with him, she said, because they had been arguing. She said she had intended to take advantage of the time alone to call an old boyfriend and leave Jerome. Instead, she went back to the Sugar Shack, just as Jerome had ordered her to do, and picked him up where he was waiting on the highway bridge near the store. From there, she had driven to Pound Gap to a convenience store just over the Virginia state line so Jerome could buy beer.

She claimed he had told her he had killed two people and gotten them some money, and she claimed he had thrown a leather pistol holster out the window of the car near Fishpond Lake, a county park about three miles from the state line.

She said he told her a couple of days after the killing that he had thrown the gun away before she picked him up.

Troopers Derek Hall and Ben McCray would put the easy part of April Boggs's story to the test immediately. They would put her in the back of a cruiser and drive her up U.S. 119 to the long straightaway at the entrance to Fishpond Lake. Once there, they would jog her memory about where exactly Jerome had thrown the holster; then they would begin beating the tall grass next to the road.

Sergeant Little would take the harder part of the task—locating the missing murder weapon. Since Jerome had been standing on the bridge when April picked him up, Little reasoned that he might have thrown the .22 pistol into the North Fork of the Kentucky River.

Police were going to have to search the area sooner or later, since Jerome Boggs had not had possession of a gun when he was arrested. April, whose name was on the lease to the apartment, had not given police permission to search there, but now she had given a statement that Jerome had thrown the gun away.

It was almost too much to wish for. Since the river begins only a few miles up the road near Jenkins, it is still a fairly small stream at Whitesburg. It is barely fifty feet wide and no more than hip deep at the deepest point. Searching the muddy bottom of the river was certainly going to be easier than searching the hillside near Blister Cook's home.

Bledsoe had talked the matter over with Danny Webb, his recently retired captain, only the night before while eating dinner at a Whitesburg restaurant.

Searching the hillside below the murder scene would
be a nightmare. That hillside was covered over with
kudzu, the persistent, crawling vine that hides mature
trees, utility poles, and whole abandoned houses
throughout the South. Not only would the dead leaves
conceal a weapon, the clinging vines and the steep
slope would make it next to impossible to walk.
Searching the thicket of clinging vines would be im-
measurably worse than searching the river, even
though it was still the middle of winter and the kudzu
was dormant.

McCray and Hall loaded April into Hall's car and
McCray squeezed his linebacker physique into the
passenger seat. Kentucky State troopers rarely patrol
in pairs, and the cruisers are set up accordingly. The
front seat, floorboard, and dash of a full-size Ford
Crown Victoria cruiser are jammed with radio, radar,
and video gear.

After an uncomfortable fifteen-minute ride, April
pointed out the location where she thought Jerome
had thrown the holster, and the troopers pulled over
onto the shoulder of the highway.

At that mile point, U.S. 119 was a mile-long ribbon
of straight, two-lane asphalt. One side of the highway
was a sheer cliff cut into the side of the mountain.
The other sloped gently down to a six-foot-wide
brook, which was the headwaters of the Kentucky
River. There were no houses in sight, and the only
road on and off the main highway led to the park and
a small cluster of houses well hidden from passing
cars.

Leaving the blue lights on, and April Boggs locked
in the backseat, Hall and McCray began methodi-
cally searching the side of the highway next to the
river.

It didn't take long for the troopers to find what

they were looking for. A brown leather holster lay in the grass just off the shoulder of the highway.

Only a few miles away at Mountain Breeze Apartments, Bledsoe had found someone who would later identify that holster.

Christopher Duff, an eighteen-year-old who hung out with Jerome, was a frequent visitor at the apartment complex and at Jerome and April's home. His mother, Kathy Clark Hall, had lived with Jerome for three months before he was sent to prison.

Under questioning by Bledsoe, Duff said he had been at the Super 8 Motel on Sunday night after the murders. Jerome and April had called him, he said, and asked him to bring them some beer. He had waited until his mother came to get him; then they went to the motel with Duff's fifteen-year-old brother.

Kathy Hall had gone inside with her older son and had made small talk and called the American Legion Club to make sure the bartender would sell her beer. Before she left, Jerome had asked April if she had shown Kathy her ring. She had not, but she readily raised her hand for Hall to examine the tiny diamond and the fourteen-karat-gold band. It had cost $600, Jerome claimed, and April volunteered that they had gotten it in Tennessee the day before. Then, Hall said, Jerome had pulled out a large roll of cash and had given her $50 for beer and gas. She and her younger son had gone to buy it at the American Legion Club at Neon, a city of about nine hundred residents between Whitesburg and Jenkins.

Christopher Duff admitted to staying at the motel and smoking pot. His mother confirmed that he and Jerome were smoking when she left to get the beer. Both said Jerome had shown them two large plastic bags with marijuana in them. Chris claimed it looked and tasted like pot he had purchased from Blister Cook before.

When Hall returned, she said, she watched part of the local news about the killings, and then left with her younger son. Chris stayed and called his girl-friend to pick him up later.

Though Chris confirmed the party atmosphere at Super 8, he had other more important information.

He told police he had been target shooting with Jerome, and Jerome had lent him a .22-caliber pistol to shoot. He described it as "a cowboy-style" pistol that held a lot of bullets. He had carried it in a brown leather holster, also provided by Jerome. Jerome, who had already been convicted of a felony and was ineligible to carry a gun, had shot a .22-caliber rifle with no stock.

Ballistics had shown that Timothy and T.J. Cook were both slain with a .22-caliber gun. The fact that Jerome had been in possession of two such weapons was interesting, though not really much in the way of concrete evidence. Almost everyone had at least one .22 in the house.

But if police could match a .22 to the bullet found at the trailer, Chris Duff might be able to identify it as the one Jerome had lent him. If Chris could do that, Jerome Boggs would be well on his way to prison.

Back in Whitesburg, Sergeant Little had decided he was going to need much more help than he could muster from the mini task force that had been created for the murder investigation.

Little's father had been a Whitesburg City Council member and a member of the Whitesburg Volunteer Fire Department for as long as he could remember. His mother had been appointed to his father's council position when he died, so the sergeant turned to what he knew. He contacted Whitesburg Fire Chief Truman Thompson and asked him to page his volunteer firefighters to go to the river to help with the search.

With the high-profile murder only four days before, a small army of firefighters, police, other city employees, and officials turned out to help search. They had little more than an hour before dark and the temperature was sinking with the sun beyond the tops of the mountains.

The lawn at Blister Cook's trailer sloped off steeply to the riverbank, and the KY 15 highway bridge was no more than 150 yards downstream. It was on that bridge that April Boggs said she had picked her husband up on February 17.

Seven firefighters, three city police officers, and the mayor showed up at the bridge to help search for the gun. Little took one group, including Chief Miles, who had brought two metal detectors from home to search, to the hillside below the murder scene. Another group waded into the thigh-deep water downstream of the bridge, careful not to muddy the already turbid water any further. They spread out across its width and began probing the mud.

Luck was with them again. Jerome Boggs had not realized that the kudzu would be a much more secure hiding place than the river. He also had apparently not realized that the river was so shallow under the bridge.

There were businesses on both sides of the highway and both sides of the bridge. Perhaps he had been unwilling to make the wild motion necessary to hurl the pistol into a less obvious place, or perhaps he had been confident enough in his past history with the courts that he didn't think he would ever go to jail. Whatever the reason, he had merely dropped the gun straight down from the bridge railing. It was lying in mud, readily visible to anyone who looked because of its imitation pearl grips.

Whitesburg Councilman Gary Mullins, a longtime volunteer firefighter, marked the spot and called to Sergeant Little. Miles and Mayor Baker headed to the scene with cameras, while Little waded into the water.

Baker, an avid shooter and gun collector, identified the make and model of the weapon while it was still in the water. When the sergeant pulled the gun from the river, he found Baker's assessment was right. It was a Harrington & Richardson 922, a nine-shot, .22-caliber revolver. Popping open the cylinder, Little found it had been fully loaded. Six shells were still live, though one had apparently been a misfire. Three other rounds had been fired.

A quick check of the model name showed it was one of forty-four models of revolver the ballistics lab had already identified as using the same type of rifling found on the bullet recovered from the crime scene. It also matched the description of a gun belonging to Boggs's father that Christopher Duff had already told Bledsoe he had fired at targets with Jerome Boggs.

Little bagged the gun to be sent to the crime lab. Since it had been in the water for several days, there was little hope of finding fingerprints, but the bullet might be matched to it by ballistics experts.

Billions of .22 long-rifle cartridges must be sold every year, but even if lab technicians could not positively match the bullet, the circumstantial evidence would be strong. The gun was similar to one that a witness had seen in Jerome's possession. It had been found in the spot where April Boggs had told police she picked her husband up a few minutes after the killings. Three of the cartridges had been fired, matching the number of shots fired inside the Cook trailer. The condition of the cartridges also spoke volumes.

A .22 long rifle caliber cartridge is one of only three rimfire cartridges still mass-produced in the United States, and one of only two available in 2002. Most large-caliber cartridges have a round primer, an explosive cap, in the center of the shell opposite the bullet. When the firing pin strikes it, it fires a spark into the smokeless powder inside, causing it to explode and force the bullet down the gun barrel. In rimfire cartridges, like a .22, the primer is built into the hollow rim that holds the cartridge in the firing chamber and prevents the entire cartridge from falling straight out of the barrel. The firing pin strikes the edge, or rim, of the cartridge and causes the spark that ignites the powder.

When the steel firing pin strikes, it leaves a round indentation in the primer of a centerfire cartridge or a nick in the rim of a rimfire cartridge. If there is no indentation or nick, the firing pin did not strike the shell.

With most revolvers, a shooter can hold the hammer with his thumb and lower it gently onto a live shell to prevent it from firing.

The nicks in the rims of the cartridges found in the gun believed to be the murder weapon led police to develop a new theory about the murders—a theory that made the shooting of the child all the more horrific.

Because of the order of the spent cartridges, police believe two rounds had been fired first, one into the father and one into the child. When Sergeant Little opened the cylinder of the revolver, he found two shells side by side that had been fired. But the next round still held a bullet and showed no mark from the firing pin, indicating that the killer had cocked the gun, then lowered the hammer. He had then pulled the trigger again, sending a second bullet into T.J. Cook's chest.

The two bullets that had been fired into T.J. Cook had not been fired on the spur of the moment. The killer had thought about it before delivering the coups de grâce. Then he had pressed the muzzle to the boy's chest and killed him.

With the holster and the gun now in the possession of police, the noose was tightening around Jerome Boggs's neck. More evidence would be needed to take the case to trial, but there was plenty of evidence to charge him with murder.

It was a bittersweet day for police. Not only had they made an arrest, they had found enough evidence to make an indictment almost a foregone conclusion. The statement by Donnie Baker the day before placing Jerome Boggs at the scene of the crime had been only a crack in the dam. The dam had broken on February 21, spilling a flood of evidence and witnesses.

With that evidence in hand, Bledsoe, Pratt, and Duff returned to Whitesburg City Hall. They placed Jerome in a closet-size interrogation room and all three went in with him. Boggs denied that he had committed the murders, but claimed to have purchased marijuana from Blister Cook two days before the murders. Police would have none of it. They took Jerome's shirt and shoes as evidence and sent them away with Pratt to show to the witnesses who had told police they had seen a man run off the hill. Both women agreed the shirt looked like the one the man they had seen was wearing. While the shirt and shoes seemed clean, the only way to know for sure was to have the lab treat them and place them under ultraviolet light. If there was a trace of blood there, it would glow.

Police bagged the items as evidence to send to the crime lab, and charged Jerome Boggs with murder, robbery, and burglary.

If convicted, he could be sentenced to die by lethal injection, the method of execution approved in Kentucky in 1998.

They charged April Boggs with complicity to the same crimes. She would not be eligible for the death penalty, but she could spend the rest of her life in prison.

Late that evening, as the sky started to darken, police perp-walked Jerome and April Boggs out of the police department in front of the television cameras. The jail was only a couple of blocks away, and Jerome Boggs would not see the outside of it again without a police guard.

Sitting in a straight-backed chair inside the booking area of the jail, dressed in a long-sleeved undershirt under a Jägermeister T-shirt, jeans, and socks, his hands cuffed behind him, Jerome Boggs told his tale to a reporter from *The Mountain Eagle*, the local newspaper.

He claimed both he and his wife were completely innocent, though he admitted to staying in the motel the night of the murders. To police, he had said only that he had nothing to do with the murders, and he only hoped that his wife was innocent. He promised to tell them his whole story the next day, after he talked to his father. The next day, Jerome Boggs had "lawyered up," refusing to be questioned without an attorney present.

April, however, was still talking. She and Jerome had stayed at another motel on February 18. This time they had picked the Daniel Boone Motor Inn, in Hazard. Again police got a copy of the receipt, again raising the question of how a couple with no jobs and no income could afford to stay in motels two nights in a row. Not only had they stayed at the motel, they had had a nice dinner at the Applebee's restaurant near the motel, and had watched a movie at a nearby theater.

Police also learned that the engagement ring April was wearing was new and had apparently been purchased shortly after Blister and T.J. Cook were murdered. Police would begin looking into that purchase as soon as possible, but it seemed doubtful that the ring really cost the $600 that Jerome had bragged of to friends in the motel room. It was a small diamond in a ten-karat-gold band. It couldn't possibly have cost more than a couple of hundred dollars.

It seemed that the $1,500 or more in cash that police believed had been stolen from Blister Cook after he was shot was spent mostly on liquor, drugs, and motel rooms. Police had receipts for two motel rooms and witness statements that Jerome had bought bootleg liquor and tried to buy cocaine. When Jerome and April Boggs were arrested four days after the murders, police found $186.40 between them.

The two zippered storage bags of pot that witnesses reported seeing at the motel room the night of the murders were also gone, or nearly gone. Police found only ashes, some scraps of marijuana from the carpets of the apartment and the Whitesburg motel room, and a pack of cigarette rolling papers.

Meanwhile, the community was breathing a sigh of relief that the man who had murdered Blister and T.J. Cook was safely locked away in the Letcher County Jail. But the mood was getting even angrier as information about Jerome and April's movements trickled out into the public.

As if people in the community were not outraged enough just because of the murders, they were even more incensed when they learned that the couple had apparently lived it up on the night of the murders and the night after them.

Court bailiffs began breaking out metal detectors, and police from every department in the county showed up in droves for the hearings. Police officers who had spent days trying to track down a killer, now had to keep him from being killed.

Chapter 9

Normally open and laid-back, the Letcher County Courthouse was a different place on February 22.

The district courtroom, where everyone who was arrested must have their first court appearance, was located behind the first door on the left inside the Main Street entrance of the building, straight across the hall from the Letcher County Sheriff's Department.

District court, which some call "the little court," is where the bulk of court cases are tried in Kentucky. The state reorganized its court system in 1973, creating the district judge positions and eliminating hundreds of magistrate courts, county courts, and city courts around the state. The district court's jurisdiction includes city ordinance violations, misdemeanors, traffic violations, small-claims suits, probate court, involuntary psychiatric commitments, and juvenile cases. It also handles preliminary hearings on felony cases and arraignments on both misdemeanors and felonies.

In Letcher County, it was a rather informal setting. Judge Jim Wood, a short, plump, bearded man who chain-smoked cigarettes in his chambers behind the courtroom, often entered court with blue jeans protruding from his black robe. Spectators roamed freely in and out of the courtroom, as long as juvenile court was not in session. Cases involving persons under eighteen years old were closed to the public.

In other cases, anyone could walk in, take a seat, and watch the proceedings. Bailiffs rarely gave them a second look.

On February 22, 2002, everyone entered the courtroom as usual and took their seats on the hard wooden pews in the gallery. Cases were heard, one by one, until the docket was cleared of all but the bond hearings of Jerome Boggs and April Boggs.

The district court bailiff was there, but it was circuit court bailiff Bert Slone who stepped to the front of the rail and addressed the crowd. He asked them politely to step back into the hallway so officers could conduct a security check.

What followed was a scene that would be repeated numerous times over the next year, every time a hearing or trial was held in the case.

Bert Slone, whose brother was the deputy who arrived first at the murder scene, herded spectators back into the hallway, then stood in front of the door with a handheld metal detector. Then, keeping up a steady string of good-humored patter to keep people comfortable during the uncomfortable process of being searched, Slone swept each person with the wand, patted down coat pockets, and emptied purses before allowing them back into the courtroom.

When the people returned to their seats, rather than finding the single deputy sheriff that usually served as bailiff, the courtroom was crawling with police. The walls were lined with Whitesburg, Jenkins, and Fleming-Neon city police officers, Letcher County Sheriff's deputies, KSP troopers and detectives, and elected constables. The wooden rail between spectators and the front of the courtroom was lined with newspaper reporters and photographers and a single television camera.

Once the courtroom was full, the door was locked from the inside, preventing any latecomers from getting past police without being searched.

Only then did Judge Wood call the case and ask an officer to retrieve Jerome Boggs from the jail, one floor below the courtroom. Like the circuit courtroom on the second floor, the district courtroom was served by its own elevator that opened directly into a holding cell beside the bench. Boggs was brought up in the elevator, then made to stand with his public defender in front of Judge Wood.

The hearing was short and to the point. Police had charged Boggs with two counts of murder, robbery, burglary, and other serious crimes; Boggs pleaded not guilty; Judge Jim Wood ordered him held without bond and set a date for a preliminary hearing to determine whether his case should be heard by the grand jury.

Lee Mueller, a longtime reporter for *The Lexington Herald-Leader*, had traveled from his Eastern Kentucky Bureau Office in Paintsville, more than an hour away, to report on the case. He would cover subsequent hearings as well. In more than thirty years as a reporter, Mueller had covered murder cases with some regularity. He said in many ways the Cook case was no different from others he had covered during his career. There was really only one thing that set it apart.

"It was not a typical situation in that a child was shot in what was basically a drug deal," Mueller recalled. "What made it typical was the anger—just the suppressed rage in the courtroom."

Boggs was standing handcuffed and shackled beside the bench, waiting to be taken back downstairs to the jail, when four members of the Cook family suddenly bolted from their seats in the audience, someone yelling, "Kill him! Kill him!" Others in the family yelled for them to stop: "We don't want to mess this up!"

Mueller, who was standing with other reporters at the rail, said he had never seen anything like that happen before.

"For some reason, they (police) didn't put anybody between the rail and the obvious," he said. "We were standing there and these guys ran past us like it was the starting gate at the Derby."

The three brothers and their father got through the open wooden fence between the gallery and to the front of the courtroom before police could react. Officers intercepted them halfway between the counsel tables and Boggs, tackling them as they made a headlong rush at the defendant.

Commonwealth's Attorney Edison Banks, standing closest to Boggs, shoved him into the holding cell just to the judge's right, slammed the door, and then ducked for cover.

In the center of the courtroom, Trooper Derek Hall dragged one of the Cook brothers to his hands and knees and straddled his back like a bull rider, finally grabbing his arms and forcing him to the floor. At the bench, Jenkins Police Chief Bill Tackett, who was seriously ill and near retirement, and Constable Jerry Fields held on to Blister Cook's father at the bench and tried to calm him down.

Trooper Ben McCray, Whitesburg Mayor Nathan Baker, who was nearing seventy years old and retired from police work, and several local police officers had subdued the two other brothers on the other side of the courtroom. Police finally took control of the situation, handcuffing the three brothers. Police arrested two of them—Donald Keith

"Keetsie" Cook and Michael Cook—and charged them with disorderly conduct.

Judge Wood ordered everyone out of the courtroom immediately, making exceptions only for police and members of the press. He again waited until spectators were gone and the doors were locked before he allowed the hearings to proceed.

In the nearly empty courtroom, April Boggs's arraignment went off without interruption.

As the hearings ended, two more television reporters arrived, carrying their cameras and asking the other reporters if they had missed anything. Those present said nothing to the newcomers, but videotape of the fight was shown repeatedly on local television news in Hazard, and stories and photos appeared in newspapers as far away as Louisville. It was one of the reasons family members cited in declining to discuss the case.

Mueller visited the Cooks after they were released from jail that evening and encountered what, he said, was a surprisingly soft-spoken couple of men, chagrined at the thought of what the community would think. They were not, they told Mueller, a violent family.

Many people in the community, however, said it was not the family, but the police who were in the wrong. They said officers should have stood aside and let the Cooks have Boggs. Some police officers—even some of those who helped subdue the Cooks and protect Jerome Boggs—agreed with that assessment.

The video was shown over and over again as the case progressed through the court system and was the topic of conversation for weeks. While most sided with the Cooks, some were more impressed that police had subdued the men without resorting to nightsticks or pepper spray. There were no injuries as a result of the melee. The only casualty apparent on the videotape was Trooper McCray's gray campaign hat, knocked off during the tussle, then crushed under the feet of the police and the attackers.

In Kentucky, grand juries consist of fourteen to eighteen members who sit on the jury until they have served thirty days in active session. Up to six of the members are alternates who do not vote, but are present in case some of the regular twelve jurors become ill or have to be excused for some other reason. Indictments by a grand jury do not signify guilt, but mean that a majority of the jurors believe that there is enough evidence to formally charge someone with a crime. Since there is no standard of "beyond a reasonable doubt," a unanimous decision is not required. Nine "yes" votes are all that are needed to bring an indictment.

A grand jury was already sitting in Whitesburg and Commonwealth's Attorney Banks had been issuing subpoenas in the case under its authority already. Though a grand jury operates under complete secrecy to the outside world, the outside world is not a secret to it. Unlike a petit jury, members of a grand jury have no obligation to avoid listening to or reading the news, so when the grand jury was called into session on February 26 to hear the case against Jerome and April Boggs, the jurors were well aware of the murders that had taken place in their community. They already knew that the couple had been arrested, and they already knew about the fight in the courtroom the Friday before.

Detective Bledsoe was the only witness to appear before the jury. He told them that Belinda Cook had called the 911 dispatcher twice, laying the receiver down during the second call rather than staying on the phone as requested. While the phone line was open, another family member picked up the receiver and began screaming and crying.

Bledsoe went through the events as police arrived, conducted their investigation and arrested Jerome and April Boggs. Banks pointedly stopped him from telling jurors the name of the witness who had seen Boggs at the trailer, citing a need to protect the witness.

The testimony was bare-bones, telling the jury only the basic facts, but avoiding a discussion of evidence collected and witnesses interviewed. Jurors seemed more interested in other aspects of the case anyway.

One juror, unidentified in the transcript of the grand jury session, asked if there were powder burns present on either of the victims. Bledsoe answered that there were burns on both of the victims, indicating that the gun was pressed against them when they were shot. But what about Boggs? The juror wanted to know if there was powder on him. Police did not check for gunpowder residue on Boggs because so much time had elapsed between the murders and the arrests, Bledsoe said. Over that period of time, he could have laundered his clothes and showered or washed enough times to remove all traces of gunpowder that might have clung to his skin.

Another juror wanted to know if fingerprints had been found on the gun, a fact that had still not been determined when the grand jury met. Another wanted to know if April Boggs had been in the trailer. She had not been at the trailer during the murders, but had been there on other days prior to the murders, Bledsoe testified.

Another juror asked the question that was on other minds in the community: Were the murders premeditated? Had Boggs gone to the trailer intending to kill Timothy and T.J. Cook? Bledsoe said he believed that at least the murder of Timothy "Blister"

Cook was premeditated, simply because April Boggs was not at the trailer. That was unusual because she had always taken him to the trailer in the past and had spoken with both T.J. and his father. On the day of the murders, she had dropped Jerome off at the foot of the hill, then had come back twenty minutes later and picked him up. To Bledsoe, that indicated that she knew something was going to happen and didn't want to be there when it did.

Banks followed up with the other question that the community had been dreading to ask: why had the little boy been shot?

Bledsoe testified that the investigation had shown that if someone went up to the house and talked with T.J. and he heard his name, he would know him "from then on." The detective noted that Jerome and April Boggs had been at the trailer before, had talked with the boy, and had even given him money.

"The reason, in my opinion, this little boy was shot, [was] because he knew who just shot his dad. So there couldn't be a witness left," Bledsoe testified. "That's the only motive and reason that I can find for the death of this little boy."

Another juror spoke up, addressing the rumors of drug dealing and questioning whether the city police or state police knew it was going on before the murders. When Bledsoe answered yes, the juror wanted to know if they were doing anything about it.

Bledsoe answered that he probably knew everyone in the county that was selling drugs, but that knowing about it and doing something about it were two different things.

"You've got to have proof," he said. "You've got to have people that will come in and help you."

He said he could not have gone to Blister Cook and bought a joint because "he wouldn't have sold it to me. He didn't know me."

Banks defended police, telling jurors that Belinda Cook had been arrested and was under indictment for prescription fraud and for trafficking in prescription drugs.

"You can draw some conclusions from that, and I'm not trying to taint it," Banks said.

A juror also wanted to know if there was any evidence that Belinda Cook had been involved in any way. Bledsoe said there was no evidence of that.

Another asked if April Boggs had confessed. Banks interrupted at that point, saying he did not want to go into the contents of her statement. It wasn't actually a confession, but Banks said her statement "confirms everything that the investigation had determined as to Jerome's involvement." But, he said, it left out a lot of the other things that had gone on after the murders.

"She didn't confirm that they planned together to go up there and he was gonna kill him or anything like that?" the juror asked. "She's not confirmed that?"

She had not, Banks and Bledsoe said. However, Bledsoe said, she had an amount of money in her possession at the time of the arrest that was unusual for her to have.

The grand jury transcript is twenty-three pages long, a small amount of testimony considering that two people had been murdered. Bledsoe was excused from the jury room. After giving possible charges to the jury, Banks also left the room so the jury could deliberate and vote.

The grand jury returned indictments against Jerome Boggs for two counts of murder, first-degree robbery, first-degree burglary, trafficking in marijuana, possession of a handgun by a convicted felon, and being a persistent felony offender (PFD) in the first degree.

It indicted April Boggs on charges of complicity to

each of the counts, with the exception of the firearm and PFO charge.

The maximum sentences ranged from twenty-five years to life for April Boggs and from twenty-five years to life or the death penalty for Jerome Boggs. The grand jury indictments were not an indication of guilt, but they did move the case into more serious territory. The exact vote was not recorded, but at least a majority of the jurors believed there was enough evidence to take Jerome and April Boggs to trial.

Both Jerome and April Boggs pleaded not guilty during the arraignments on March 20 in Letcher Circuit Court. Unlike their first court appearance, the arraignment was uneventful.

The next day, the grand jury returned another indictment, charging Belinda Cook with hindering apprehension for calling the wife of Donnie Baker and telling her that police were looking for her husband.

Shortly after that, Banks served notice on defense lawyers for Jerome Boggs that he planned to seek the death penalty.

Trying a murder case in a small county is never easy. Everyone knows everyone else, and with large extended families on either side of a case, a misstep can mean the end of a prosecutor's career at the very least. Still, trying Jerome Boggs would be comparatively easy. Police either had the evidence already or were confident that they would obtain the evidence to convict him. He was already despised in the community because of what he had done to Paschal Fields. No one believed his previous prison sentence had been enough to qualify as justice.

The case against April Boggs presented a considerably larger challenge. For one thing, it was not as clear-cut as the case against her husband, and there was always the possibility that a jury might be sympathetic toward her because she was a woman. And she was unknown to the public at large. She had no major black marks against her, and both her mother's family and her fathers' family were large and well liked. Prior to the murders, the only thing most people would hold against her was the bad judgment of marrying Jerome Boggs.

But there was a more immediate problem for Banks. Family trees in a place like Letcher County often converge or take unexpected twists, causing entanglements that cannot be seen except by those with an intimate knowledge of family history. And those with knowledge of Banks's genealogy knew that the branches of his family tree and April's had intertwined.

April Boggs's uncle was married to the prosecutor's sister.

It was not a direct connection. In most parts of America, it would not be a connection at all, but in a community where "Who's your daddy?" is the first question many people ask of new acquaintances, Banks had what could be deemed a personal conflict in the case.

He notified the Kentucky Attorney General that he planned to step aside from prosecuting April Boggs because he had discovered he had an almost familial relationship to the accused.

Chapter 10

The first four days of the investigation into the deaths of Timothy Louis Cook and Timothy James Cook had given police little in the way of information about the murders. The second four had given them a wealth of knowledge into what happened before, during, and after the killings.

Laboratory evidence was trickling back into Post 13 and witness statements were coming together like the pieces of a puzzle. A picture was beginning to form. It was still fuzzy in places and parts of it would be disputed later, but the basic facts had fallen into place.

According to the account pieced together by police, the events of February 17 and after had gone something like this.

April and Jerome Boggs had been arguing over money and their living situation in general. They had been married for only two months and they were living with Jerome's parents. Neither of them had a real job, though Jerome's father had agreed to pay April $150 a month to clean house. She also babysat for a few people.

On February 17, they had driven to Whitesburg in Jerome's parents' green Geo. The reason for the trip was disputed, but both police and April Boggs's defense lawyers agreed that the trip had been made. Police claimed the trip was made in order to rob someone. The defense said that April thought they were returning wedding presents to a store.

The two argued in the car and at some point Jerome hit April. April dropped Jerome off at Sugar Shack. He gave her strict orders to come back within twenty minutes, and then sent her on her way. Again the reason was disputed. Police said the only reason April would have dropped him off, rather than waiting for him, was because she knew he was going to rob and possibly kill the Cooks and she didn't want to be there when he did. April's defense lawyers would claim that she dropped him off because she was trying to get away from him and saw it as an opportunity.

When she left, Jerome walked toward Blister Cook's driveway, careful to watch out for anyone who might see him. He even went inside the Pentecostal Faith Tabernacle to see if anyone was in a position to see him walk up and down the driveway to the murder scene.

After leaving the sanctuary of the church, which was empty when Jerome went in, he apparently threw caution to the winds. He walked past the pickup truck where Paul Williams Jr. was sitting in the passenger seat and then walked into the trailer. Blister Cook was on the phone and Donnie Baker was sitting beside him on the couch. T.J. was playing with toy cars in the floor in front of the coffee table.

Jerome wandered around the living room, waiting for Baker to leave. All the while, he was careful to keep his face turned away from Baker. When Blister had hung up the telephone and Baker had left the trailer, Jerome continued to wander around the room, probably making small talk until he heard the pickup truck leave the driveway. Possibly he told Blister he wanted to buy some pot so he would get it out for him. Then, standing behind the couch, Jerome Boggs drew his father's .22-caliber pistol from its holster, stuck the muzzle against the back of Blister's head, so he couldn't miss, and pulled the trigger.

Blister slipped off the front of the couch onto the floor, still alive, but apparently unconscious, since Jerome did not feel the need to shoot him a second time. The main threat, Blister Cook, had been eliminated. No one else could stop the robbery, but someone else had seen the murder and could pinpoint Jerome as the killer. As T.J. jerked to look at his father, Jerome fired again, the bullet striking the boy in the chest. T.J. fell on his back on the floor, but didn't die immediately. Instead, he began crying. Jerome Boggs cocked the gun and pointed it, but then hesitated. Maybe he had second thoughts about killing the child or maybe he thought T.J. had already died. Whatever the reason, the third shell in the revolver's cylinder showed no indentation, meaning the firing pin had never struck it. Either the gun's firing pin had jammed or Boggs had lowered the hammer slowly to prevent the gun from going off.

But there were still six bullets in the revolver. Jerome Boggs stepped around the couch, pressed the gun barrel against T.J.'s tiny chest, and fired again.

Police believed that Jerome then went about the task of finding the money and the drugs, something that apparently wasn't very difficult, since the house had not been ransacked. Officers thought Jerome was being distracted by T.J.'s presence, however; he took time to drag him into the bedroom and close the door. There was a blood trail on the carpet and on the baseboard near the bedroom door.

Then Boggs grabbed Blister's wallet and two plastic

bags of marijuana, stuffed them under his shirt, and made his escape.

Houses were close by and three shots had been fired. It had taken time for him to steal the money and drugs and drag T.J. into the other room. He was in a hurry to leave and ran down the steep driveway past the church. He probably took the shortest route, through the U-Haul parking lot, a route that would also provide him some concealment from the convenience store next door. When he got to the highway, April was not there.

Jerome walked to the bridge between the U-Haul store and the Wendy's restaurant and stood on the sidewalk, waiting for his ride. When no cars were coming, he removed the gun from its holster and slipped it over the edge of the steel railing, letting it fall straight down into the river.

Then he stood on the bridge and waited.

April drove back from the direction of Isom, a small community to the west. She picked him up and started into Whitesburg. Jerome told her to take the bypass.

April Boggs drove on the bypass around Whitesburg to U.S. 119 and continued north on that road toward the Virginia border. As the car approached the isolated stretch of the two-lane near Fishpond Lake, Jerome unfastened his belt, removed the leather holster, and threw it out the passenger window of the car.

Then, April later quoted him as saying, he told her, "I got us some money. I just killed two people."

The two drove on to Pound Gap, the pass through Pine Mountain where U.S. 23 crosses into Virginia, and stopped at a convenience store a few feet on the Virginia side of the line, only to realize the store did not sell beer on Sunday.

April then drove Jerome to two more stores before they found one at the foot of the hill that had its beer coolers unlocked. They bought beer, then turned the car back to Kentucky, this time with Jerome driving.

From Virginia, police believed the next stop was the Super 8 Motel. The receipt showed the two checked in there at 3:14 P.M. and paid $88.16 for a room. Jerome paid with two $50 bills.

Police believed that when the couple got to the room, both Jerome and April sat on the sofa, ate supper, and watched as police conducted their investigation and as funeral home employees carried the bodies out of the trailer.

They had left the motel for a while—possibly to buy a ring for April—but returned after only a short while. At some point, they ordered more pizza, had it delivered to the room, and called friends to come down and party with them. Jerome gave one woman $100 to go to the local American Legion Club and buy more beer and liquor.

People came in and out of the room until far into the night.

The Boggses checked out the next morning, paying another $1.36 for local phone calls and collecting their phone deposit. They then drove to Hazard, about forty miles to the northwest, and spent the day and night there. The taped statement that April gave to police on the night of her arrest showed she and Jerome went to Applebee's Neighborhood Grill and Bar just off Kentucky Highway 15, and the nearby Hilltop Cinema to see Britney Spears in *Crossroads*. That night they stayed at the Daniel Boone Motor Inn, a cheap, run-down motel tucked back from the road on the outskirts of the city.

The next few days were not yet as clear. Jerome Boggs kept an appointment for a group session at the mental-health clinic at Isom. April Boggs signed the lease on the apartment at Mountain Breeze in

Jenkins, and the couple spent the next few days moving in.

They were still moving in when police arrived to arrest them on February 21. April's mother had been helping them move, and the back of her truck was filled with furniture and other items.

Some of the details might have been off, but police believed the basic theory was sound. They had much of the proof already—plenty to keep Jerome and April Boggs in jail until they could find the rest of what they needed.

Chapter 11

Even though Jerome and April Boggs had been arrested, police still had a lot of work ahead of them. Criminal law requires that a jury believe beyond a reasonable doubt that the person being tried is guilty, but jurors in murder trials themselves often impose an even tougher standard of "beyond a shadow of a doubt."

Police and prosecutors had to be sure there were no holes in the case before they presented it to a jury, and to do that, they would have to thoroughly test their theories ahead of time. If there was an alternative theory of what happened, police and the prosecutor had to try to find it and find a way to disprove it. Jurors might be looking for another explanation and the prosecutor had to be ready to show them why no other explanation was plausible. Once the jurors sat down in court, it would be too late to find a way to disprove alternate theories that the prosecution hadn't thought of.

There was evidence still to be collected and evidence that had already been sent to the crime lab had to be examined and analyzed. Police and prosecutors would then have to go over the reports and see how they fit into the framework they had already built.

Witness statements—even those from people who seemingly had no ax to grind—had to be viewed skeptically until other evidence could be found to back them up.

April Boggs's statement was especially subject to scrutiny, since she was one of those accused in the case. Though the gun and the holster had been where she said, police were still very skeptical of her story. Why had she stayed with Jerome Boggs for four days after he told her he had killed two people? Why had she sat on the motel room couch and had pizza while she watched police investigate the murders she knew her husband had committed?

April Boggs knew the little boy. She had sat in the car and talked to him while Jerome was inside buying marijuana. Was it really believable that she could watch his body be carried out of the trailer and not go to the police, unless she had not known about or helped plan his murder?

Police investigating the crimes weren't buying the line that she was an innocent bystander—at least not without some proof. Bledsoe set out to check on her story the next day. Neighbors had told him the night of the arrests that April had a new engagement ring and that the ring had apparently been purchased the evening of the murders. April had never mentioned the ring to police. If the neighbors were right, then April must have known that the ring was being purchased with blood money. The big question was whether they were right. Where could an engagement ring be purchased on a Sunday night in Whitesburg, Kentucky?

Most stores in Whitesburg close down at 4:30 or 5:00 P.M. on weekdays and don't open at all on Sunday. The only jeweler in town did mostly wholesale work and only opened his shop when someone asked him to. The big national chain jewelry store had closed many years before.

There was only one logical place Bledsoe could think of where a couple could go to buy an engagement ring on a Sunday evening in Whitesburg: Wal-Mart, located on the opposite end of Whitesburg from the scene of the murders in the Ermine section of town.

If traffic was light, it was a short, five-minute drive around the KY 15 Bypass, then up old U.S. Highway 119 North to the shopping center. On a busy day, it might take three times as long. On a Sunday evening, such as the day the Cooks were murdered, the trip would have been on the short end of the scale.

Unlike most towns in rural America, Whitesburg didn't have a Super Wal-Mart. Residents regularly speculated on who was responsible for blocking the world's richest retailer from getting what it wanted in Letcher County, but no one really knew where to point a finger. For whatever reason, store employees said the company had never been able to purchase the property it needed to expand.

So instead of the giant box store with a supermarket and department store in one building and a gas station out front, Wal-Mart had a relatively small "Discount City" in Whitesburg.

Bledsoe contacted managers at the Wal-Mart store and asked them to review surveillance tapes from February 17. The security manager confirmed that the videotapes showed a couple matching the descriptions of Jerome and April Boggs in the store shortly after seven o'clock that night, and provided police with the original tape. Bledsoe watched the tapes and confirmed that it was Jerome and April walking out of the store.

Store cash register tapes and printouts of sales that day showed a ring had been sold at the jewelry counter about the same time that the video showed the Boggses were there.

Bledsoe took the ring police had confiscated from April Boggs to Gail Cook, the jewelry department manager and a cousin of April's, to see if she could identify it. While Cook, not related to the murder victims, could not say who had bought the ring, she confirmed that the vendor's mark inside the ring showed it had been sold by Wal-Mart. The ring, a simple gold band with a marquise diamond setting, was priced $99.97, plus tax, for a total of $104.94.

The printout of receipts from the jewelry counter showed only two engagement rings had been purchased that day. The receipt didn't give the name of the purchasers, but it did give the details of the transactions. Whoever bought the ring, like the one Bledsoe brought to the store, gave the clerk $110 in cash.

Bledsoe felt sure the ring was purchased with money stolen from Blister Cook. It would not be returned to Boggs. Instead, it would be placed in a zippered plastic bag and placed in the evidence locker at the state police post. The facts that the ring was purchased on the evening of the murders, and that Jerome and April had appeared so calm and normal on the videotape from the store, would be valuable evidence at a trial.

Police also had to be sure that the gun they found in the Kentucky River had belonged to, or had been in the possession of, Jerome Boggs. Bledsoe took it and the holster to Chris Duff, the eighteen-year-old who had told Bledsoe he had been shooting with Jerome. Duff confirmed that the gun looked like the one Jerome had given him to shoot, and noted that the holster had the same kind of stitching and was made to slip onto a belt, just like the holster he had used.

That was not enough to be sure that the gun was

the same as the one Duff had borrowed from Jerome, but Bledsoe would have to put it aside temporarily. Letcher County Deputy Jailer Tim Rose contacted him and told him that an inmate at the jail, Robert LaCrone, had come to him with information that Jerome had confessed to the crimes while the two were in cells next to each other. The letter not only implicated Jerome, but also Belinda Cook.

Bledsoe picked up the letter from the jail and looked into it, but he and prosecutors soon dismissed it as being of no use in the case. Even if the letter were true, LaCrone was a thief and jurors would place little faith in his credibility. Jailhouse informants constantly go to their jailers with supposed confessions and other information in hopes of earning preferential treatment while in lockup, or in hopes of having their sentences reduced. On top of that, a background investigation showed that LaCrone had once worked with Blister Cook's brother, and that brother had even visited him in the Letcher County Jail.

Even if LaCrone's statement were true, it would be of little use in a murder trial. The defense could claim that any testimony LaCrone gave was tainted by his relationship to the Cooks and his criminal record. LaCrone's letter was filed away with the case file, but police gave it no credence.

It had simply been another false trail in a case that had so far been replete with them. It had taken up police time and effort, but had yielded nothing of value.

Officers instead chose to focus on the statement that April Boggs had given to Detectives Pratt and Duff on the night of her arrest.

In that statement, April Boggs said after picking Jerome up on the bridge near the Cook home, she had driven him to Virginia to buy beer. Kentucky

State Police could enlist the help of police in Virginia to check out the statement, but instead they chose to call in help from a former colleague.

Jeff Baker had been a state trooper at the Hazard post before he took a job as a special agent with the federal Bureau of Alcohol, Tobacco and Firearms (ATF). Eastern Kentucky was part of his area, and as a federal agent, he had jurisdiction across state lines. It would also be helpful that he was with ATF because the investigation led to the beer stores in Virginia and because Jerome was a convicted felon who had been in possession of a firearm on at least two occasions that police could prove.

Baker made the two-hour drive to Letcher County from the ATF field office in the Reagan Federal Courthouse in Ashland and then headed into Wise County, Virginia.

Like the rest of Virginia, Wise County, directly east of Letcher County, just across Pine Mountain, was a "wet" area. Letcher County residents frequently go there to buy alcoholic beverages and to eat in the kind of restaurants that won't locate in areas where alcohol sales are prohibited.

Under Virginia alcoholic beverage laws, privately owned stores can sell beer and wine, but liquor is only available at government-owned "state stores." If Jerome Boggs had bought liquor, there was only one place that he could have gone—a state store in a shopping center at Norton, about a forty-five-minute drive from Whitesburg. But he was alleged to have bought only beer on his trip to Virginia. He could have gone to any one of dozens of convenience stores or beer stores, but police doubted that he would have passed up very many stores before stopping.

Anyone driving from Kentucky to Virginia on U.S. 23 must go through Pound Gap, a pass though the ridge of Pine Mountain discovered by explorer

Thomas Walker in 1751, and used extensively by early settlers led by such historic names as Christopher Gist and Daniel Boone.

The modern four-lane passes through a three-hundred-foot-high cut that exposed rock strata normally hidden two thousand feet below the surface of the earth. As travelers cross through the ridge line, the mountain opens up to a panoramic view of Virginia's blue mountains. A convenience store sat just in front of that panoramic view, its parking lot bisected by the state line.

Baker collected surveillance tapes from that store, another two hundred yards farther into Virginia, and a beer and tobacco outlet at Pound before finding a tape that showed Jerome and April.

The tape came from Wholesale Tobacco and Beverages, a thriving beer store about five miles from the Kentucky border on U.S. 23. The store was a favorite of Letcher County residents because it opened on Sundays and offered a large selection of beer and wine.

The tape showed Jerome and April entering the store together. April stood by the counter looking at knickknacks and lottery tickets, while Jerome went to the coolers in the back and took out a case of beer. He paid the clerk cash and then he and April went back to the car. The tape showed him putting the beer in the trunk, then climbing into the driver's seat and leaving the parking lot toward Kentucky.

The tape left more questions about April Boggs's story: If she was scared of her husband, why did she not ask the clerk at the beer store for help? Why didn't she ask the other customers in the store? Why did she wait patiently for him to get beer, instead of running while he was at the other end of the store?

* * *

Bledsoe had been using his time to get a search warrant for Jerome and April Boggs's apartment in Jenkins. The apartment had been closed up and locked since police arrested the couple, and Bledsoe thought he might be able to find valuable evidence inside. The search warrant said he was looking for clothing worn during the murders, firearms, ammunition, illegal drugs or drug paraphernalia, cash, or anything else taken during the murders and robbery.

At 4:30 P.M., on February 27, Bledsoe and Agent Baker took the warrant to Mountain Breeze Apartments and opened up apartment 327 for the first time.

The apartment had little in it, but April and Jerome had obviously been staying there for a few days. There was a bed, a kitchen table, and a few other pieces of furniture. There were clothes in the closet, some folded and lying on the floor.

One of the first things Jerome and April Boggs had done was hang pictures on the walls. A place of honor over the bed had been reserved for a certificate. It wasn't a high-school or college diploma, however. The certificate over Jerome Boggs's bed was the "restoration of civil rights" certificate signed by the governor after Boggs served out his last prison sentence. A picture of his mother was tucked into the frame with the certificate.

Bledsoe confiscated the certificate and kept searching. If the certificate was meant to restore all of Boggs's rights, including the right to carry a gun, then one of the charges against him would have to be dropped. Bledsoe would check with the governor's office later to see what the certificate really meant.

At that time, the governor routinely restored the rights of convicted felons, with the exception of the right to possess firearms, once it was shown that they had successfully completed their sentences. Since

Jerome Boggs had served out his sentence, he was eligible for reinstatement of his rights simply by submitting an application.

By the time Bledsoe and Baker left the apartment, they had taken two T-shirts, a receipt from the Whitesburg Wal-Mart store, a Dollar Store receipt, twenty wedding photographs, a black baseball cap, two packs of cigarette rolling papers, five handwritten letters, including love letters between April and Jerome, and a ceramic ashtray, which was later shown to contain marijuana residue.

Police were looking for blood on the clothing. The letters would show whether the newlyweds were really fighting as April had said.

With the items from the apartment in hand, Bledsoe headed back to Whitesburg. There were more forms to fill out and the evidence had to be shipped to the state police crime lab in London for examination.

While the evidence picked up that day seemed unremarkable to the naked eye, the visit to Mountain Breeze once again raised questions about April's story. The application for the apartment had been filled out and the lease issued in her name because Jerome, as a convicted felon, was not eligible to live in the housing project. She had told the apartment manager that he would not be living at the apartment, and she told police that she and Jerome had been fighting and that she was going to leave him. In spite of that, his belongings were all over the apartment, and his "restoration of rights" certificate was given a place of unusual prominence.

Police had already been wondering whether they could really believe that April Boggs was what she said—an innocent bystander, a young girl caught up in a murderous plot developed and carried out by a low-life husband from whom she had grown apart in only two short months of marriage.

With the evidence from the apartment, the video-tape from the beer store, and the statement from the motel desk clerk, more questions had been raised. Police had now thrown the innocent-bystander story out the window. April Boggs had had ample opportunity to run or to call police, Bledsoe concluded. She had been out of reach of Jerome at the beer store, and she had moved him into the apartment, despite having the opportunity to move in alone and separate from him. Most important, she had been out of the motel room alone, waiting for a pizza to be delivered. If she had disapproved of the murders as strongly as she said, she could have run out of the lobby of the motel or used the desk phone to call the police, and Jerome would have been none the wiser until officers burst through the motel room door. If she was afraid to call police, she could have called one of her parents. Her mother lived less than twenty minutes away and her father lived less than ten minutes away.

April Boggs, police were sure, had some role in the murders of Timothy and T.J. Cook. In Bledsoe's mind, the question now was not of innocence or guilt, but of degree of guilt.

Investigators now had to determine which of two new scenarios was true—had April simply been glad to get the money, no matter if a child and his father had been murdered to get it? Or had she had a more sinister role? Had Jerome kept his plans quiet, or had April helped him hatch his scheme? Had she dropped him off at Blister Cook's house, thinking he planned to buy marijuana, or had she left him there, knowing full well she was to be the getaway driver after a murder?

For now, police and Commonwealth's Attorney Edison Banks chose to take the most extreme view. April Boggs was to be considered a cold-blooded murderer—as guilty as if she had pulled the trigger herself—and the charges of complicity would remain in force until something—or someone—proved them false.

Chapter 12

April Boggs was born April Dawn Banks, the oldest child of Darrell and Bonita Banks. By the time she started school, her parents were divorced and she was living with her mother, a cook at Parkway Restaurant, a motel eatery just outside Whitesburg.

As she was finishing high school, her father took a job with the Letcher County government. A completely new set of local officials took office in the 1993 election, a change fueled by a corruption scandal that saw several county officials charged with felonies. The new judge/executive, a reform candidate, hired Darrell Banks to enforce new antilittering and mandatory garbage collection laws. He was officially the county's litter control officer, answerable to the county judge, but he was also made a special deputy sheriff. That designation would allow him to carry the weight of the sheriff's department with him when he served court summonses and oversaw the people sentenced to pick up litter from the roadsides to pay for their own filthy habits.

While her father lived at Little Cowan, a tiny, cloistered hollow just outside Whitesburg, April grew up eight miles outside the county seat at Isom.

As small and close-knit as Whitesburg is, Isom is

even more so. Isom was once the center for the livestock industry in the area, but that changed when
the state built a new Highway 15, rerouting it around
the old town. The stockyards closed in the early
1970s, and the show horse ring closed soon after
that. But the town itself didn't die, it just scooted
over. Gas stations opened up on the main road, while
the ones on the old main street closed. The post
office moved from the old false-front building to a
new building by the new highway. By 2002, the unincorporated town, which was too small for the
census bureau to even list, boasted two small shopping centers, a supermarket, two banks, two gas stations, a doctor, a dentist, a lawyer, and assorted other
businesses, most owned by local entrepreneurs.

In a place like Letcher County, family relation-
ships intertwine like the honeysuckle and kudzu
vines that creep over trees and unused hillsides.
Most of the residents in Isom and the surrounding
communities belong to a handful of extended families, often interrelated, and April was no exception.
Though her parents were divorced, she wasn't the
product of a classic broken home. Her father had
her every weekend and her mother reported no
problems with him after their divorce. April grew up
among family and members of a community that
were as close as family.

When it was time for her to go to school, she had
to travel five miles west to Letcher Elementary
School, the same school her mother had attended.
When she finished eighth grade, she had only to
walk up the hallway to Letcher High School.

It was a small school—no more than three hundred students in the whole high school—and that's
why most parents liked it. It was comfortable. It was
like home. The faculty at the elementary and high
school, like the community, were often family or as

close as family. Most had taught their entire careers there and had either taught April's mother or had been among her classmates. Even if they didn't know April personally when she entered high school, they had seen her in the hallways for the eight years that she was in elementary and middle school, and it would not take long to attach a name to a face. Teachers there talked among themselves, and if they did not know a student, they soon would, by questions like "Whose girl are you?" or "Didn't I go to school with her mommy?" By the time April finished her freshman year, every teacher would know her and all of her classmates by name and by family association.

April was not an exceptional student, but she wasn't terrible. Family members rated her performance as "fair," but her participation in outside activities was pretty much nonexistent. She invited friends to stay at her house, but she didn't stay at theirs, instead preferring to sleep at home.

Her senior photo shows a neatly dressed girl, somewhat overweight, but with a happy smile, seemingly no different from her classmates. But April was apparently not as happy as she appeared. She had only one boyfriend when she was in school and that relationship was short-lived. She had a few friends, but was far from the most popular girl in school. When a favorite uncle committed suicide, she went through extensive counseling and went on antidepressant medication, which she was still taking at the time of her trial.

April Banks led a quiet, protected—some would say boring—existence. She had one other boyfriend after graduation, but once again the relationship failed within a few months. She tried attending a business college in Pikeville, forty miles to the northeast of Whitesburg, but she dropped out after a half semester when winter set in and slick mountain roads became too much for her.

She worked odd jobs, instead—babysitting or cleaning house. She also worked a series of more regular jobs as a clerk at a Texaco gas station and at a Food World IGA store in Whitesburg, and as a dishwasher at the Courthouse Café, which sits catty-cornered across Main Street from the county courthouse.

After high school, she moved in with her father at Little Cowan, and she spent much of her spare time in front of the television.

It was there that she met Jerome Boggs.

Jerome's brother Lindsey was a friend of Darrell Banks and he brought Jerome with him to watch a ball game on television soon after Jerome got out of prison.

Darrell Banks wasn't thrilled with Jerome, but Jerome swore he had changed and would never do anything to go back to prison. So while Lindsey and Darrell watched sports on television, Jerome and April played cards at the kitchen table. They were, seemingly, friends. Darrell Banks would later tell the jury deciding his daughter's fate that he had no idea that they were romantically involved until April came to him and told him she was getting married.

Her father asked her to be sure before she married Jerome; her mother asked her flatly not to marry him. But April was twenty years old—old enough to marry without her parents' permission—and she was determined to marry. She wanted a husband—this husband—and a place to live.

It didn't matter that Jerome had been out of prison less than six months, or that he didn't have a job, or that he lived with his parents. She was going to get married one way or another, and she did. The wedding was December 15, 2001, two months and two days before the murders. It was held in the living room of her father's mobile home.

April had found someone to love and someone to love her. After the wedding, they moved into Jerome's parents' house just up the road from her father's home. Things began to go downhill rapidly.

Family members never saw her alone; she stopped taking pride in her appearance and started showing up in public in dirty clothes and without taking a shower. Wherever she went, Jerome was at her side. Her parents worried that he was "smothering" her, but there was little they could do.

She called her mother often, but they never really got a chance to talk about the problems in her marriage. Whenever she would go to her father's house, Jerome was with her and there was no opportunity to ask her if she was okay. If there had been an opportunity, it is unclear what the answer would have been. April's defense lawyers were building a case that she was an abused spouse who wanted to get out of her marriage, but was too scared to leave Jerome—especially after he told her he had murdered two people. Police, however, questioned whether she was really that scared of Jerome or if she was even really repulsed when she learned of the murders.

They could find no evidence that she had tried to call anyone, that she had tried to ask for help, or that she had tried to leave Jerome after learning what he had done.

In fact, the evidence they could find showed she had ample opportunity to run away from him. Instead, she waited for him outside the mental-health clinic for hours while he attended a group therapy session. If she was scared of him, or if she really condemned what he had done, why had she not driven off then and gone to police?

The answer to that question might have been in

one of the most damning pieces of evidence against her: a handwritten love letter to Jerome, which police recovered from her apartment and which her lawyer would later describe to jurors as "pitiful" and "dumb."

The letter was erroneously dated six months before Jerome Boggs was released from prison, but was thought to have been written a month before the murders. In it, April proclaimed how happy she was to be Mrs. Jerome W. Boggs. Like a giddy school-girl, she wrote that she knew Jerome did not like for her to write him letters, but said she was so happy that she couldn't help herself. She ended the note with the words: "I love you, I love you. Love, April."

Chapter 13

The case against Jerome Boggs was becoming as solid as the cut-stone retaining walls that line the streets in Whitesburg.

Bledsoe's case file was over three hundred pages long now, plus stacks of photographs of the crime scene, the autopsies, and the motel room where Jerome and April had stayed. Commonwealth's Attorney Banks had taken his copy of that case file and broken it down into tabbed and cross-referenced sections and subsections, stored in three-ring binders to allow him instant access to any information about the case that he needed.

The case file showed that Jerome Boggs had the means, the opportunity, the motive, and the history to be a murderer. He had been in possession of the gun—police were sure of that now. Even though the river had washed away any fingerprints that may have been on the revolver, Jerome's own brother had identified it as their father's gun. Ballistic tests, while inconclusive when it came to making an absolute match of the gun to the bullet recovered at the scene, showed that it was consistent with the weapon that fired the fatal shots. It was also found straight down from the spot April had said Jerome was waiting for her on the bridge.

Witnesses put him at the scene at the time of the murder, and statements from April and her mother were beginning to show that Jerome was in a violent mood the afternoon of February 17.

Bonita Collins, April's mother, had taken the two shopping the day before and had taken them home after she became unnerved by Jerome's behavior. He had hung around the counter at a discount store in Jenkins, and the clerk had been visibly nervous. He had acted "weird" during the trip to Jenkins and back, and Mrs. Collins finally took them home and told her son-in-law to get out of the car, refusing the take him anywhere else that day.

She was cooking at the Parkway Restaurant the afternoon of the murders when April came in with a mark on her face, apparently caused by a blow from Jerome's hand. Mrs. Collins had gone to the car and had a talk with him then about his behavior before the couple left.

Police were unsure whether the trip to the Parkway Restaurant was first, but at some point that early afternoon, Jerome and April drove to the Family Dollar Store in Whitesburg, about a quarter of a mile from the Cook home. An assistant manager there, after seeing the two on television following their arrest, came forward to tell police that she had seen Jerome and April at the store the day of the murders.

The Family Dollar Store was in the Parkway Plaza, the oldest strip mall in Whitesburg. The shopping center at that time included a bank, a couple of insurance agencies, a dentist's office, a veterinary clinic, a couple of community action agency and social service organizations, a handful of small shops, an alternative school, a supermarket, and the Family Dollar Store. On the day of the murders,

Family Dollar and the supermarket were the only businesses open.

The Family Dollar was the first store in the shopping center, just past the bank. The murder scene was hidden from the parking lot only by trees.

When Bledsoe went to the store to interview the assistant manager, she said April had been in the store and left, but Jerome remained. The woman told Bledsoe she remembered him because he had scared her so badly. A clerk had been at the counter and called her up from the stockroom in the back of the store because she thought Jerome Boggs was acting strangely and might be a shoplifter. The assistant manager took her place at the counter so she could watch him.

She said Jerome had been browsing through the hardware aisle of the store and then came toward her at the counter, staring at her and smacking a claw hammer into the palm of his hand. When Jerome had gotten to within a few feet of her, the front door flew open and April came back in.

"Is my husband in here?" the woman quoted her as asking. Odd that she would ask, the clerk told police. The counter was less than ten feet from the door and Jerome was in plain sight, only five or six feet away from the counter.

Almost within striking distance.

But when April came in, Jerome turned away, returned the hammer to the shelf, and the two left the store. The clerk watched as they went outside and walked to a little green car on the other side of the almost empty parking lot. The store employees noted the incident and considered calling the police, but did not.

An hour later, the clerk said, she heard sirens as police, ambulances, and firefighters converged on the trailer at Susan Cook Drive.

To police, the incident showed that Jerome Boggs was intent on robbing someone on February 17. The clerk's account of him coming toward the counter with a hammer, slapping it into his hand, was eerily reminiscent of the Paschal Fields robbery. Fields had been clubbed with a hammer during the robbery for which Jerome Boggs had already spent time in prison, and the hammer was a found item—he didn't bring it with him. Fields had been using it prior to the robbery and had left it lying in the garage office, where Boggs picked it up.

The fact that the car was parked on the opposite side of the parking lot, when there were plenty of empty spaces right in front of the store, also spoke to an intent to rob the store. Since Family Dollar was the only store on that end of the parking lot, an ordinary customer would probably have parked right out front so they could have a short walk through the frigid parking lot. But if Jerome Boggs planned to rob the store, it would make more sense to park far away. If the car was parked right in front, someone could have seen it and connected it to a robbery. If it was parked far away, it might escape notice.

Again, moving the car to an obscure place was something Boggs could have learned from the Fields robbery. In that case, he had parked his car directly in front of the garage and police had gotten a description of it as soon as they answered the call.

To police, the statement given by the store clerk lent even more credence to the theory that Jerome had planned to rob someone that day, but April had interrupted him. Had she genuinely wondered where he was, or had she known and become scared? Had that been the cause of the argument that led to him hitting her? Or had the two argued beforehand about money, leading Jerome to seek out a new source of cash?

Whatever the case, one thing was clear to Commonwealth's Attorney Edison Banks: Jerome Boggs deserved to die. Banks served notice that he intended to seek the death penalty.

The fact that a child was killed made the death penalty seem to be an obvious choice to anyone, but under Kentucky law, there must be very specific aggravating circumstances before the death penalty can be imposed. The age or the defenselessness of the victims were not included in the equation.

In order for Banks to seek the death penalty, one of the following had to be true: The accused must have been convicted of a capital offense before, or must have had a history of violent offenses. He must have been committing another crime, such as robbery, burglary, arson, rape, or sodomy, all in the first degree. He must have used a destructive device. He must have committed the murder for hire or for some other form of profit. He must have been a prisoner who murdered a prison guard. He must have intentionally killed more than one person. He must have intentionally killed a police officer, or other public officials during the exercise of their duties; or he must have murdered someone who was protected by an emergency protective order, domestic violence order, or other similar court order.

Only one of those circumstances had to apply for Boggs to be eligible for lethal injection. In his case, three applied. He had already been convicted of a violent felony, the murders occurred during the commission of a robbery, and more than one person was intentionally killed.

Seeking the death penalty was a no-brainer. Any elected prosecutor who did not seek the death penalty for a case like this would never be reelected. Even if Banks had been appointed, the public sentiment along with the obvious legal support for execution would have made ruling out the death penalty a politically indefensible decision.

The death penalty was a foregone conclusion. But seeking such a draconian penalty brought with it unavoidable and unwanted consequences as well— namely in the form of delays. The case was progressing rapidly, and it appeared as though Jerome Boggs would get the speedy trial guaranteed by the Constitution. Not only was it what the Constitution called for, it was what the public demanded—a speedy trial and an equally speedy execution.

But since this was a death penalty case, appearances would be deceiving. The prosecution was not dealing with a petty theft and the defense lawyers were not from the local public defender's office, run by former Letcher County commonwealth's attorney and long-time private defense attorney Peyton Reynolds. Though Reynolds would no doubt put on a tenacious defense, the resources of the local office were reserved for more mundane cases. Instead of working against a local lawyer whom he knew, Banks would be dealing with Reynolds's bosses from Frankfort. The decision to seek the ultimate sentence would mean a long, involved trial that would tax the public patience and the victims' family's emotional strength.

Third-world countries have death squads; Kentucky has a death penalty squad. Properly known as the Capital Trials Branch of the Kentucky Department of Public Advocacy, it was available to assist anyone who was charged with a capital crime. Since Jerome Boggs was indigent—he had no job, no property, no source of income—the death penalty squad was automatically assigned to work on his case.

Two attorneys, Capital Trials Branch manager Bette

Niemi and Trial Division manager George Sornberger, and an investigator descended on Whitesburg. A flurry of paperwork was filed in the case, and Banks, the prosecutor, dutifully answered each motion. He made evidence available, sent heads-up memos about impending events, and in general played nice with the new lawyers. He said he had no intention of giving the appearance of stonewalling, on which they could base an appeal. Even with a preponderance of evidence, it would be tough going, considering that Banks's office consisted of only himself, one assistant, and some secretaries.

Though attorneys for the Department of Public Advocacy were notoriously overworked and underpaid, they did not lack for resources. The department was involved in every death penalty case in the state and the lawyers knew what they needed to do to save their clients' lives. In contrast, the attorney general's office was of little help to local commonwealth's attorneys, generally becoming involved only in the appeals process.

"The AG's office gives us a little help every now and then, but we don't even get a checklist saying this is what you need [for a death penalty case]," Banks said.

The public defenders were present when the ballistics lab ran tests on the bullets. They took pictures of the evidence as it was laid on a conference table at the Kentucky State Police Post in Hazard. They had access to everything possible to save Jerome Boggs from lethal injection. When he was convicted—and there was little doubt that he would be—the death sentence would be appealed automatically. Not only would the resources of the state be available, but the resources of national organizations dedicated to opposing the death penalty would also be there for Jerome Boggs.

Timothy "Blister" Cook and T.J. Cook lived minutes after Jerome Boggs sentenced them to death. Jerome Boggs would live years and probably decades after a court sentenced him.

While the Department of Public Advocacy was doing everything in its power to save Jerome Boggs, Bledsoe and nearly every other police officer in the area were doing everything in their power to get a conviction and an execution.

The one obvious piece of evidence that police had not seen was the car that Jerome and April Boggs had been riding in the day of the murders. They had seen the white car the two were in on the day of their arrest, but witnesses placed them in a green car on the day of the murders. Bledsoe obtained a search warrant for a green Geo Metro, which belonged to Jerome's mother.

On March 26, Jeff Baker, the ATF agent and former state trooper, was back in Whitesburg, this time with ATF chemist Leanora Brun-Conti. They and Bledsoe showed up at Jerome's home with the search warrant and also obtained permission from his father, Lee Boggs, to search the house and property.

Investigators found nothing of value to the investigation in the house, but there were stains in the floor of the car that could have been blood. Officers cut three pieces of carpet from the car and sent them to the laboratory for analysis. It would be some time before police could determine what the substance was, but there would be plenty to keep them busy in the meantime.

Chapter 14

As summer was winding down, prosecutors were almost prepared for a trial. They had what they felt was an ironclad theory of what happened, they had the murder weapon, they had witnesses who could place Jerome Boggs at the scene, and they had the circumstantial evidence of the money being spent after the murders and robbery. But there were still some key pieces of evidence that had not come in.

The crime labs in Kentucky were managed through the Kentucky State Police Technical Services Branch, Division of Forensic Services. There were six laboratories around the state that conducted everything from polygraph examinations to firearms testing and forensic biology work. Only one lab—the Central Forensic Laboratory in Frankfort—conducted DNA testing.

The laboratories were backed up with work on other cases, and test results from samples of blood, or what was thought to be blood, from the carpet of the car and a cushion from the motel still had not come back. Police had also sent Jerome's shirt and shoes to the lab to determine whether there was any blood on them, and that test also had not been completed. If any of those tests were positive for bloodstains,

additional testing would have to be done to determine whether that blood was human, and whether it
belonged to either of the victims.

In the meantime, the defense was gearing up to
put the police on trial. Niemi, the public advocate
from Frankfort, the state capital, had made her first
major court appearance on Jerome Boggs's behalf
shortly after the murders. From that first appearance, it was clear that this was not going to be a con-
genial battle of wits between two colleagues in the
legal profession. Niemi was trying to save Jerome
Boggs's life and one of her first court filings was a
broadside at the prosecutors and police, who were
trying to take his life.

The motion asked for thirty-four items from the
prosecution, including psychological examinations
and criminal background checks of all the witnesses
the prosecutor planned to call, notes and memos
written by all of the police officers involved, and a
secret hearing to seek money for expert witnesses.

She also wanted notes taken by anyone who might
have talked to Jerome Boggs after his arrest, including the local newspaper.

Banks slammed on the brakes. Most of the items
she asked for either didn't exist or were items to
which she was not entitled, Banks argued. Besides, he
didn't even have any control over items owned by
other people. He could give her evidence lists and
taped statements—and he would go out of his way to
do so. He could not, however, make the newspaper
turn over notes of its jailhouse interview with Jerome
Boggs. Similarly, police officers were under no obligation to give her preliminary case notes that had
not been filed with their agencies.

Letcher Circuit Judge Sam Wright agreed with
Banks. He gave Niemi access only to those items under
the direct control of the commonwealth's attorney.

That meant witness statements, lab tests, evidence, and the like were fair game. Any other items, Wright ruled, would have to be sought separately by the defense.

He did grant the secret hearing, however, and gave Niemi permission to seek expert witnesses for the defense. Because the documents were filed under seal, it was not clear what experts Niemi intended to employ, but based on later court hearings, one was apparently a psychiatrist who examined Jerome Boggs to determine whether he was mentally fit to stand trial. The psychiatrist said he was mentally fit, though he was unable to do a valid IQ test to determine Boggs's exact level of intelligence.

The sparring between lawyers continued throughout the summer. Banks, a soft-spoken, slow-moving, and methodical man, was becoming increasingly frustrated with Niemi's sometimes abrasive manner and the tone of the motions filed by the defense. He noted more than once that he had given Niemi everything he had and had worked diligently to make sure that she had no reason to accuse him of withholding evidence.

Indeed, the defense requested and was granted permission to attend some lab tests. Laboratories were also ordered to preserve enough evidence that independent testing could be done if necessary. Banks wrote a letter to everyone involved in the prosecution, drawing their attention to the order to make sure no one slipped up and violated it. Evidence was removed from the vault at the Kentucky State Police Post at Hazard and moved to a guarded conference room, so defense attorneys for Jerome and April, whose cases were separated, could examine it and photograph it. Police officers went with the defense to the Cook residence twice. Niemi went everywhere with a Department of Public Advocacy investigator in tow, and was often in the company of another lawyer in court.

The court file rapidly filled with briefs and motions, and the court calendar filled with hearings for Jerome and April Boggs, as well as cases filed against Belinda Cook for hindering prosecution and against Blister Cook's brothers for the attack in the courtroom.

After the initial flurry of findings after police arrested Jerome and April Boggs, new developments in the murder and robbery case began to slow down. But the differences between Jerome and April Boggs's court cases became more pronounced. The cases were separated because of their divergent interests and April Boggs was moved to the jail in neighboring Pike County to keep her away from her husband, who was still housed in the Letcher County Jail in the basement of the courthouse. That would keep them from sharing information so readily, and it would protect her in case Jerome Boggs was unhappy about the statements she gave police. Jerome Boggs was kept in solitary confinement in the Letcher County Jail, ostensibly for his own protection.

The charges against April Boggs were reduced from complicity to facilitation, a big step down in severity.

Complicity means that the person charged is just as culpable as the person who actually committed the crime. It is usually used for people who conspire with others to commit a crime, or who physically assist while the crime is in progress. Sometimes, when police are unable to determine which of two people present actually committed a crime, both are charged with complicity.

Facilitation means that the person charged provided the means for the person to commit a crime, while knowing that a crime would be committed. But

while the law says a person must know that a crime
is going to be committed, case law says only that a
person must be able to infer that a crime is to be
committed. The charge against April Boggs stemmed
from her own statement that she had driven her husband to the scene of the crime and had picked him
up later. Though she maintained that she didn't
know why he wanted her to drop him off, police and
prosecutors said she should have known or at least
suspected that he intended to commit a crime.

It was September, just before Labor Day and seven
months after the murders, when the case took another unexpected turn. Banks had to have the DNA
evidence and he called the lab to ask for a rush. He
recalled that the analyst who did the DNA tests at the
Central Forensic Laboratory promised to finish the
work on the Cook case, even if it took working on her
own time. Finally the testing was done, and on September 4, 2002, Bledsoe made the drive to the Frankfort crime laboratory to retrieve the last of the items
he had submitted for blood analysis.

During the autopsies, the blood of the two victims
had been typed and then tested for DNA in hopes
that some evidence would turn up later that would
link Jerome Boggs to the crimes. It had already been
matched to samples taken from the trailer to help
police reconstruct the location of the victims when
they were murdered.

The evidence being returned now was from the
apartment rented by the Boggses, the car they had
driven the day of the murders, the motel room they
had rented that night, and the clothing of the accused man himself. April Boggs had told police he
was wearing the same pants, shoes, and button-up
shirt at his arrest that he had been wearing the day
of the robbery and murders, and that she had not
done any laundry since that day. Careful not to lose

anything, police made Jerome Boggs strip the night of his arrest and give them the items of clothing that his wife identified.

The lab had examined the clothing, the carpet samples cut from the car the Boggses had been riding in on the day of the murders, and a couch cushion taken from the motel room where the Boggses had stayed on the night of the murders. The cushion from the Super 8 showed no trace of blood. The same was true of the T-shirts. If blood had spattered on Jerome Boggs during the crimes, the clothing confiscated was either not what he was wearing during the crimes, or it had been meticulously laundered, contrary to April's statement. The carpet samples showed blood in initial testing, but its more detailed testing was inconclusive. The most that could be said was that the stains found on the carpet were inconsistent with the blood of either of the victims.

The only thing left was Jerome's white athletic shoes. If the clothes had been laundered, he had not been as meticulous with his shoes. From a search of the house and the statement of his wife, police believed the shoes they took from Jerome Boggs on the day of his arrest were the only ones he owned. He had to have been wearing them the day of the crimes. Police detectives interviewing Boggs on the night of his arrest saw some small spots that could have been blood on the shoes and made him remove them for testing. Lab technicians found what police were looking for. A tiny stain trapped between the top edge of the rubber sole and the white leather upper part of the sneaker was so small, it could barely be seen with the naked eye, but laboratory equipment picked it out and showed it was indeed blood. And further analysis showed it was not only blood, but it was human blood.

Though the spot was almost microscopically small,

forensic science has ways of compensating for the size of a DNA sample. Experts use one of two different processes—polymerase chain reaction (PCR) or the older and less effective restriction fragment length polymorphism (RFLP)—to duplicate DNA and create samples large enough for testing.

During PCR, a process available since the early 1990s, scientists split the double helix of the DNA, and immerse it in an enzyme mixture that causes the split thread to reconstitute itself into a complete strand of DNA. A single strand produces two strands, those two strands produce four, those four produce eight, and the chain reaction continues so that within hours there are millions of DNA strands available for testing.

When the sample has produced enough DNA for testing, scientists begin looking at unique markers called short tandem repeats (STRs) that occur in thirteen areas of each DNA strand. Each STR is made up of a sequence of four nucleotides, the basic proteins that build DNA, which can be combined in different ways. Since the combination of proteins in each STR is different in each individual, the sequence of those markers can be used to identify the person from which the sample was obtained.

Forensic scientists can compare the markers from an evidence sample, such as the blood from Jerome Boggs's shoe, to the markers in a known sample, such as blood collected during the autopsies of Blister and T.J. Cook, and give a qualified statement of whether the two samples match. That statement is presented as a statistical probability based on population.

Statistically speaking, there were not enough people on the planet for there to be another person with a DNA signature that similar to the blood collected from Jerome Boggs's shoe. Scientists, prosecutors, and police were absolutely sure: the blood in the shoe sole belonged to one person and one person alone—T.J. Cook, the defenseless, thirty-two-pound victim.

Police felt that the DNA proved beyond any reasonable doubt that Jerome Boggs had been at the murder scene after T.J. and his father were killed, and if he had been at the scene, they reasoned, he had to have committed the murder.

Still, police worried at first that Boggs could argue he had gone to the trailer to buy marijuana, had found the bodies, and had run away because he was a convicted felon and was scared he would be blamed for the murders.

There was only one thing wrong with that argument. The location of the blood showed he could not have simply walked through the blood on the carpet. The stain was in the top of the rubber sole, where the molded sole of the athletic shoe wrapped around the sides of the leather upper, and it was on the inside of the rubber—sandwiched between it and the leather. There were only three ways police could think of that the blood could have gotten there: if Boggs had waded through puddles of blood over the top of the sole; if blood had spattered there when T.J. was shot; or if it had dripped there from above.

There were no puddles of blood that deep in the trailer and there were no discernible footprints in the blood that was there. That left only two possibilities: blood spatter or dripping. Spatter was a definite possibility because of the proximity of the killer to T.J. With the little boy lying on the floor and the gun pressed against his chest, it was entirely possible that blood could have spattered Jerome's clothing and shoes. Dripping was also possible, since T.J.'s body had been moved.

Since April Boggs claimed the clothes had not

been washed, and the rest of her statement had proven to be true, police believed dripping was the most logical explanation for the blood in the shoe. If that was so, there was only one way blood had gotten on Jerome's shoe—when he dragged T.J. into the bedroom and out of his way.

Jerome Boggs had no way out. He could dispute any other fact presented by the prosecution, but the DNA evidence was decisive. It was too much in the news; too much in the movies. Even if DNA did lie, no juror would ever believe that it did. Its infallibility was as ensconced in the American mind as the infallibility of fingerprints or the uniqueness of snowflakes.

Presented with the DNA evidence, jurors would undoubtedly convict Jerome Boggs of the murders. And everyone involved believed that if the jurors found him guilty, they would also sentence him to death.

Police officers thought most jurors would, at least to some extent, figure that Blister Cook was shot during a drug deal and would not necessarily vote to execute Boggs for that killing. But T.J. was innocent. There was no excusing that killing—no mitigating the horror of murdering a four-year-old child. It was on that death that the prosecutor planned to dwell. The commonwealth would hammer that death into the jury from opening statements, through direct and cross-examination, and right into the penalty phase.

Jerome Boggs had watched Timothy Louis Cook and T.J. Cook die. Now he was watching as his case died. His defense attorneys got the lab results over the Labor Day holiday. Negotiations began shortly afterward.

On November 7, 2002, Edison Banks presented two "housekeeping" matters on which Letcher Circuit Judge Sam Wright was to rule: The first was to admit into the case record a written order of discovery based on Wright's oral ruling on March 21, requiring Banks to make available to the defense all of the evidence under his control. The second was to admit into the record a listing of items provided to the defense.

Niemi, at the table with Jerome Boggs and with another attorney from the Department of Public Advocacy, had no objection, verifying for Wright that the prosecution had, in fact, given her all of the things she had asked for, including allowing her into Timothy and T.J. Cook's residence on two separate occasions so they could examine the crime scene.

Wright admitted both items. When he asked if either of the attorneys had any motions for consideration, Niemi had only one to present: she asked that Jerome Boggs be allowed to change his plea to guilty.

Nine months after the murders, Jerome Boggs had finally owned up to his crimes. The only question left for him was whether the judge would accept the guilty plea or force him to face a jury.

Judges are under no obligation to accept a plea agreement. Even if the prosecution and the defense agree, the judge can still throw out the arrangement and make the accused stand trial. They can do so because they feel the prosecution or some third party has in some way coerced the accused into pleading guilty, or they do it because they feel the sentence is too lenient.

A judge can also accept the guilty plea, but not the punishment recommended by the prosecution. One of Wright's predecessors had done exactly that in an early murder case in Letcher County, imposing the second harshest penalty available. No matter what penalty the prosecutor recommended, the judge could go over and above that—even to the point of imposing the death penalty.

Still, the chances of a judge imposing the death penalty unilaterally were remote—much more remote than a jury recommending that sentence. If Boggs's plea was not accepted, he would have to face a jury that would almost surely convict him. And if convicted, his only option would be to beg mercy for killing a baby. His chances of succeeding were slim, to say the least.

The plea agreement was virtually his only chance at survival. The judge would have the final word.

Chapter 15

Until the DNA evidence came to light, Jerome Boggs had little reason to plead guilty. Police had a lot of circumstantial evidence, a lot of theories, but they had no "real" evidence.

They could place him at the scene of the crime, but big deal—it would have been easy to admit buying pot, but deny the crime. Besides, there were two more people who had admitted to being there. They could just as easily have committed the crime.

Then there was the gun. It was his dad's gun, but it could have been stolen. No one had claimed to have seen him with it on the day of the murders, and there were no fingerprints on it. The state crime lab couldn't even positively match it to the bullet recovered from the trailer. Even if he admitted to having used it in the past, that would do nothing more than get him a conviction on possession of a handgun by a convicted felon. That wouldn't buy much prison time, even for an ex-con like Jerome Boggs.

The most damaging thing by far up to that point was the statement by April Boggs. She placed him at the scene, had heard him confess, had led police to the gun and the holster—she had even told police how they spent the money. Despite that, she was also Jerome Boggs's wife. Under spousal privilege laws, police could not make her testify if she didn't want to, and the defense might be able to get the judge to exclude her testimony just because Jerome didn't want her to testify.

He had little to fear from April Boggs's testimony as long as he was still married to her.

Even if the case did seem strong to police, it was not impregnable. It could be attacked from any number of different directions. There might still be a conviction, but a jury might be more reluctant to sentence a man to death if they didn't have any more direct evidence than that.

But the DNA was different. The DNA evidence could only be attacked from one direction—that the blood had gotten onto Jerome's shoe in some way other than during the murder of T.J. Cook. That was an argument that simply would not fly. When football star O.J. Simpson was tried for the murder of his ex-wife, his defense attorney famously said of a glove used in the killing, "If it doesn't fit, you must acquit." In Jerome Boggs's case, it could be said that if the shoe fit, the jury must convict. And there was no question that the blood-spattered shoe was his. There was no plausible argument that could be made to explain away the blood.

God help Jerome if the jury thought he had killed that little boy. T.J. Cook was four years old—still a baby, really—and there wasn't a jury anywhere that would cull the death penalty for a baby killer. If the jury saw those shoes, saw those test results, Jerome's final destination would be a medical gurney and a deadly IV drip.

In common terms, Jerome Boggs was screwed. His only possible choice was a guilty plea. He could plead out and buy himself time. Maybe, sitting behind bars, a solution would arise. Maybe he could file appeals based on careful thought rather than on desperate attempts to avoid meeting the executioner.

When Boggs's attorneys began negotiations with Edison Banks on a plea agreement, they had nothing to bargain with except the slim sliver of common knowledge that juries are entirely unpredictable. Every time a lawyer goes before a jury, the only certainty is that the outcome is uncertain.

It was barely possible that if Banks took the case to trial, a jury or a judge would find a way to let Jerome Boggs go. It was a bare chance, but it was there. Maybe Banks would prefer to plea-bargain than take any risk of losing the slippery Mr. Boggs again.

But in this case, the uncertainty of juries was more of a worry to the defense than to the prosecution. It was much more likely that the jury would find Jerome Boggs guilty and sentence him to death than it was that a jury would take pity on him. He wasn't rich; he wasn't handsome; he wasn't downtrodden. He was a short, overweight son of a college professor. There was nothing remarkable about him, other than his propensity to commit more serious and more violent crimes with each passing year. Jerome Boggs could take his chances with a jury, but it would be like playing Russian roulette with six bullets, and hoping one was a dud.

The case was Banks's to lose. It would take a monumental screwup or a monumentally stupid jury not to convict Jerome Boggs of murder. The only thing that made Banks worry was not the unpredictability of a jury, but the unpredictability of the appeals courts. If Jerome were convicted and received the death penalty, he would get an automatic appeal. That appeals process would go on for years while Jerome sat in safety, away from the rest of the prison population on death row at the Kentucky State Penitentiary at Eddyville.

In the end, a judge somewhere might find that a lower court had erred and the whole process would have to start over again. He thought of the autopsy photos being shown to the court, of the testimony from the medical examiner, of the endless details of death and suffering. Then he thought of the family sitting in the hard wooden benches behind the rail in the courtroom. Opal and Riley Cook, Blister's parents and T.J.'s grandparents, were getting on in years. They would have to sit there and listen to that testimony and look at those horrible, bloody pictures not just once, but possibly again and again. They might die without ever knowing for sure that the man who killed their son and grandson had been properly punished.

Banks went ahead with negotiations and worked out what he thought was the best possible deal. Jerome Boggs would spend the rest of his life in prison with no possibility of parole—ever. In return for the generous offer of life in prison rather than lethal injection, Jerome Boggs would waive his right to appeal, precluding any high-court judge of ever second-guessing his sentence. He would also sit down with Detective Bledsoe and give a complete statement of what he had done. With no more fear of the death penalty, he would fill in the blanks for police and let them know if anyone else was to blame for the deaths of Blister and T.J. Cook.

Before he signed off on the deal, however, Banks wanted the family to sign off on it. This was a major, high-profile case and he had lots of reasons for making sure the victims' family was happy with the deal. First and foremost, human decency demanded that he ask the family to approve before he allowed

Jerome Boggs to escape the state-paid Grim Reaper. But there were personal motives as well.

Commonwealth's attorneys are elected officials. Banks had seen his predecessor, the brother of T.J.'s preschool teacher, undone by accusations that he had made too many plea deals and let criminals get away with sentences that were far too lenient. That prosecutor, William Lewis Collins, had not had victims sign to show that they agreed to the pleas, and when he challenged the sitting circuit judge during the last election, he was painted as soft on crime and unsympathetic to victims and their families. He lost miserably.

Banks didn't plan to let the same thing happen to him when he ran for reelection, or if he decided to seek higher office someday.

So before Jerome Boggs was allowed to plead guilty, Banks invited all of the Cook family to come into his office in the Whitesburg City Hall and discuss the case with him. He went over the possible outcomes of the case, he went over the evidence, and he talked about the torture the family would have to go through during the trial.

This would not be a short, easy process. The trial would likely last a week or two, but the appeals could go on for years. There were no assurances that Jerome Boggs would ever keep his appointment with the executioner, even if the judge and jury set such an appointment.

The Cook family agreed just before Halloween. They signed the plea agreement right under Banks's signature, and Banks completed the agreement with the defense attorneys.

It was the same week Jerome Boggs received another unpleasant notice from the court: April Boggs had filed for divorce on October 24, saying her marriage was irretrievably broken. Had he not signed the plea agreement, his spousal privilege would not have protected him at trial.

The court set a hearing during the court's motion hour on Thursday, November 7, to take up the criminal case.

The 47th Judicial Circuit was a relatively small circuit, comprising only Letcher County. Its only judge was Samuel Tilden Wright III, the last of a politically powerful family to hold office in Letcher County. His clan traced their familial and political lineage back through the legendary "Devil John" Wright, a Confederate veteran, feudist, U.S. Marshal, and outlaw who patrolled the region in the last years of the nineteenth century.

Sam Wright had been in private law practice—mostly civil law—until he was appointed to fill the unexpired term of the district judge after that judge was elected to the circuit court bench. When the newly elevated circuit judge resigned after being indicted on felony bribery charges, Wright was elected to replace him. When the Cook murder case came before him, it was in his first full six-year term as circuit judge.

The day of motions began normally enough. Case after case droned on before Judge Wright. Lawyers lounged in the wooden pewlike seats, talking about other things while cases that didn't concern them came before the bench.

The Letcher circuit courtroom is on the second floor of the newly remodeled courthouse. It is a large room, but capable of holding less than a hundred people. The seating was purposefully limited to meet security guidelines from the Kentucky Administrative Office of the Courts, an agency of the supreme court that oversees all court facilities and personnel in the state.

The pale yellow walls of the courtroom were lined

with portraits of former judges and a common-wealth's attorney who died while in office. The judges occupied the left wall as spectators entered the courtroom. Wright's immediate predecessor, the only sitting judge ever to be indicted in Kentucky, was notably missing from the lineup, and a portrait of Wright, with his black hair parted on the side, his sharp features, and smallish chin, had not yet been placed.

The painting closest to the bench, the one that caught the eye, was of the late Judge F. Byrd Hogg, a twenty-year jurist famous for his unconventional courtroom demeanor. Hogg chewed tobacco on the bench, harangued out-of-town lawyers as "flat-landers" and "carpetbaggers," and routinely invited the press to attend in-chamber discussions with lawyers that were no more than excuses for the bored judge to recharge his batteries with a long session of swapping lies. He was also known for appearing to sleep during trials. But woe be to the attorney who failed to make his case in an efficient and intelligent manner. He would learn very quickly that the closed eyes and the dribble of tobacco juice on the judge's chin did not indicate sleep. Judge Hogg was merely thinking—usually about a way to trap and embarrass the hapless counselor before him. Despite his eccentricities, Hogg was rarely over-turned on appeal and presided over some of the most hotly contested cases in the eastern end of the state.

Hogg, his face disfigured by German shrapnel during World War II, looked down at the courtroom with the sneer of disdain that he often turned on those lawyers who failed to meet his exacting legal standards. The tobacco stain was missing from the painted lips, but the mischievous glint was plainly evident behind his steel-rimmed spectacles.

Opposite Hogg, on the right side of the gallery, was the masterpiece—the 150-year-old oil portrait of Governor Robert P. Letcher, the man for whom the county was named. The oval portrait was blackened by years of hanging in coal and wood-heated buildings, but the stern countenance of the late governor and ambassador could still be seen glaring out of the gold-painted frame from under a layer of soot.

The antique frame and dingy portrait stood out in sharp contrast to the clean, contemporary design of the oak furniture and railing. The judge's bench, custom built a foot taller than state specifications at Judge Wright's insistence, towered over the witness stand and the counsel tables, and was made even more imposing by the massive oak cornice suspended from the ceiling above it.

Despite the stately appearance of the room, the atmosphere during motion hour was informal at best. People wandered in and out of the courtroom, checking on the progress on the docket, then wandered back out again.

Motion hour before Judge Wright was more of a private affair than public court. Attorneys were encouraged to stand at the bench and discuss their cases quietly, out of hearing of curious onlookers and the occasional member of the press. Anyone who wanted to know what happened at the bench must request copies of videotapes created by the closed-circuit TV system, which were kept under lock and key in the judge's office.

The normal routine continued through most of the day as the judge disposed of one motion after another, sometimes holding a mini hearing, but mostly just listening to the two sides as they shuffled their feet and huddled around the microphone on the front of the bench that recorded their words for the video transcript.

The atmosphere changed abruptly about four o'clock P.M. that afternoon. When Wright called a recess in the proceedings, the courtroom was closed and Deputy Bert Slone ushered everyone out of the room. Since the near riot in the district courtroom during the first court appearance by Jerome Boggs, Slone had made the security sweeps a routine during hearings in the case.

Using a long-handled mirror, Slone scanned the bottoms of the pews and the two attorneys' tables for weapons, and made sure no one had left a briefcase or bag sitting anywhere in the courtroom. When he was finished, he went back out into the second-floor hallway, where the Kentucky Administrative Office of the Courts had supplied a large, walk-through metal detector, like those used in airports across the country.

From there, spectators had to line up down the hallway and wait their turn. One by one, Slone had them hand him their purses and jackets, empty their pockets onto a chair, and step through the detector. He then searched coats and purses by hand. If the detector went off for any reason, Slone would scan each person with a handheld wand. Invariably, the handheld detector would squeal as it reached the floor. It was, Slone explained repeatedly, the steel re-inforcement bars in the concrete floor.

Nonetheless, he would manually feel the pants cuffs of men and sometimes have them take off their boots to satisfy him that there were no weapons inside.

Once the search was complete, they were allowed to go inside the courtroom. If they needed to go to the restroom or forgot something, they would have to go back through the metal detector again. If they waited until court started to go out of the room, they would have to stay out.

The courtroom, which had been devoid of law enforcement with the exception of the red-haired deputy, was suddenly teeming with uniforms. By the time the hearing began, ten officers from the state police and four other agencies lined the aisle between the two sets of pews, guarded the door, and stood next to the defense table.

At 4:09 P.M., Judge Wright called for the bailiff to bring Boggs from the holding cell next to the jury box, where prisoners were to get off the private elevator that ferried them from the basement jail to the second-floor circuit courtroom. As court began, Banks presented his "housekeeping" requests, and Niemi, subdued at this hearing, agreed that, to the best of her knowledge, she had received all of the evidence that the commonwealth had.

Though the general public may not have expected Boggs to plead guilty, the announcement by Niemi that he was moving to change his plea was not much of a bombshell to those in the courtroom. Everyone in the room knew why the hearing had been called.

Immediately after Niemi made the motion, Banks presented the judge with the Commonwealth's Offer of Plea Agreement, and informed him that the family had agreed to the terms. The judge asked members of the family present in the courtroom if they had approved, and Riley Cook, Blister's father and T.J.'s grandfather, confirmed that they had.

With those preliminaries out of the way, it was time for Jerome Boggs to answer for himself whether he had really committed the crimes with which he was charged.

Boggs, wearing a jail-issue sweatsuit, shower shoes, handcuffs, and leg irons, shuffled to a podium set before the bench and began answering questions from the judge.

Boggs, whose hair had grown long during his 8½ months in jail, answered in a monotone voice, rarely saying anything more than, "Yes, Your Honor" as Wright grilled him on whether he had signed the plea agreement, whether he understood the crimes he was charged with, and whether he understood the penalties. He answered, "No, Your Honor" as Wright asked if he had been threatened or coerced in any way to make the plea agreement.

When Wright asked if he murdered Timothy L. Cook and Timothy James Cook, Boggs again answered, "Yes, Your Honor."

The only times he varied from those three-word answers were when Wright asked his age and his education. The question about his education apparently took Boggs off-guard. He fumbled for an answer before replying simply, "Seventh grade."

When the judge asked whether he was mentally competent, Niemi answered for him. He was, she said, at the moment, and he was at the time the crimes were committed, though he had been treated for mental illness in the past. According to Niemi, diagnoses included schizophrenia, anxiety disorder, and several other mental illnesses. She said the defense had employed its own psychologist, however, who had pronounced him mentally fit at that time. Boggs was not taking medication for mental illness and said he was not under the influence of any other drugs or alcohol during the hearing, or when he signed the plea agreement.

When asked whether he could tell the judge the sentence to which he was agreeing, Boggs said that he was agreeing to life in prison.

"It's a little more complicated than that," Wright said before reading the plea agreement back to him.

Under the agreement, Boggs would plead guilty to two counts of murder, first-degree burglary, first-degree robbery, possession of a handgun as a convicted felon, trafficking in less than eight ounces of marijuana, and being a persistent felony offender, a charge that would enhance the penalties attached to the other charges, but carried no penalty by itself.

In Kentucky, charges can run either concurrently or consecutively. If two 10-year sentences run concurrently, the accused has a total sentence of ten years. If they run consecutively, the total is twenty years.

For the murders, the commonwealth recommended that Boggs serve two life sentences, which would run concurrently. He would not have a chance of probation or parole. For the other crimes, he would receive a total of 111 years, though state law limited the time he could actually serve on those charges to seventy years. Those sentences would run consecutively to each other, but concurrently with the life sentences.

He would never be eligible for parole or probation, and in order to get the deal, he would have to give up his right to file an appeal. Boggs said he understood those sentences, he understood waiver of appeal, and he answered affirmatively when the judge asked if he thought his lawyers had done their best for him.

Though Wright accepted the motion to change Boggs's plea to guilty, he delayed formal sentencing. Under the Kentucky law, the Department of Probation and Parole must prepare a presentencing report prior to sentencing.

Wright was still not bound by the terms of the agreement. He could accept or reject the commonwealth's recommendations.

Jerome Boggs would have to stew in the Letcher County Jail for two more weeks while Wright contemplated his fate.

A novel sign welcomes visitors to "friendly" Whitesburg.

Whitesburg is usually a sleepy town where not much happens.

Detective Chuck Bledsoe headed the murder investigation.
(ID Photo)

Businesses ring the entrance to the murder scene.

The front page of *The Mountain Eagle*, the local newspaper, on the week of the murders.

Newspaper photo of the crime scene.
(Ben Gish, The Mountain Eagle*)*

Timothy "Blister" Cook and his four-year-old son T.J. were buried together in the same casket.

The gravestone includes an engraving of the father and son and their favorite possessions: A Ford Mustang and a weed trimmer.

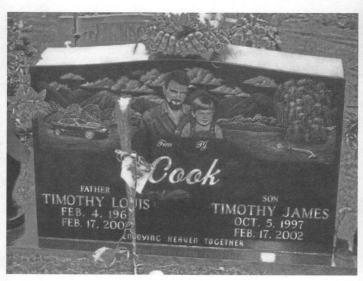

FATHER
TIMOTHY LOUIS
FEB. 4, 196
FEB. 17, 200

SON
TIMOTHY JAMES
OCT. 5, 1997
FEB. 17, 2002

ENJOYING HEAVEN TOGETHER

Cook

Blister Cook, who police say sold marijuana, was also a
veteran of the U.S. Army.

The apartments in Jenkins where Jerome and April planned to live.

COMMONWEALTH OF KENTUCKY

PAUL E. PATTON
GOVERNOR

To all to Whom These Presents Shall Come, Greeting:

Whereas, It is represented to me that the conduct of Jerome Boggs has been of an exemplary nature and merits the restoration of all civil rights lost by reason of conviction of a felony.

Now Know Ye, That in consideration of the premises and by virtue of the power vested in me by the Constitution, I do hereby grant unto the said

Jerome Boggs
ALL THE RIGHTS OF CITIZENSHIP

denied in consequence of said judgment of conviction, and I direct that all officers of this State respect this restoration.

In Testimony Whereof, I have hereunto set my hand and caused the seal of the Commonwealth of Kentucky to be affixed at Frankfort this 31st day of August, 2000.

By the Governor

Secretary of State

The certificate, signed by the governor, granting Jerome's restoration of rights after he finished his first prison sentence.

Whitesburg City Hall, where the police interrogated the suspects.

The interrogation room at the Whitesburg Police Department.

Trooper Adam Hall and Detective Chuck Bledsoe with Jerome Boggs handcuffed between them. *(Ben Gish,* The Mountain Eagle)

Detective John Pratt led April Boggs into the Letcher County Jail and Jerome Boggs sat shoeless inside.
(Ben Gish, The Mountain Eagle)

Jerome Boggs in his mug shot. *(Kentucky Department of Corrections)*

April Boggs as a senior at Letcher High School. *(Yearbook photo)*

April Boggs in her mug shot. *(Kentucky Department of Corrections)*

Jerome Boggs had just gotten out of prison for robbing and beating 88-year-old Paschal Fields, who lived in this house next door to his gas station.

Jerome Boggs waited for his wife on this bridge after murdering Timothy and T.J. Cook.

The gun used in the murders was found in the Kentucky River, under the bridge where Jerome Boggs had stood.

The murder weapon, a Harrington-Richardson 922 revolver.

The holster that Jerome Boggs threw from the car on his way to Virginia to buy beer after the murders.

A car crosses the state line into Kentucky. Jerome Boggs tried to buy beer at the convenience store on the Virginia side after the murders, but could not because it was on a Sunday.

Super 8 Motel, where the killer spent the night of the murders. The trailer now on the site of the murder scene is on the hill to the rear of the motel.

Jerome Boggs paid for the motel room with two $50 bills.

While partying at the motel, Jerome and April Boggs showed friends this engagement ring purchased with money stolen during the robbery.

Jerome and April Boggs stayed in the Daniel Boone Motor Inn in Hazard the next night after the murders.

The killer and his wife watched Britney Spears in the movie "Crossroads" at this theater the night after the murders.

The Letcher County Courthouse.

The judge cleared the courtroom after members of the victims' family attacked Boggs at his arraignment. This photo of the fight appeared in the newspaper. *(Ben Gish,* The Mountain Eagle*)*

Jerome Boggs is sentenced for the murders.
(The Mountain Eagle)

April Boggs sits at the counsel table with her lawyer as police look on. *(Sam Adams, The Mountain Eagle)*

In the meantime, he would be required to submit to an interview with an officer from Probation and Parole so the presentencing report could be completed. He would also have to tell Kentucky State Police about the planning of the crime.

Chapter 16

Whitesburg might have been a quiet town with few major crimes, but Letcher County had seen its fair share of murders over the years.

The last murder to take place in the city limits of Whitesburg happened within view of the Cook trailer, near what is now the commercial strip. But unlike the Cook murders, robbery was not the motive. The last murder was the result of a domestic dispute that went especially bad.

It was August 1984 and Juanita Hatton, a longtime employee of a downtown restaurant, had been canning green beans in the basement of her home on the opposite side of the Kentucky River from the Cook home. Whitesburg was a smaller place then. West Whitesburg, where the home was located, had little of the commercial development that it has now, but Hatton's home was right behind the Long John Silver's restaurant.

Hatton's son-in-law, William Pennington, was out of work and had been drinking all day. He told the court he had had an entire fifth of whiskey between 11:00 A.M. and 6:00 P.M. When his wife, Sharon, did not come home from her nursing job on time, he went berserk. Two phone calls had set him off. He had ripped the instrument out of the wall and thrown it into the yard, then blasted it twice with a ten-gauge shotgun. He knew that his wife was planning to stop at her mother's house to borrow money, but Pennington was insanely jealous. He was also humiliated by being a "house husband," staying at home while his wife went to work every day.

He got in the car and drove three miles to his wife's parents' house, but he later told police that he couldn't remember driving there. When he pulled into the driveway, he saw Sharon Pennington outside, next to her aunt's car—a car just like the one he was driving.

Pennington parked behind her and got his .357 Magnum revolver out of the glove box. He would later say that he loved guns more than he loved women. He proved it by taking aim at Sharon Pennington as she stood by the car and pulling the trigger. He missed his wife and her aunt, who ducked down in the seat to avoid him. Sharon Pennington ran to the back bedroom of the house and grabbed the phone to call police. Her husband stalked inside after her.

He was looking for her in the kitchen when her mother opened the basement door. William Pennington turned and fired a hollow-point bullet into Juanita Hatton's head. A city police officer and a state trooper were parked nearby talking and heard initial shots and headed off in different directions looking for the source. The city policeman happened to see Pennington coming out of the house with the gun and pulled into the driveway. Pennington dropped his weapon on the ground the third time the officer ordered him to do so.

A jury found him guilty of murder and retired to the jury room to decide his penalty, but Pennington denied them the opportunity. He pleaded guilty before the jury could return with its sentencing recommendation. He was sent to prison for life without the possibility of parole for twenty-five years for Hatton's murder, twenty years for the attempted murder of Sharon Pennington, another twenty years for burglary, and five years for first-degree wanton endangerment.

Though that murder occurred probably within one hundred yards of the Cook murders, most of the killings in Letcher County have occurred outside Whitesburg. Among the worst were the murders of Casper and Marie Collins at Buck Creek in rural Letcher County.

A neighbor found the elderly couple shot execution-style in the living room of their home on June 2, 1985, and then-state police Lieutenant Danny Webb was one of the officers assigned to investigate. It was Webb who would be elected sheriff in 2002. He was the candidate who had seen Belinda Hall walking toward the Cook trailer and fixed the time of her arrival by his grocery receipt.

At seventy-three years old, Casper Collins was a mean old man who enforced his No Trespassing rules with a rifle. He had been indicted three times for killing or almost killing men and had spent time in prison once for voluntary manslaughter. He had been indicted in 1930 for murder, but the charge was later dropped. He was convicted of assault in 1983 for shooting a man, but avoided prison because of his age and health. In contrast, diminutive sixty-three-year-old Marie was pleasant, friendly, and liked by everyone.

There was no indication of what Casper Collins did to make money, but he had shown a friend $18,000 in cash only a few days before he was killed. It was widely believed that someone found out about the money and killed the Collinses because they thought the money was hidden in the house. In fact, police found $9,000 hidden in the back of a radio, but Collins's wallet was missing and there was no other money in the house. Several guns, a satellite television system, and other items popular with thieves had not been touched. A .38-caliber revolver was missing, however.

When police began putting together the clues, they pointed not to strangers but to someone very close to the Collinses. Marie Collins kept an immaculate house. When she cooked, she washed the pots and pans. When she ate, she washed the dishes. When she washed the dishes, she put them away immediately. Evidence showed she was scrubbing the stove with Windex just before she was killed.

There was one problem with the scene at the house. Lieutenant Webb noticed that the freshly washed dishes were still in the drainer on the kitchen sink, meaning Marie Collins had been murdered right after breakfast, before she could put them away. Trying to get a clear picture of what had happened, Webb took out the dishes and set the table.

There were three plates and three sets of silverware. Casper and Marie Collins's murderer had let them cook breakfast for him before he killed them. He had sat at the table and eaten with them.

The murderer had known them.

The investigation showed that two nephews and two cousins had come to visit from Tennessee. One of the nephews, then eighteen-year-old Bobby Holland, pleaded guilty to killing the couple in order to rob them. Police said there were also indications of a dispute over family property. The prosecutor had recommended Holland be sentenced to life in prison, but then Circuit Judge F. Byrd Hogg overrode the recommendation to sentence Holland to life without parole for twenty-five years. At that time, it was the harshest sentence available short of the death penalty.

The most talked-about case in recent years had

happened two months later, in Fleming-Neon, another of the small towns in Letcher County.

The cities of Fleming and Neon merged in the 1970s after the population of the towns dropped so low that neither was a viable city anymore. Fleming had been a coal camp, built for the express purpose of housing miners for the Elkhorn Mining Corporation. Most of the houses were crumbling duplexes built around 1914, when coal was booming in Letcher County.

Dr. Roscoe J. Acker's house was an exception. The house was a rambling yellow-brick ranch that sat behind a low wall right beside the main highway through Fleming. It was just down the street from the Boone Fork Senior Citizens Center and across the street from a Little League park.

Acker was a Boston native who moved to Kentucky to work as a doctor for the United Mine Workers of America. He had been a physician in Fleming-Neon for decades, though not the most reputable one in the area. He was the doctor to go to if you needed a clean bill of health on a physical exam for school or work, and one of a couple to go to for "nerve pills" without questions. He was also involved in the financing of mining equipment for some of the smaller mines that could not go to banks for money for fear of drawing the attention of state and federal regulators. Still, Acker was well regarded among a certain group of people in the county. He had two pretty blond daughters with matching Porsche cars, one a student at the University of Kentucky and the other an employee there.

It was August 1985 when three men posing as FBI agents knocked on the door and conned their way into the Acker home. Roger Dale Epperson, from Hazard, knew people in the mining business and knew that Acker supposedly had a lot of money in the home. He and his partners, Benny Lee Hodge and Donald Terry Bartley, had already been involved in the robbery and murder of an elderly couple in South Central Kentucky, and Acker looked like an easy second target.

After entering the home, the men forced Acker to open his safe. Exactly who did what next was in dispute, but Bartley rolled over on his two friends, telling police that he had stood watch while the others did the dirty work. While one man strangled the doctor with the electrical cord on his daughter's curling iron, the other stabbed his college-aged daughter Tammy eleven times with a butcher knife. The killer stabbed her so hard that the blade of the ten-inch knife was embedded between two slabs of the marble floor beneath her body.

The three men made off with an estimated $2 million in cash from the doctor's safe. Police later arrested them in Florida. Dr. Acker survived the attack, but died a few years later. Epperson and Hodge are now on death row in Eddyville, Kentucky. Bartley is serving a life sentence without the possibility of parole for twenty-five years.

In 1987, an elderly Perry County couple and their adult retarded son were burned to death in their daughter's home at Isom in Letcher County. Police said at the time that Sie Shepherd, seventy-six, his wife, Judy Shepherd, sixty-five, and their thirty-eight-year-old retarded son, Buster Shepherd, had been invited to spend the night with the Shepherds' daughter, Carolyn Smith. The Shepherds had adopted Smith's two-year-old granddaughter legally and brought the child with them. Police said the couple were beaten and left in the house, along with Buster, while Smith and her husband kidnapped the baby and fled the state. The husband was accused of setting the trailer on fire before they left, burning all three victims to death.

The Smiths were convicted of murder, and received life sentences.

There have been other murders in the county as well. Mothers have killed their newborn babies, wives have killed their husbands, drunks have killed their drinking buddies, and at least two murders have never been solved. Each had its own unique features, and some—in the long mountain tradition—were forgiven because the victims "got what they deserved."

But murders were still rare enough in Letcher County that the community was shocked when one occurred and residents were not forgiving of the perpetrators. Like the proverbial elephant who never forgets, the murders of the past were indelibly scribed on the collective memory of the county. One was even memorialized in the law library that occupied a tiny office at one end of the second-floor hallway in the old courthouse.

There were whispered rumors of at least two lynchings in the early 1900s—one in which the victim was pulled by his neck through a hole chopped in the roof of the jail. But history records only one legal hanging in Letcher County, and it was that event and the crime that it punished that county officials have made sure residents remembered—however vaguely—for four generations.

For nearly ninety years, the circuit clerk's office kept on display in the library the noose used to conduct that one legal execution. Even given a best-selling true crime book about the Acker murder and the public rage over the death of Juanita Hatton, within Letcher County's borders, the 1907 murder of Ellen Flanary was the most infamous crime in history. And like the murder of Timothy and T.J. Cook, it was committed by a young man from Little Cowan.

Chapter 17

The most notorious murder in the history of Letcher County occurred on May 21, 1907—ninety-five years before Jerome Boggs killed Timothy and T.J. Cook.

It was at once the most whispered-about crime in the history of Letcher County and the least talked about. Few of the Flanary family remain, and many of the murderer's family still object to any mention of the crime. It has become legend—the unspeakably horrible murder of a young woman, and the conviction and hanging of a young man. With it came superstitious whisperings of the strange storm that struck the night of the execution and of the terrible weight borne by the executioners.

No local newspapers have survived from the year of the murder, and most of what has become known locally came not from records but from word of mouth and deduction. The only local news account that remained was from the day Floyd Frazier was executed. And curiously, though public officials and local society wanted the community to remember what happened, they didn't want it to remember too much.

The only two sure facts known by most people

were that Mrs. Ellen Flanary was murdered on Pine
Mountain, and Frazier, of Little Cowan, was convicted of the crime and hanged.

The scene was easy to imagine. The mountain
would have been covered in old-growth forest with
trees so large a man couldn't reach around them.
There would be little underbrush, most of it being
choked out by the shade of the tall trees or ridden
down and trampled by free-ranging pigs and other
livestock. Some of the hillsides might have been
cleared for farmland, with cairns of sandstone and
limestone thrown from the furrows to make plowing
easier. Perhaps it was from those piles of discarded
stone that Floyd Frazier formed Ellen Flanary's
tomb, and from the farm fields that he filched his
murder weapon.

Regional news accounts at the time and the appeal
record showed that Mrs. Flanary's body was found
covered with a pile of rocks in a ravine at Pert Creek,
which connected to Little Cowan at the gap between
Cowan Mountain and Pine Mountain, about two
miles from Whitesburg. She had been stabbed over
and over again with a harvesting knife and her
clothes had been ripped from her body. In addition
to the multiple stab wounds, her head had been
crushed with a rock.

It was a horrible crime by the standards of any time,
but in the puritanical mountain culture of 1907, it was
as lurid as they came—a young wife ravaged and
killed, hidden on a hillside only to be found by men,
her naked body exposed for all to see. It was not only
frightening, it was positively scandalous.

The only local newspaper account that survived is
from *The Mountain Eagle* dated May 26, 1910, a week
after the twenty-four-year-old Frazier was executed.
The long, rambling article covered the entire front
page under a headline and two subheads:

GOES TO THE SCAFFOLD

Floyd Frazier, the Young Man Convicted
of the Murder of Mrs. Ellen Flanary on
May 21, 1907, Pays Extreme Penalty
of the Law on May 19, 1910.

OVER 3,500 WITNESS AWFUL PAGEANT

The article was written by a court stenographer
who stayed with Frazier during his march up the
steps of a gallows, which had been built on College
Hill overlooking Main Street, the later site of the
largest high school in the county. Though his job
was to record the proceedings, the stenographer
omitted much of what happened at the request of
the condemned man.

The newspaper, rather than cover the execution
itself, printed the stenographer's notes in their entirety, also at Frazier's request. The only photograph
was of Frazier himself in collar and tie, as he had
asked that the newspaper take no photographs of his
hanging. The article ended with a vow of silence that
many others in the county still take to heart a century
after the murder: "Now that this matter that has so
long agitated the minds of our people is all over, we
trust our readers will excuse us if we refer to it no
more in future issues of this paper."

It also included a flowery editorial cryptically con-
demning the execution, and defending its standing
to do so by noting that Ellen Flanary was related to
the editor. Though the newspaper left the details to
the imagination of the reader, it made oblique reference to Frazier's mental capacity, and Flanary's
"death struggle . . . over in that little lonesome
ravine."

Frazier was put to death by the county sheriff, by
coincidence named Lewis Cook, after three years of

appeals had run their course. The execution took place in the presence of several deputies and doctors, and U.S. Marshal Sam Collins, the grandfather of T.J. Cook's preschool teacher nearly a century later.

When Frazier's body was cut down from the scaffold, he was placed in a coffin, loaded in a carriage, and taken to his mother's home on Little Cowan. He was buried in a cemetery there.

Like the murder of Ellen Flanary, the murders of Blister and T.J. Cook were something family members on both sides would rather forget. But in the Flanary case, the noose used to hang her murderer was taken to the courthouse as a reminder of the crime and of the punishment. When the courthouse remodeling project began in 1998, the circuit clerk became afraid that someone would steal the grisly relic. She finally locked it in a cabinet, where it remains today.

Floyd Frazier stood trial and went through three years of appeals before he eventually was executed. Jerome Boggs's plea agreement, if accepted, would allow him to escape the death penalty. If the public had its way, there would be a second noose on display.

Formal sentencing for Jerome Boggs was set for November 21, 2002. His guilty plea had been accepted and there was little chance that the judge would sentence him to anything other than life in prison, the penalty recommended by the prosecutor. But it was the only opportunity the victims' family members would ever have to face the man who had murdered Timothy and T.J. Cook, and the family intended to make the most of the opportunity.

Chapter 18

It had been two weeks since Jerome Boggs stood before the judge and admitted to killing the Cooks. Since that day, he had sat in isolation in the Letcher County Jail waiting for the judge to pass final sentence.

Boggs's lawyers had asked early on that he be moved from the Letcher County Jail to a facility in another county, where he would be safe. The jailer, however, assured the court that Boggs was protected. He had been kept in isolation, able to communicate with other prisoners only by talking through the door of his cell, since his arrest nine months earlier. Nothing would change as long as he was in the Letcher County Jail.

The only difference now was that Jerome Boggs was not waiting to learn when his trial would be; he was waiting to see what his sentence would be. When the day finally arrived, he would not have to wait anymore. He would be at the front of the line of defendants set to attend hearings.

Hearings for high-profile or very serious cases, like murder trials, were usually set as the first or last item of the day, when they would not interfere with other motions and hearings.

Jerome's case was set for 9:00 A.M., but it would not

be his first stop when he left his tiny jail cell. The first stop was the interrogation room at the Whitesburg Police Department. Police drove him there, still in handcuffs and shackles, where he met his lawyers and Detective Bledsoe. It was time for Jerome Boggs to live up to his part of the deal.

Boggs confirmed what police already knew. He had gone to the trailer, he had killed both of the Cooks, and he had used the gun police found in the river. He admitted to everything. He also told police that he had acted alone—neither April Boggs nor Belinda Cook had had anything to do with the murders. He said he had planned and carried out the crimes without help or encouragement from anyone.

He would not, however, answer the one question police were most eager to ask: why had he killed T.J. Cook? Bledsoe said he wanted to hear the answer from Jerome, even though he knew in his own mind what the reason had been. T.J. Cook had been too smart, too observant for his own good. He had seen Jerome Boggs before. He had asked Jerome's name. He would have remembered without question that the man who killed his father was "Romey" who had come to the house before. Though Jerome Boggs would not answer the question, Bledsoe was satisfied in his own mind that T.J. died because he was a witness.

One other area of questioning was fruitless for police. Jerome denied being involved in or knowing anything about the other robberies around Whitesburg. Bledsoe had hoped the fact that Jerome was already going to spend his entire life in prison would make him cough up the information on the other crimes, but either he honestly was not involved or he wanted to continue to conceal his involvement. Bledsoe got no satisfaction in those cases.

While Jerome was answering questions, Deputy Bert Slone was setting up his metal detector outside the doors of the courtroom again. The hallway was beginning to fill up as participants in the sentencing hearing waited to follow the long security process to which they had become accustomed.

Wright was about fifteen minutes late for the 9:00 A.M. hearing, citing corrections that had to be made to the presentencing report before the hearing. As the time set for sentencing approached, then passed, Jerome Boggs sat in the tiny holding cell beside the jury box, hidden from the courtroom.

With the questioning completed and the motion to plead guilty already made, he might have been expecting a quick sentencing. What else could be done? The deal had been struck; so far, he had lived up to his end of the bargain.

But the sentencing hearing was not going to be quick and easy. The family of the victims had not had their say. They gave Banks a long list of relatives who had things on their mind that they wanted Jerome Boggs to hear.

With police officers lined up along the aisle again, Commonwealth's Attorney Edison Banks began calling members of the victims' family to the front of the courtroom to give "victim impact statements" about the deaths.

Impact statements had already been submitted in written form and were part of the presentencing report. The oral statements at the hearing were more of a way to give the family the opportunity to get their feelings off their chests. Rather than reading the statements already in the court record, each family member, in turn, stepped to the podium and unloaded on the man who had killed Blister and T.J. Cook.

A steady parade of sisters, brothers, parents, in-laws, other relatives, and friends came to the front of the room and stood near the prosecution table to

berate Boggs and make known their wishes that he
would "burn in hell."

During the emotional hour-long hearing, Wright
ordered Boggs to stand up and face the families of
the victims as they spoke.

Boggs stood between his lawyers, his back against
the witness stand, his head hung down as the victims' family members screamed, cried, threatened,
and cursed Boggs. The hearing nearly devolved into
a repeat of the first arraignment in February when
family members attacked Boggs.

Pamela Collins, who called her brother "Timmy,"
was the first to speak. Her back ramrod straight, the
tall, slender woman was the picture of forced com-
posure as she walked up to the front of the room,
her short dark hair carefully combed and her chin
held high. Collins had at least some of her comments written down and she started off her time at
the podium by reading them.

"'There's so many mixed emotions that I can't
begin to describe how I feel,'" Collins said.

Instead, she told of events in her life. She kept her
voice calm as she told of raising her two-year-old
niece, T.J.'s sister, and of having the little girl's birthday party just two months after the murders. Unlike
her first party, her brother and father weren't there
to share it with her.

Collins said after everyone left her home that day
she took out the videotape she had made on the
little girl's first birthday and watched it.

"'There was little T.J. helping,'" she said.

"'You could hear him in the background saying,
"Daddy, can I open this one next for Sissy?" And his
daddy was saying, "Just a minute, baby."'"

Collins said the girl was too young to understand
what had happened; she only knew that her daddy

and T.J. were in heaven with the angels, and she pretended to talk to them on the telephone.

Collins said she would have to explain what had happened someday, and she did not know how she would do that. Collins described what she believed happened that day in the trailer, how her brother "'didn't know what hit him. Maybe he was caught totally off-guard. But little T.J.—how terrified he must have been.'"

She said she thought often about T.J., but she tried not to think about his last moments alive.

But, she said, she hoped Jerome did think about them. She wanted him to remember those moments for the rest of his life.

"'When you're laying in bed at night, do you ever see his little face? Do you ever hear his little voice? Did he ask you your name before you left? Did he ask you if you had a WeedEater?'"

She pulled a tiny marble from her pocket designed like a globe. She said T.J.'s teacher gave it to her, and it would have been given to T.J. if he had graduated from kindergarten. The marble was to symbolize that he would have had the whole world in his hands.

Sitting at the table beside the podium, Edison Banks wiped his eyes as Collins spoke.

Finally she made one unscripted plea to Jerome Boggs before she returned to her seat in the gallery.

"I pray to God that you think about what we say here today," she said. "We want you to realize how what you have done has affected us. I also pray to God if there's anything else you know on anyone else involved in this, you'll come forward and you'll talk."

A brother, Shawn Cook, was not as calm, telling Jerome "if we had a piece of rope, we'd take you out and hang you, but that'd be too good for you.

Maybe in prison you'll get what you deserve." He spoke for only a few seconds before sitting down again.

Blister's sister-in-law, Debbie Cook, was even more distraught. She cried uncontrollably as she showed Jerome a photograph of Blister and T.J. in matching motorcycle jackets, T.J. cuddled in his father's left arm as the two lay in their casket. Most of her statement was so emotional that it was not understandable.

"Every night when I try to sleep, I see this little baby and his daddy laying in a coffin," she screamed.

"Timmy was my brother-in-law for twenty-seven years and he was good to me," she sobbed.

In contrast, she said she had never heard anyone say anything good about Jerome.

A niece, Brandy Baker, also cried as she stood at the front of the room and spat out her words at Jerome.

"I've thought so long about what I'd say to you— how bad I hate you," she said.

The pretty, slim blonde, her face contorted with anger and grief, recounted how she had been at home eating with her family when a cousin came pounding on the front door, crying, and telling them that Tim was dead and they couldn't find T.J.

"My husband is a nurse and he ran down there and found T.J. and he wiped the tears from his eyes," she cried. "Did you know he cried while he laid there?

"And did you know that I had to tell my two little boys, who loved T.J., what you did to him? And that T.J. wasn't coming up to play with them anymore."

Even the sight of the trailer where she had so often picked up T.J. was hurtful, she said.

"I have to drive by there every day and look. Some days I almost forget and I look for T.J. to come out and say, 'Hey! Stop and let me come up and play for a while.' He did that all the time," she said. "I hate you. I have never hated anybody like I hate you."

Baker said she was a Christian and that she should not hate anyone. But she said she believed Jerome Boggs's crimes were so horrible that God would forgive her for hating him.

She said it gave her satisfaction to know that Boggs, whom she called a monster, would never leave prison except "in a box.

"I get more satisfaction knowing that in your second life, you'll be bound and tied and thrown in a lake of fire and you're going to burn for eternity."

Patsy Cook, a sister-in-law of Blister's, said she had raised T.J. for two years and "I loved him just like a son."

Thin to the point of being bony, with long, straight blond hair, she looked as though she carried the weight of the world as a result of the murders.

"Every day I look for T.J. to knock on my door and say, 'Let me come in and play, Auntie.' But he won't. You know why, Jerome? Because you killed him! I'd just like to know how anybody can kill a four-year-old baby," she screamed. "And Tim—Blister—he was good to everybody. He never did anything to anybody."

She nearly ran back down the aisle to her seat.

Opal Cook, Blister's mother, mirrored the dignity of her daughter, Pamela Collins, as she questioned how Jerome Boggs felt after admitting what he did.

"Do you feel like a big man today because you murdered a little baby and his daddy?" she asked.

She talked about how smart T.J. was and said she was sure that's why Jerome had killed him.

"You turned the gun on T.J. and you shot it. Not once, you shot it twice because you knew he could identify you."

Most of the family confined their comments to Jerome, but Opal Cook voiced the belief that others

so far had not—that Belinda Hall Cook had somehow been involved in the crimes.

"Hate was never part of my vocabulary, but there
are three people I hate, and that's you, your wife,
and Belinda Hall, and they will pay for whatever part
they had in this, you can take that thought to prison
with you," she told Boggs.

Her husband, Riley Cook, stood with her during
her comments, telling Boggs, "If it had been left to
us, you wouldn't be standing there today, but we
didn't get to do it. I hope when you get to prison,
they treat you like the scum you are."

He wheeled back toward Boggs as he left the front
of the courtroom, but he was blocked by a burly
Whitesburg City Police officer.

Mark Cook, another of Blister's brothers, told
Jerome Boggs that somebody would be waiting for
him in prison—somebody who hated baby killers.

"Every time you look over your shoulder, he's
going to be there," Mark said.

He, for one, said he was thankful that the law had
done its job and put Boggs in prison. The fact that
the system had worked had saved others in the Cook
family and in the community, Mark Cook said.

"There was a lot of people in this community and
this family that was willing to sacrifice their lives to
take your life," he said.

He also berated Boggs for committing the murders for a little money, telling him that if he wanted
money, "Get a job, man."

He said he had worked of his life, and that Jerome
would not have needed an education to get an honest
job in Letcher County.

"Nobody don't have to rob and steal and kill to
make money," he said. "You make your own destiny,
buddy. You can make as much money as you want to
in this county and do it right."

When Mark Cook sat down, his brother Donald Keith "Keetsie" Cook took his place. Obviously distraught, Keetsie glared at Boggs from under his dark mullet haircut as he walked to the podium, telling him, "You know what I got for you." He pointed at the defendant and shouted at him to look at him when he spoke and to "talk up" and answer his questions about how long they had known each other.

He said the two had even run around together some, though Keetsie declared Boggs was "the most retarded SOB I ever saw." He said he had hated Jerome Boggs even before the killings.

"You're a damn thief and a chickenshit coward," he said.

Keetsie Cook, shaking with anger, became more wild and threatening as he told Boggs the police "can drag me to hell right here with you," saying he wanted to choke Boggs and break his neck.

"I'll kill you if I ever get ahold of you, if I have to go to prison myself to do it," he said.

"That boy was like [a son] to me—a second chance for me to raise a boy, and you're the lowlife that took him. I might be the lowlife that takes some of your family," he said.

As Keetsie Cook stepped toward Boggs, threatening him and calling him "a sorry bastard," police officers converged, grabbing Cook as he screamed for them to let him go, and shouted curses and threats at Boggs. Family members yelled from the audience for him to stop. "He's not worth it," they yelled.

Police officers dragged him away from Boggs as he uttered one last threat: "I want to break your damn neck and I will get your family!"

Police officers dragged him out of the courtroom as his mother hurried out of her seat and followed them through the double doors. Members of the family continued to shout at Boggs, telling him he was "not worth it." Wright said little about the outburst, except to ask the spectators to remain seated. He told them that he understood the emotion, but "we have to proceed in a certain manner."

Keetsie Cook's testimony was followed by a heavy-set man identified on the witness list as "Robert Chumley." But when he walked to the front of the room, he identified himself as Porky, a friend of Blister's who had talked with him on the phone just before the murders.

Banks didn't seem to react in the courtroom, but he said later that he had not known who the man was and accepted the name on the witness list at face value. When he heard the nickname Porky, he realized that "Chumley" was actually James Wiley York, a friend of Blister's whom Banks had had a prior problem with over the phone. York had spent a good part of the past nine months hurling threats and insults at anyone he perceived as standing between Jerome Boggs and the death penalty.

Banks said the statements were supposed to be confined to family members, and if he had known who York was, he would have stopped him from speaking out at the sentencing hearing. If the police officers present had known him by sight, Banks said, they would have prevented him from entering the courtroom. But he got into the room, and he got to the front of the room, to the podium, where the others had spoken.

York followed Keetsie Cook's lead, telling of his fantasy that someone would catch Boggs in the shower in prison and "shank" him. When they did, he told Boggs, he would go to the funeral home and "kick the embalming fluid out of you."

York, slurring his words as he yelled at Boggs, spoke of changing T.J. Cook's diaper and treating him like a son. He said Blister and T.J. were like family to him—the only family he had.

He said that after the murders he had to see psychiatrists to keep from killing Boggs or his family.

He, too, was led away by two police officers after telling Boggs, "When I go to Eddyville, it'll be for more murders than you ever thought about doing and it'll be your family," he said. Eddyville, Kentucky, was the location of Kentucky's death row. York was not charged for the threats.

Though he still made no comment on the threats, Wright warned York and the others that they must remain at the podium while they made their remarks. York had started walking toward Boggs when police intervened. He stayed a fair distance away from the defendant, however, and made no attempt to shrug off the police officers who took him by the arms and led him out of the courtroom.

Johnny Collins, married to Pamela Collins, was the last family member to speak, asking Boggs why he had committed the murders when he knew he had been seen near the trailer. Collins, dressed neatly in casual clothes and hair clipped short, spoke in a low, controlled voice, and unlike the previous two speakers, he made no attempt to move toward Boggs.

But like the others, he also had dire warnings for Boggs, calling him a coward and telling him that people in prison were just waiting for a baby-killing coward like him to show up.

"Have you ever been a girlfriend before? You will be," he said.

While Collins stopped short of making direct threats to Boggs, he told Boggs to take a good look, so he would remember his face, and know what he looked like in case Boggs ever got out of prison. He said if "the wheels of justice ever stop turning" and

Jerome ever got out of prison for any reason, he wanted him to come and visit him.

"If you ever get out, I hope you come to see me first thing, because there's things I want to say to you that I can't say in the courtroom."

Boggs showed no emotion during the hearing except fear, when police had to intercept Keetsie Cook and drag him out of the room. When the witness statements were over, he remained silent, saying nothing and showing no reaction when Niemi apologized on his behalf to the Cooks and to his own family for what he had put them through. He didn't look up when Niemi thanked the court and asked that Wright place Boggs behind bars for the rest of his life.

Wright listened to the remarks, then took his own turn when Niemi was done. Glaring down at Boggs through the thick glasses set on his hawklike nose, Wright gave Boggs his blunt assessment of his character.

"Jerome Watson Boggs, you disgust me."

Wright said the only reason he allowed the plea agreement was that the family had agreed to it and wanted to move on with their lives without the uncertainty of a trial and appeals. If he could impose a harsher sentence, Wright said, he would gladly do so.

"If anybody ever deserved the death penalty for the crimes they have committed, you do."

The judge sentenced Boggs to the penalty agreed to in the plea agreement. He would have to serve the rest of his life in prison, without the chance of probation or parole, "at hard labor."

Wright told Boggs he was "not fit to be in the company of decent people" and told the Letcher County Sheriff's Department to take Boggs to the nearest state prison as soon as possible.

Wright said nothing to the Cooks and to York for

their threats, instead telling them that he sympathized to some extent with their emotion.

Wright's own words and his inaction in the face of the threats made during the hearing would come back to bite him later, endangering the plea agreement that had been so painstakingly negotiated.

Though the term "hard labor" used by Wright was the same phrasing used by Banks in regard to Boggs's sentence, Kentucky law has no "hard labor" provisions. Boggs would spend his life in a cell, at least part of it in the Green River Correctional Complex, a medium/minimum-security prison at Central City, two hundred miles from Whitesburg.

The prison held 982 prisoners. Forty-four could be kept in the maximum-security isolation unit, and fifty in a minimum-security dormitory. By far, the majority of prisoners were kept in 444 two-bunk cells built for medium-security inmates. Jerome Boggs was placed in one of those.

That fact in itself was enough to raise the ire of some, who saw a medium-security prison, which had only two doors between a prisoner and freedom, as too soft a place for Boggs to spend his life.

Green River was only eight years old, and if not for the razor wire fences, its brick dormitories would have borne as much resemblance to a community college as to a prison. It had a reputation among those skirting the law as a place where guards arbitrarily punished prisoners, locking them "in the hole" for even minor infractions. But the general public saw a much more lenient picture painted by the statewide press.

A story had broken in the newspapers only three months before Boggs was sentenced that state officials had banned satanic worship services at Green River. Prisoners had been allowed to practice devil worship after some inmates had claimed Satanism as their religion and requested that they be allowed to exercise their First Amendment right to practice their religion.

Most people would have preferred that Boggs be placed in the Kentucky State Penitentiary, a maximum-security prison dubbed "The Castle" by some because of the stark, medieval appearance of its cut-stone walls, guard towers, and turrets. More often, it was known simply as "Eddyville."

Opened in 1886, the prison at Eddyville was the oldest in the state, and the most feared.

The Kentucky State Penitentiary housed 856 inmates—the worst of the worst of Kentucky's criminals—including the thirty-five men who were awaiting the death penalty. Placing Jerome Boggs there would have been a constant reminder to him of the penalty he had so narrowly avoided.

Green River, some people feared, would be almost a vacation compared to Eddyville. No one believed that Jerome Boggs needed a vacation.

Most of the community would have gleefully placed him in a chain gang, if Kentucky had chain gangs, until the day they could march him to the execution chamber and sit him in "Old Sparky," the electric chair the state had now stopped using.

The consensus seemed to be that no punishment was bad enough to fit the crime of killing T.J. Cook.

Chapter 19

With Jerome Boggs on his way to prison, Edison Banks now had only April Boggs's trial left to worry about. There were no other murder cases on the docket, so the criminal court was fairly quiet with only the run-of-the-mill drug cases and property crimes to consider. The charges against April Boggs had also been reduced. She had been charged with complicity to each of several charges: murder, robbery, burglary, and trafficking in marijuana. All of the charges—except the trafficking charge—had been reduced to facilitation, a much lesser offense.

All of the charges to which Jerome Boggs had pleaded guilty were either capital offenses or Class A felonies, with the exception of trafficking in less than eight ounces of marijuana, which is a Class A misdemeanor for the first offense and a Class D felony for a repeat offense. Complicity means that a person is responsible for the crime of another and would be subject to the same consequences.

With the reduction of charges, April Boggs would be facing only a fraction of the time that she would have faced under the complicity charges.

Under Kentucky law, facilitation of a Class A or B felony, or a capital offense, was a Class D felony, punishable by up to five years in prison. Facilitation of a Class D felony was a Class A misdemeanor punishable by up to twelve months in the county jail. April Boggs theoretically would now face a maximum of fifteen years, and even that would be limited by state sentencing guidelines.

The charges against her were serious, but not as serious as those her husband faced. Still, in its own way, April's case presented more problems for the prosecution than Jerome's. While the DNA and April's statements provided solid links from Jerome to the murders, there were no solid links to April, except her own statement, and that did nothing to show that she *knew* what was to happen before she left her husband at the foot of the hill below the Cook residence.

There was no DNA evidence because there was no indication she had actually been at the scene of the crime on that day. On top of that, Jerome Boggs told police just before his final sentencing hearing that April had nothing to do with the crime. To be sure, the statement of someone like Jerome Boggs would carry little weight with a jury, but it was still possible that it could have an effect.

While April Boggs's own statement was not a confession, it did show unequivocally that April Boggs had driven her husband to the crime scene, and had picked him up. But it was also a two-edged sword. While a jury might find it reprehensible that she had partied with the money her husband got from the robbery, they might also sympathize with her as she wept on tape over the death of the little boy. Also, she claimed not to have known what was going to happen beforehand. Her lack of a criminal record and the fact that police were able to verify at least most of her statement might also lead a jury to have sympathy for her.

Worse than the lack of evidence was that Banks had what some considered to be a personal conflict involving April Boggs. Banks's sister had married April's uncle. It was a tenuous relationship at best, but it could be enough to lend an appearance of impropriety and make prosecuting her akin to walking a tightrope. Those against April might think he was going easy on her because of his sister. Those for her might think he was betraying his own family. If she were convicted, a good lawyer might be able to make something of the family connection on appeal, even though most would say a family relationship would be more likely to make Banks favor acquittal for April.

Banks asked the then-attorney general Ben Chandler to rule on whether he should step down from the case and get someone else appointed. Chandler's office, however, noted that Kentucky law only recognized immediate family members, aunts, and uncles as relatives and therefore no conflict existed.

Instead of granting Banks's request to be removed from the case, Chandler offered him help in prosecuting it. Banks accepted readily and the attorney general appointed 30th District Commonwealth's Attorney Rick Bartley, from neighboring Pike County, to assist Banks in preparing the case.

Bartley and Banks made an odd couple at the prosecution table. Bartley—tall, stringy, and bespectacled—was to be the courtroom voice of the prosecution, even though the stout, bearded Banks was technically the lead attorney. Together they would develop a courtroom strategy to handle the case, but Banks was to be the boss. And while Bartley was to question witnesses and make opening and closing statements in the trial, Banks would handle the legal arguments when it came to motions and objections.

Unlike Jerome, April Boggs was not facing the death penalty; so in some ways, the case would be easier. She was not represented by the death penalty squad, but she did have a public defender from the Hazard Office of the Department of Public Advocacy, and a private attorney retained by her family.

Again, the appearance of the team of attorneys was somewhat of an odd match. Barbara Carnes, blocky with her dark, bobbed hair and dark, solid-colored suits, was a veteran public defender in the Hazard office. Jane Butcher, slender with stylish auburn hair and flashy clothes, was a private attorney from Williamsburg, a tiny conservative hotbed one hundred miles away. But their courtroom styles were complementary. Carnes handled the opening and closing statements and some of the nonconfrontational questioning. Butcher handled the tough cross-examinations, sometimes hurling sarcastic remarks at witnesses and hammering police. Both lawyers sometimes baited the prosecution with caustic remarks in the judge's chambers.

One of the first acts by the defense was to ask the judge to bar the victims' family members from bringing photographs into the courtroom. The family was making sure no one forgot the victims in the case. They had been wearing homemade pins with photographs of Tim and T.J. Cook attached whenever there was a hearing. They wore them around the hallways of the courthouse, while waiting on Deputy Bert Slone's security checks, and when they went into the courtroom and took their seats.

The attorneys reasoned that the pins would have a prejudicial effect on the jury and asked Wright to order them not to bring the pictures to court.

Family members stopped the practice voluntarily before the judge could rule, though they continued to place advertisements in *The Mountain Eagle* each week with photographs and written memories of the murder victims. Jerome Boggs's case file included copies of twenty-three such advertisements, complete with photos of T.J. playing with cousins and of Timothy Louis Cook in his army uniform, fresh out of basic training.

Jerome Boggs was sentenced on November 21, 2002, but with pretrial motions, holidays, and schedule conflicts, April Boggs would not come to trial for another 5½ months.

That didn't mean she wasn't busy. April Boggs had filed for divorce in October, and the case was languishing on the docket. Jerome Boggs had filed a response opposing the divorce and asking for a reconciliation conference.

April Boggs had answered with an affidavit saying she had tried to borrow money from her parents before her arrest so she could divorce Jerome, and that she had no desire to see him or anyone representing him at a reconciliation hearing.

The judge accepted her argument on February 11, and denied Jerome's motion. That cleared the way for the domestic-relations commissioner to hear the case. On May 2, 2003, Jane Butcher filed a deposition by April in the divorce.

It was a bare-bones document, stating only the facts: that the couple were married December 15, 2001, that they had accumulated no property and no debts, that they had no minor children, and that she was not pregnant.

It said they had been separated since February 21, 2002, and restated the grounds in the original petition—that the marriage was irretrievably broken.

In a sense, the divorce was a race against the clock. If April Boggs could be divorced from Jerome before her trial, she would be able to show that she was not willing to be married to a murderer. But there was a problem—the trial was only three days away.

Court began on May 5 with a motion by Carnes to delay the trial further. She waved a copy of an article from *The Community News-Press*, a tiny paper at Cromona, an unincorporated community about fifteen miles east of Whitesburg, as the basis of her motion.

According to Carnes, the publication had quoted Edison Banks as saying that the jury should find April Boggs guilty. She maintained that it was improper for the prosecutor to make such a statement in the case because of its potential to prejudice jurors before they ever showed up in the courtroom.

Banks, however, said he never made such a statement. He said the reporter had called him on the phone, and he had only quoted the elements of the law on complicity to her. He pointed out that the statement to which Carnes was referring was not enclosed in quotation marks, as were statements attributed to other individuals in the story.

He also noted that the *News-Press* primarily covered what he termed the "upper end" of the county and that few people outside its immediate area of publication read it. He contrasted it to *The Mountain Eagle*, which covered a much wider area.

Wright overruled the motion for continuance and proceeded with jury selection.

Because of the notoriety of the case and the family ties in the community, Wright had two jury panels available from which to select. The courtroom was crowded with potential jurors, and for a while, it appeared as if there might not be enough. Of the first thirty-four people called, twenty-seven knew witnesses that were to be called, and twenty of those were excused for that reason. Among the twenty-seven were potential jurors who were related to April Boggs, some who lived in the small community where she had grown up, some who worked for the city of Whitesburg or for Wal-Mart's security department, and at least one with a direct relationship to the case. Gary Mullins, one of the jury pool, was the city councilman and volunteer firefighter who found the murder weapon.

Several other jurors said they had small children of their own and could not give a fair trial to someone accused in connection with the murder of a four-year-old boy. Another said his father had been killed and the person accused had been acquitted. He said he did not have enough confidence in the legal system to be a juror. Still others brought medical excuses.

It took six hours for the court to finally seat fourteen jurors who did not profess to have already formed an opinion about the case.

Though those jurors had already sat in the courtroom since 9:00 A.M., they would have to sit in the jury box before the end of the day.

Opening arguments began at 4:20 P.M.

Bartley, arguing for the commonwealth, took only a few minutes to lay out the case against April Boggs. And when he did, he focused very little on the murders themselves, instead telling jurors about the argument Jerome and April Boggs had before the murders. That argument was over money, he said, and the fact that they didn't have any. He talked of Jerome thumping a hammer in his hand as he approached the clerk at the Family Dollar Store, of the murders, then moved on to after the murders.

It was the four days between the time Timothy and T.J. Cook were killed and Jerome and April Boggs were arrested that Bartley detailed most closely for the jury. It was the drinking, the drugs, the parties, and the pizza on which Bartley focused, because he said it raised the key question in the trial: why had April Boggs not gone to police when she found out what her husband had done?

It was the same question police had been asking for more than a year.

Barbara Carnes, in providing the defense's opening statement, answered that question for the jury. April Boggs had not gone to police because she was scared. She knew what Jerome Boggs was, and she knew what she was. He was a predator; she was his prey.

Carnes's statement lasted scarcely five minutes. At 4:51 P.M., the newly selected jury stood up, placed their badges in their chairs, and shuffled out the back door of the courtroom. The trial was to begin in earnest the next morning at nine o'clock.

That was not to be. Though the jury had heard the opening arguments and was primed to hear the first witness, the day before had been a false start. Jurors who expected to begin court at 9:00 A.M. had to cool their heels, instead, in the jury room while lawyers again wrangled over evidence.

The lawyers and the judge gathered at a long table in the judge's conference room with the prosecution on one side of the table and the defense on the other. It was the same table where Wright had denied the defense's motion for a continuance the day before.

Before the first witness could be called, the defense called into question the photographs that the prosecution planned to present as evidence. Among them were gruesome photographs taken by Bledsoe during the autopsy of T.J. Cook.

The defense claimed the photos would play to the jurors' emotions and would prejudice them against April Boggs. Wright agreed, throwing out all the autopsy photos. Banks said he wanted to show the contact wound to explain why he thought April Boggs did not want to be at the trailer that day, but Wright excluded that photo as well.

He also ruled the prosecution could not show the contents of the child's toy box or a photo of T.J. in a body bag, though he did allow photos of T.J. and his father at the crime scene, before their bodies were removed.

The defense also asked the judge to suppress any evidence concerning the apartment at Mountain Breeze, claiming that since April Boggs was not charged with federal housing fraud, the prosecution could not introduce evidence that she had lied on her application for housing. At the same time, they asked that Wright suppress any testimony about the Family Dollar Store visit by Jerome and April Boggs, since she had not been charged with complicity to attempted robbery.

Pike Commonwealth's Attorney Rick Bartley, however, said the apartment application was relevant because the defense was claiming that April Boggs was afraid of Jerome Boggs and was trying to get away from him.

"We think the fact that they were moving into an apartment together showed she was not fearful of him and that she wanted to continue the relationship with him," Bartley said.

Butcher, the private defense attorney, claimed there was nothing to show they planned to move in together. But Bartley pointed out that Jerome and April Boggs had been moving his belongings from his parents' home when police arrested them.

Wright overruled the motion to suppress that evidence and the evidence of the incident at the Family Dollar Store the day of the murders. Wright said no crime was alleged to have occurred at the store, so the evidence was not prejudicial.

But while the defense didn't want the evidence of

the apartment and the Family Dollar Store incident admitted, they were clearly desperate to keep love letters between April and Jerome out of court.

Carnes claimed that the defense had never been given any love letters as part of discovery and that no love letters were listed among the evidence.

Banks contradicted that, saying the defense team spent an entire day at the state police post in Hazard examining and photographing evidence, along with Jerome Boggs's defense team.

"Their investigator had every opportunity" to examine the letters, Banks said.

Butcher, however, said the letters were not on the search warrant return. She maintained that their investigator took pictures of everything that was made available, and there were no letters in the photos.

Bartley pointed out that the search warrant did list five handwritten letters and pointed out that the evidence bag containing the letters plainly had "love letters" written on the outside. The envelope was in photos of the evidence lying on the table in the state police conference room.

"These were not taken out (of the envelope); they were not made available," Butcher argued.

Wright allowed the defense time to read the letters, but overruled the motion to suppress them.

Butcher continued to argue against the letters, saying that Jerome Boggs's attorney's name was on the notice of service of the letter setting up the meeting on evidence, but hers was not.

Wright again overruled the motion, but Carnes attacked the letters and a telephone book taken from the motel room where Jerome and April Boggs stayed the night of the murders from another perspective. She claimed that the letters and phone book were hearsay evidence, because no handwriting expert or other evidence was to be introduced identifying the writing as April's.

She also claimed there was no proof that the "Dwayne" whose name and phone number were scribbled on the phone book was April's brother. She also said there was no proof that the note reading "I love Jerome" scribbled on the book referred to April and Jerome Boggs, and that even if it did refer to them, there was no proof of who wrote the notes.

Wright ruled that the phone book could not be admitted without something to establish who had written on it.

Apparently energized by the decision, the defense again attacked the letter from April. By this time, the lawyers had read the letters and noted the date of one was more than a year before the crimes were committed.

Banks said the date was in error, since Boggs was still in prison on the date listed on the letter and had not even met April at that time. He was "sure" that the date was intended to be January 12, 2002, not January 12, 2001.

"Are we sure, Judge?" Butcher asked sarcastically.

Banks's response was uncharacteristically sharp.

"Unless your client is an idiot. It makes reference to the fact that they were married and their first Christmas together. I'm assuming that means 2002."

"That's a lot of assumption," Carnes responded.

The judge ended up allowing the prosecution to introduce the letters from April Boggs to Jerome Boggs, but requiring them to provide some sort of legal foundation before using Jerome's letter to April.

The letters were the final obstacle to the trial. By the time the jury heard the last case, it had been more than a year since Timothy and T.J. Cook were murdered.

Chapter 20

For more than a year, Letcher County had been captivated by the story of the double murder in Whitesburg. Newspapers had covered every hearing, and television cameras had been a regular fixture in Whitesburg in the aftermath of the killings.

There had been interviews with the family of the victims, a jailhouse interview with Jerome Boggs, and myriad details of the spending spree. Everyone had read about the motions filed in court and had seen the videotape of the arrests and the hearings. But while the information had been out there in the public for months, many felt they had been denied a chance to peek into the real story of the murders.

Some felt they couldn't believe what they read. Others felt there was more than had been told. Many felt that there were other people involved in the slayings or that more money had been stolen than police knew about. Others debated why police had found no evidence of drug dealing at the trailer. Had everything been stolen? Had the rumors of drug dealing been wrong? Had someone else removed everything before police could arrive? There had been plenty of rumors to fuel the speculation, but nothing had come out in court yet. Jerome Boggs had pleaded guilty in exchange for his life, so there had been no public testimony about what had really gone on the day of the murders and the days that followed. Many in the community felt cheated. They would have been much happier if Boggs were on death row, and even happier still if the Cook family had been allowed to reach him in the courtroom.

April Boggs would have to be the surrogate for her husband, even though she was divorcing him and the community was divided on her culpability in the crimes. Was she an innocent, sheltered young girl dragged into a murder plot by her Svengali-like husband? Or was she the Svengali in the marriage— encouraging her unbalanced husband to commit the crimes for her so she could have the money she longed for? Perhaps she was an opportunistic gold digger, satisfied with the money her husband stole, no matter what the expense.

The trial was an opportunity to find out.

In the courthouse, the mood was tense. Though most police officers at the time said they did not believe April Boggs was in danger, they and the court were taking no chances. They remembered all too well the near riot in the courtroom downstairs, and no one had any desire to repeat it.

In the hallways, the two families were separated, with April's family sitting on one side of the double doors that led to the vestibule of the courtroom, and the Cook family sitting on the other. The metal detector was between them, and when Deputy Bert Slone did his security check, one family was asked to sit while the other was searched and let into the courtroom. Once inside, the heavy police presence was not as apparent as it had been during the Jerome Boggs hearings. However, the court had requested and received additional state court security officers from Frankfort. The officers were less obtrusive than patrolmen, but in their identical slate gray slacks and navy blue blazers, they were nonetheless in uniform.

An officer stayed outside the double doors in the back of the courtroom and another sat inside, his chair blocking the doors. Witnesses were required to stay outside in chairs lining the hallway until they were called to testify. Even police officers, with the exception of Bledsoe, who had been designated as the commonwealth's representative, were not allowed in the room if they were on the witness list.

The jury had its first taste of what was to come, on May 5, when Bartley unfolded his long legs from under the counsel table and ambled up to the podium facing the jury box. He began his opening statement by assuring jurors that they would not have to make a decision on sending a woman to her death. The charges against April Boggs were facilitation to murder, facilitation to robbery, facilitation to burglary, and complicity to trafficking in marijuana.

If the jurors were disturbed that they might have to find a penalty of death for April Boggs, they had nothing to worry about. The charges she faced did not carry the death penalty.

But while they were not capital crimes that could deprive her of life or of freedom for the rest of her life, they were serious crimes. Bartley began by telling jurors how April and Jerome Boggs had married and lived with Jerome's parents for the two months before the murders. But April had applied for an apartment at Mountain Breeze, lying on the application by saying that Jerome Boggs would not be living with her. He was a convicted felon, and as such could not live in the federally funded housing project.

Bartley said on February 17, she and Jerome had argued about money. She had argued that they had no money because he had no job.

So, Bartley said, Jerome said he would get her

some money and the two went to Family Dollar. But
as Jerome walked toward the clerk with a hammer,
April had burst in and stopped him, yelling, "Have
you seen my husband?"

Then they went to the mouth of Susan Cook Drive,
and April dropped Jerome off there at the Sugar
Shack. That, Bartley argued, proved that she knew
what was going on. She had been to Blister Cook's
home several times before and had waited in the car
while Jerome bought pot, Bartley said, but this time
was different. Why? Bartley questioned. They were arguing because they didn't have any money, but she
dropped Jerome off at the trailer to buy pot. Bartley
said April thought he had $20 or $30 in his pocket,
hardly enough to buy any pot at all.

He came back with two bags of marijuana and
over $1,000 in cash. He told her he had killed two
people, but instead of going to the police, Bartley
said, April Boggs took Jerome to buy beer, checked
into the Super 8 Motel, and began calling friends to
come and party with them.

The friends would testify, Bartley said, that April
Boggs was "rubbing on Jerome, saying what a good
fellow he is." Those actions, he maintained, were not
the actions of a woman in fear for her life.

Bartley went over the next few days in great detail.
He talked about the couple renting a room in
Hazard, eating at Applebee's, watching a movie,
buying things at Kmart and Wal-Mart, and about
April sitting in the car for "two or three hours" while
Jerome attended a group therapy session at the local
mental-health agency.

His presentation was short and to the point. He
wasted no time and gave jurors only a bare sketch of
the testimony they would hear.

But if Bartley's opening statement was stripped
down, Carnes's statement was positively bare-bones.

She took only a few minutes before the jury, ridiculing Bartley's opening and the prosecution case in general.

She called it "ludicrous" that anyone would say April Boggs had goaded Jerome Boggs into the murders with the argument over money. She was scared, Carnes said. She didn't report him for what he had done because she "wasn't a hero." But, Carnes noted, April Boggs cooperated with police as soon as she was sure Jerome Boggs was safely locked away.

April Boggs was not guilty, Carnes told the jury.

"She married a monster," she said.

Chapter 21

The opening arguments had been a fair picture of how the trial would proceed. When jurors were finally led into the courtroom an hour late on the second day of the trial, the prosecution's first witness wasn't much of a surprise.

It was Robbie Campbell, the deputy coroner who had pronounced Timothy and T.J. Cook dead. A coroner's job is to investigate and determine the cause of death and pronounce persons dead. In Kentucky, they are elected officials, and neither they nor their deputies are required to be doctors. Most, like Campbell, are funeral directors. Both coroners and deputy coroners are required to take basic training during their first year in office, and at least eighteen hours of continuing-education courses each year to keep their certifications.

Since a coroner is a peace officer, as well as a medical official, most of the classes deal with legal issues, evidence preservation, and death investigations. Campbell had been a deputy coroner in Letcher County since 1986, serving six coroners, and had taken his classes every year to maintain his certification. In addition to his official duties, Campbell, who was in his early fifties, had worked at funeral homes

as an ambulance driver, funeral director, and embalmer since he was seventeen years old. Few people
in Letcher County knew more about death than the
bespectacled, good-natured deputy coroner.

The only thing surprising about Campbell's testimony was the amount of time he stayed on the
stand. With a wealth of knowledge, Campbell could
have been expected to give lengthy testimony on the
manner and time of death.

Instead, he was a quick witness, remaining on the
stand for only eight minutes. There were no autopsy
photos to identify, but Campbell did identify photos
of both Timothy Louis "Blister" Cook and T.J. Cook
lying in the trailer, as they were when he arrived. He
also identified the death certificates of the two victims
and gave the cause of death, as listed on those certificates. T.J., the death certificate showed, died of multiple gunshot wounds to the chest. His father died of
a perforating projectile injury to the brain caused by
a single gunshot wound to the left-posterior supra-
auricular parietal region.

Campbell's testimony was matter-of-fact and straight-
forward, right down to the self-deprecating chuckle at
his own failure to pronounce "supra-auricular parietal"
on the first attempt. But while Campbell might have
had trouble with the pronunciation, he had no trouble
pointing out a spot behind his left ear to illustrate to
the jury where Blister Cook had been shot.

The defense asked him no questions. His testimony had done nothing more than prove to the
jury a fact that no one disputed—Timothy Louis
Cook and Timothy James Cook had been shot to
death.

Detective Pratt was next, and the early part of his
testimony was no more earthshaking than that of
Deputy Coroner Campbell's. Pratt, a KSP officer for
eighteen years, had been a detective for the past

eight years. He was assigned the task of investigating the crime scene and taking photos.

The first part of Pratt's testimony revealed nothing new. He testified that nothing seemed to be disturbed in the trailer, and testified to the location of the bodies and the number of gunshot wounds—things already established in Campbell's testimony. Pratt explained that troopers and detectives were trained in blood spatter examination and other techniques to determine the location where a crime had occurred. This investigation led him to believe that Blister Cook had been sitting on the couch when he was shot. But in examining T.J. Cook's body, he could find no projectile under his body, even though the bullet had exited.

Pratt said he investigated further and found a blood trail leading to the child's body from a spot about two feet in front of the coffee table in the living room. A small-caliber bullet, which Pratt described as "in the range of a .22 or a .25 caliber," was lying in the carpet at that spot, indicating that the child had been shot in the living room, and was then dragged into the bedroom.

Bartley also had Pratt describe the location of the trailer, the stores, church, and other features around it, and describe the location of the Super 8 Motel.

Pratt also identified a photo he had taken showing the window in room 101 of the motel and the trailer on the other side of the river.

But Pratt's main purpose was to introduce the audiotape of April Boggs's statement.

Though the tape could have been a problem for the prosecution, it was clear from the time it began playing that it had a profound effect on those in the courtroom. No one in the gallery made a sound and the hiss from the tape began coming out of the public-address speakers on the walls. Pratt's voice went from slow and deep to fast and squeaky as Commonwealth's Attorney Banks adjusted the speed on the dictation machine in which he played the tape. When it was adjusted correctly, he rewound it and started it over for the jury.

The tape was noisy and scratchy, but the jury and spectators could make out most of what April Boggs said as prosecutors set the Dictaphone on the table, directing its speaker at a microphone.

Pratt's voice was first, identifying the day, the time, the place, and the names of those present at the interview. He read April her Miranda warning and narrated as he gave April a KSP-96 form to sign, waiving her right to remain silent.

Her sobs could be heard clearly on the tape as she answered preliminary questions about her name, birthday, and address. She told Pratt that when she had dropped Jerome off at the Sugar Shack, he had told her to be gone for no more than twenty minutes or she would "have to deal with him."

She said she left him at the Sugar Shack and went to Dry Fork to try and call her ex-boyfriend from a pay phone there, but she could not reach him. She returned to Whitesburg hurriedly to pick up Jerome.

When she got there, she said, he got in the car and told her to drive him to Pound, Virginia, and told her he had killed two people. When they reached Fishpond Lake, a county park about three miles from the state line, he threw a holster out the window.

She maintained that she did not know exactly what had happened until they returned to the motel room at Super 8 and looked out the window.

"I saw all those police cars and I knew what had happened," she said.

Then, in answer to Pratt's questions, April Boggs rattled off a list of things for which they had spent the money—the motel room at Super 8, her ring, two pizzas, liquor from the American Legion Club, dinner at Applebee's in Hazard, a $38 motel room in Hazard, more beer, movie tickets to see Britney Spears in *Crossroads,* and $50 worth of clothing at Kmart.

Pratt's voice crackled through the speakers, firing a rapid series of questions at April Boggs, forcing her to clarify what she meant. He finally asked what they spent the rest of the money on.

"He spent it on drugs," April Boggs said.

April's voice became hard to understand as she began to cry again and the interview continued, but she acknowledged going to Blister Cook's house before the day of the murders, and said she knew T.J.

"I would sit in the car and the little boy—he would not let you sit in the car. He had to talk to you," she said.

Pratt asked if Jerome ever showed remorse for the murders.

"He does cry at night," she said, breaking down completely herself.

Pratt called an end to the interview at that point, and prosecutors turned off the tape.

Pratt testified that while April was at Whitesburg City Hall, he had her sit at a table with him while he emptied her purse and inventoried it. He said he found about $200 in cash and some credit cards, but nothing out of the ordinary. She could not account for $53 of the cash, but said that Jerome had given her some of the money he took during the robbery. She said she had been paid the other $150 by his father for some work she had done.

Pratt's testimony also introduced to the jury the fact that Jerome and April Boggs had stopped at Kentucky River Community Care, a local mental-health and substance-abuse agency, on the Monday and

Tuesday after the killings. He also outlined the evidence that he collected at the scene of the murders, including blood samples, a pellet gun, and a bottle.

When Carnes began the cross-examination, she drew attention from the boy to his father, asking almost immediately if there was evidence of drug trafficking at the crime scene. Pratt said there was not. She then moved on to the issue of money. The prosecution objected to her question about whether April had mentioned an argument over money in her statement, saying that everyone in the courtroom had already listened to the tape. The judge overruled them, however, and Pratt confirmed that there was nothing in the statement indicating that she had wanted Jerome to get them money.

He also confirmed that there was no evidence that April was in the trailer on the day of the murders, no evidence she had anything to do with moving the body, and that the evidence showed Jerome Boggs, not April, had checked them into the motel.

Carnes also emphasized that April Boggs had cooperated with police.

"She was cooperative in the taped interview, yes," Pratt answered.

He also answered affirmatively when Carnes asked if the police found the gun used in the murders as a result of the information she gave them.

Bledsoe, the only witness allowed to remain in the courtroom, was next. All through Pratt's testimony, he had sat at the prosecution table, his knees bouncing wildly as he jiggled his heels and fidgeted. On the witness stand, he suddenly became the picture of relaxation, lacing his fingers in front of him and slowly swiveling his chair.

Bledsoe had been in the KSP for about twelve years at the time of the trial, and had been a detective since December 2000. His first task on the witness stand was to explain the difference between a trooper and a detective.

Though not covered in his testimony, a trooper and a detective in the KSP are the same rank and get the same pay. The only difference is that detectives received an annual clothing allowance instead of uniforms.

Bledsoe explained to the jury that troopers drove marked vehicles, wore uniforms and visible badges, and their primary duties were to enforce traffic laws, investigate accidents, and answer complaints. Detectives' primary duty was to investigate serious crimes, such as burglary, robbery, and murder. Both troopers and detectives were trained to investigate the same things, but troopers had so many daily duties with complaints and patrol duties that they didn't have the time to devote to major cases. That's where detectives came in.

When a major crime was committed, a trooper was the first representative of the state police on the scene. It was the trooper's job to secure the scene and evaluate the situation, and then to make a preliminary report to a supervisor—either a sergeant or a lieutenant—at the local KSP post.

The supervisor then decided whether to assign a detective to the case, and if so, which detective to send.

In the Cook case, a WPD officer and a Letcher County deputy sheriff were the first on the scene, followed quickly by Trooper Rick Watts. Watts did a preliminary assessment of the situation and notified the Hazard Post. The post dispatcher then contacted Bledsoe to investigate.

As with Pratt, Bartley had Bledsoe describe the area around the crime scene, from the Sugar Shack beside the highway to the church next to the entrance to Blister Cook's driveway; up the hill past

Keetsie Cook's trailer, past the garage, where Blister worked on his beloved black Mustang, and into the driveway at his trailer. His testimony took the jury up the steps to the wooden porch, where two police officers stood guard at the door, and an emergency medical technician (EMT) stood just inside.

If someone parked at the Sugar Shack and walked, Bledsoe estimated, it would take no more than two minutes to make the trip.

He then took jurors inside the trailer, describing the layout of the rooms and the location of the bodies again to jurors, as Campbell and Pratt had already done.

Bledsoe said he did not touch the bodies then, because they were waiting for Campbell to arrive, but they did examine them visually. Once the bodies were removed, he said, officers began feeling around on the carpet, looking for bullets that might have exited. One of the bullets that had passed through T.J. Cook was located in the carpet on the living-room floor. The other bullet was never found, even though Bledsoe said he searched the trailer twice, and Whitesburg Police Chief Paul Miles and ATF Agent Jeff Baker searched it a third time, even taking the couch cushions to the Mountain Comprehensive Health Corporation's Whitesburg Clinic for X-rays. There was still no trace of the bullet.

Bledsoe's testimony about the crime was only slightly different from Pratt's in that he said T.J. had either crawled or been carried into the bedroom. He testified that it was possible that the child had crawled there because it was his bedroom and he could have seen it as a haven from more harm. However, outside the courtroom, Bledsoe said later that he believed the position in which the child was lying was unnatural and that he must have been placed there by another person.

Bartley then had Bledsoe walk the jury through the development of the case, beginning with the information that Blister Cook's brother gave him about a visitor at the trailer. Bledsoe was not allowed to tell the jury the details of what Keetsie Cook had told him, but he did testify that the KSP's intelligence branch had helped track down a truck that he eventually determined was owned by Donnie Baker.

Bledsoe was also not allowed to explain that Baker had seen Jerome Boggs in the trailer, only testifying that the information Baker had given him led him to Jerome Boggs.

Bledsoe told the jury that he went first to Jerome's father's house and information he received there led Trooper Derek Hall and Sergeant Claude Little to Mountain Breeze Apartments at Jenkins. While they were on their way, Bledsoe and Lieutenant Vic Brown waited at one end of the road leading to Jerome's parents' house. Pratt and Detective Ken Duff waited at the other end.

As it turned out, Little and Hall found Jerome first.

"On first contact, he was observed driving, his license was suspended, and he was arrested for driving on a suspended license," Bledsoe said.

April Boggs was not arrested immediately. Instead, she was taken to Whitesburg City Hall voluntarily, where she signed the waiver of rights form and made the taped statement that had already been played for the jury. Bledsoe had not been present when the statement was taped. He had been in Jenkins interviewing another resident of Mountain Breeze Apartments—Chris Duff. Bledsoe testified that Duff gave him the information about the Super 8 Motel that led Pratt and Detective Duff, who is no relation, to investigate room 101 at that motel.

Bartley had first asked Bledsoe to tell the jury

"what was going through your mind" about the crime before Jerome Boggs's name surfaced as a suspect, but April Boggs's defense attorneys objected to that line of questioning. Instead, Bartley asked Bledsoe to tell the jury how the case developed.

"When we first got there, we had two bodies and didn't know who did it. Naturally, the thing we do is start looking within and then move outward," Bledsoe said.

He said police first began looking at Belinda Cook as a suspect because she was the person who had called 911, and she and Blister Cook had been having trouble. He said police eventually discounted that theory and began pursuing Donnie Baker, who had been seen at the trailer shortly before the murders.

When Baker gave them Jerome Boggs's name, Bledsoe said police began looking at Boggs and realized that they had the right person. They located Jerome and April and continued the investigation by interviewing their neighbors and associates and doing searches of places they were known to have been around the time of the murders.

Bledsoe discounted the importance of April's statement in finding the murder weapon or finding out about the motel stay on the night of the murders. Bledsoe said he learned of the motel from Chris Duff, while April was en route to Whitesburg with the Jenkins police chief, and someone had stopped Whitesburg Chief Miles and given him information about the motel about the same time.

He said he had already been planning to search the area where the gun was found, and he was confident that officers would have found it even without April's help. Bledsoe said, on the night before the arrests, he had been talking with former captain Danny Webb, who, by the time of the trial, was the newly elected

Letcher County sheriff. Webb had prompted him on what he had to do next.

"I said, 'Yeah, I have to search that whole hillside all the way down and see if anybody threw the gun over the hill or in the creek,'" Bledsoe recalled.

Bledsoe testified that the gun was found directly below the bridge railing, where April Boggs had said, but also where police had already planned to search. He said it would have been found without her cooperation.

At Bartley's request, he also showed how the holster Jerome had used worked. The stitching that held the two sides of the leather together had been cut by lab technicians, but Bledsoe explained that the loop on the back of the holster was intended for a belt to slide through. Anyone using it would have had to unbuckle his belt and slide it through that loop, or shove the holster loosely down into his waistband. Bledsoe stood at the witness stand and demonstrated, shoving the holster into the top of his pants, and then sticking the gun in the holster.

For the prosecution, this indicated that April Boggs would have had to have seen Jerome put the holster on in the car, or would have had to have seen him wearing it.

It was nearing lunchtime and Bartley focused Bledsoe's testimony on how a revolver operates, first questioning what happens to the empty cartridge case after the gun is fired, and then whether any empty cases were left at the scene of the crime.

Bledsoe explained that unlike a semiautomatic weapon, which ejects the empty cases each time a bullet is fired, a revolver retains the empty cases. In the case of the gun used to murder Blister and T.J. Cook, a pin must be removed from underneath the barrel and the cylinder must be removed completely from the gun. The empty cases could then be shaken out into one's palm or onto the ground.

The gun used in the murders was a nine-shot, .22-caliber revolver. It was also a double-action revolver, meaning that a shooter could fire it one of two ways. He could pull the trigger, which would cause the cylinder to rotate and move a new shell under the hammer and cause the hammer to pull backward, then snap down against the firing pin. The other option was to pull the hammer back to a locked position, then pull the trigger, allowing it to snap.

Either way, the firing pin would hit the primer of the shell beneath it, causing the shell to fire.

Bledsoe told the jury that the gun was fully loaded with nine hollow-point bullets when it was found, but three of the bullets had been fired. Bartley then wanted to know the sequence of the fired cartridges. Two had been fired, one was unfired, then another was fired.

Though Bledsoe had already testified that he was not present when April made her taped statement to Detectives Pratt and Duff, he told the jury he had talked to her later.

Bledsoe recalled that he had taken April across the hall from the Whitesburg Police Department and into the commonwealth's attorney's conference room so officers could put Jerome in the interrogation room. It was there, Bledsoe said, that April had expanded on her taped statement about the argument she had with Jerome before the murders.

"She said they were arguing over the fact she was not happy with where they were living, they didn't have any money, and she was going home to her mother," Bledsoe testified.

The defense allowed that testimony to pass, but when Bartley asked if she had said anything about the

Family Dollar Store, attorney Barbara Carnes objected.

"We have not been provided with any of this material. Thirteen months after his investigation is complete, we get a letter from Edison alluding to an oral statement," Carnes complained at the bench conference with the judge. "The more we hear about it, the bigger it gets, and we ask that he not be allowed to testify about his late memory of things April supposedly said. It's not in the grand jury; it's not in his report; it's not even in that letter."

The judge ruled in her favor, directing the jury to disregard the question.

Bledsoe continued his testimony, with Bartley leading him through his investigation of the engagement ring, the search of the apartment, the search of the car, and the discovery of blood on Jerome's shoes.

Bledsoe testified that April had said nothing about buying the ring, but he learned through his investigation that it had been purchased the day of the murders. Since it was Sunday, Bledsoe said, he started thinking of where the couple could have purchased a ring when most stores were closed.

There were no retail jewelry stores in Whitesburg and few stores of any kind that would carry an engagement ring. Bledsoe headed to Wal-Mart and asked to see the store's surveillance tapes from February 17, 2002.

Bledsoe scanned the tapes, narrowing down the time period to after the time of the murders. It didn't take long to find what he was looking for. Bledsoe said the tape showed Jerome and April come out of the store, stop, and then go back inside.

Bledsoe then checked the store receipts to see if an engagement set had been sold that day. It had— ten to fifteen minutes before the tape showed April and Jerome leaving the store for the second time. Bledsoe said he went back to the jail and got the ring out of April's personal effects. He showed it to a woman working at the jewelry counter to make sure it was a Wal-Mart ring.

"The lady took out an identical ring," Bledsoe said.

Bledsoe testified that April did not appear to be restrained when she left the store. He said she and Jerome Boggs were walking two or three feet apart, side by side, out into the parking lot.

The detective also told the jury he had learned from interviews with other people that Jerome and April had gone to the Family Dollar Store in Whitesburg the day of the murders to return wedding presents. Bartley did not continue on that line of questioning, except to extract testimony that Bledsoe had visited the store and interviewed an employee about that visit.

Bartley's questioning mostly followed the investigation in chronological order, moving from Family Dollar to the liquor stores in Virginia. Bledsoe testified that ATF Agent Jeff Baker had gone to several liquor stores in Virginia and had picked up security tapes trying to confirm whether April and Jerome had been there.

Bledsoe testified that only one tape showed the couple. Bledsoe said it showed a green car pull up outside the business, then showed Jerome and April get out.

"Jerome Boggs goes back to the cooler and gets what looks to be about a case of beer. April stands at the county looking at lottery tickets or whatever's on the counter," Bledsoe said.

He said April stood beside another man at the counter for a few minutes; then he left. The couple then stood in line while another customer paid for

a purchase. When they paid and left the store, April
got into the passenger seat, while Jerome put his
beer in the trunk. He got into the car and drove
away. The tape was consistent with what April Boggs
had told police in her taped statement.

Bledsoe had testified earlier that he did not search
Jerome and April Boggs's apartment on the day of
their arrests because she had not given him permission to do so. However, he did obtain a search warrant and returned to the apartment later. It was on
that visit that he found Jerome's "restoration of
rights certificate," signed by the governor, framed
and hanging on the wall.

Bartley introduced that certificate and a paper
that Bledsoe said he found in a box in the bedroom.
That paper was a statement from Jerome's father,
Lee Boggs, saying he would pay her $150 a month
for cleaning his house.

There were many items that were not confiscated.
Bledsoe said he left some clothes that appeared to
belong to Jerome and some baseball caps. He said
there was also a small amount of furniture in the
apartment, including a kitchen table, a television, and
a bed. Bledsoe said he could not be sure if there was
either a sofa or a chair in the apartment when he
searched it. Bledsoe was looking for possible bloodstains on clothing in the apartment. There were a
couple of items that were sent for testing, but did not
test positive for bloodstains. There were also some
folded clothes that had apparently been washed and
stacked on the floor of the closet.

That was not the only place police searched for
bloodstains. Bledsoe testified that he, Agent Baker,
of the ATF, and an ATF forensic technician had
searched Jerome's parents' car—the car he and
April had been using the day of the murders. Bledsoe characterized the car as "very clean," and said it

smelled of ammonia and other cleaners. He said it appeared to have been vacuumed and the carpet appeared to have been shampooed. Still, he said the forensic technician located what appeared to be bloodstains on both sides of the front floorboard. Police collected a floor mat and some carpet samples from the car and sent them for testing.

However, Bledsoe testified under cross-examination that while the initial testing showed the stains were blood, lab tests could not match it to anyone connected to the Cook murder case.

The same was not true of all of the items tested in the case. Bledsoe said Detective Duff noted some small droplets that appeared to be blood on the white athletic shoes Jerome was wearing on the day of his arrest. The shoes were confiscated and sent to the state police laboratory for testing. The stains did prove to be blood.

"It belonged to T.J., the four-year-old baby," Bledsoe testified.

Butcher, April's private attorney, cross-examined Bledsoe. She moved first to the shoes, noting three times that the shoes belonged to Jerome and eliciting three yes answers from the detective to emphasize that the blood showed no connection between April and the murders. She also elicited testimony from Bledsoe that blood found on the carpets of the car Jerome and April were driving the day of the murder was inconsistent with the blood of both of the murder victims.

Though the questioning began cordially enough, it turned hostile quickly. Was Bledsoe sure the "restoration of rights" certificate was hanging on the wall and not in a box?

Bledsoe paused, then answered more carefully. The certificate was either hanging on the wall or leaning against the wall, he said. Was he sure it wasn't in a box?

"You're not even sure now whether it was on the wall or against the wall?" Butcher asked.

"It was on the wall. It was not in the box," Bledsoe said.

Belinda Cook was at the murder scene before police, wasn't she? Yes. She could have moved things or taken things away from the scene, couldn't she? Maybe, Bledsoe acknowledged, but he could not say that she had. He could not say that the scene was undisturbed, either, could he? No, he could not.

The questions jumped from one subject to another, but kept returning to two points: Belinda Hall Cook had been in the trailer that day, and Blister Cook had sold marijuana. The defense seemed to have two intents in asking those questions: Butcher obviously wanted to raise questions in the jurors' minds of whether anyone other than April Boggs had helped Jerome Boggs. She apparently also wanted to marginalize the importance of Blister Cook's death by playing on jurors' possible prejudice against anyone who sold marijuana.

In answer to the question about Belinda Cook, Bledsoe said that she did have blood on her jacket when police arrived at the scene, and the blood belonged to Blister Cook.

Though Butcher steered clear of asking how the blood got there, police had determined earlier that she had gotten the blood on her when she arrived and found her husband dead. Belinda had called 911, and during the conversation, she had informed the dispatcher that she was a nurse and would check to be sure that her husband was dead.

Butcher then turned to the layout of the area again, asking Bledsoe if "there was a church located close to where this drug dealing was going on?"

There was a church at the foot of the hill, Bledsoe answered.

Butcher also wanted the jury to think about the fact that Blister's brother Keetsie lived, as Bledsoe testified, within seventy-five yards of the trailer, where the murders occurred. She pressed Bledsoe to say that he could have seen anyone going in and out of Blister Cook's trailer. Bledsoe, however, would not oblige her.

"If the brother was looking out watching, yes," Bledsoe said.

She also questioned whether Belinda Cook had been injured the day of the murders, answering her own question by saying an EMT had treated her on the site.

She had been injured, Bledsoe said, in a fight with Blister's brother.

Butcher tried to establish that April could not have driven on the hill that day because Blister's black Mustang and Donnie Baker's four-wheel-drive pickup were already there. She went back to Bledsoe's earlier testimony, asking him if he had not testified earlier that no one else could park on the hill if Blister's car and Baker's truck were both there.

Bledsoe, however, would not budge. He said another vehicle could have parked on the hill because there was a garage halfway up where people could park if the driveway at Blister's was full.

From there, Butcher turned her attention back to the adult victim, pointing out repeatedly that the visitors just before Jerome Boggs had been there to "purchase marijuana." The first question was aimed at the fact that Bledsoe had filed no charges against Donnie Baker and Paul Williams Jr., but its real intent seemed to be pointing out to the jury again that Blister Cook sold pot.

She asked why Bledsoe didn't charge Baker and

Williams with purchasing marijuana. Bledsoe answered that he had not charged them with buying marijuana because neither man purchased it.

"Was Mr. Blister . . . Cook . . . giving marijuana away that day?" Butcher sneered.

"He did to them that day," Bledsoe answered.

Bledsoe testified earlier that Detective Pratt had known Donnie Baker from an earlier case, but Butcher seemed confused on the point. She spent several minutes asking a series of questions that left both her and Bledsoe questioning each other repeatedly about what the other meant. Butcher's questioning revolved around whether Pratt had known Jerome Boggs and why Bledsoe had not gone to Boggs's parents' home to question him. Bledsoe had gone to Boggs's parents' home and had learned that he and April Boggs were in the process of moving.

The questions then wandered to Mountain Breeze Apartments and the day that Jerome and April were arrested. Who had been at Mountain Breeze Apartments to arrest Jerome Boggs? Bledsoe named the six officers working on the case that afternoon— himself, Sergeant Little, Lieutenant Brown, Trooper Hall, a Jenkins police officer, and the Jenkins police chief. Butcher repeatedly asked if there had been more and who those others were.

"If you think there's more, give me the names and I'll tell you if they were there," Bledsoe finally said.

Butcher offered no other names, instead asking if using six officers was excessive to arrest one man.

"Depending on if you think that person has committed murder, no," the detective answered.

"Particularly if you think this person is very dangerous, isn't that right?" Butcher asked.

Bledsoe acknowledged that she was correct.

"I assume you would classify Jerome Boggs as a very dangerous person?" Butcher asked.

Bledsoe looked at Butcher as though she were exceedingly dense.

"Yeah—he killed two people."

"At this time, you didn't know that. You didn't have any information to support that. Isn't that true?" Butcher asked.

Bledsoe acknowledged that it was.

While on the surface, the questions may have seemed designed to belittle or exasperate the detective, the questioning actually played a role in the overall theory that the defense was asking the jury to accept—that April Boggs was too scared of Jerome to turn him in.

She questioned whether Bledsoe had received a notice of Jerome's release from prison, but Bledsoe did not recall. He said he assumed he had received a notice, and when he was asked the charge for which Jerome had been in prison, he turned the question back to Butcher.

"Theft, wasn't it?"

Boggs was serving a prison sentence for theft, though he had first been charged with first-degree robbery in the beating of Paschal Fields. Butcher did not delve into that, instead saying impatiently that she didn't want to get into it. She then asked whether Bledsoe knew how many times Jerome Boggs had been charged with felonies.

Bledsoe did not, but Butcher put the number at six, again asking Bledsoe whether he would agree or disagree with that number.

"He's been a thief all his life," Bledsoe said.

"If somebody said Jerome Boggs didn't have the tendency to commit a crime—that he had to be urged on—that wouldn't necessarily be true, would it?"

"No," Bledsoe replied.

Again the question was at the heart of the defense's case. The theory laid out in the prosecution's opening statement was that April Boggs's complaints about money had led her husband to murder the Cooks during a robbery. The defense's theory, however, was that Jerome Boggs needed no one to push him to commit robbery or murder. In the defense's version of the truth, April Boggs knew nothing about what Jerome had planned. She found out after the fact—when it was too late to stop it—and she was too scared of her husband to leave him or to notify the police about what he had done.

The testimony Butcher had just elicited from Bledsoe was part of the foundation for that argument. Jerome Boggs was a dangerous man—so dangerous that police felt it necessary to take six men to arrest him. How could one woman be expected to fight back against someone that even burly detectives, like Bledsoe, were afraid to go after alone?

Once she had established that Jerome Boggs—an admitted murderer and robber—was dangerous, Butcher returned to Blister Cook's history, questioning Bledsoe extensively on whether he knew that Cook had sold marijuana and why he had done nothing about it.

Was Jerome Boggs a "regular" customer of Blister Cook's? Bledsoe said he had information that Jerome Boggs had been at the Cook residence "a couple of times," but he said he did not know what a "regular" meant.

"You're not denying there was drug dealing going on up there, are you?"

No, Bledsoe replied. State police had received reports of drug dealing at the Cook trailer.

Butcher wanted to know if those reports had come to Bledsoe personally, but the detective said they had not. The reports had come to him through the state police post.

But couldn't the state police have assigned a trooper to help him with a drug buy? Butcher's line of questioning assumed, and tried to lead the jury to assume, that a detective was a detective, and Bledsoe could have done an investigation of drug deals at the Cook trailer himself.

However, as Bledsoe explained, he probably would not have been the person assigned to investigate a drug deal at that time, even though he was the only detective assigned primarily to Letcher County.

Bledsoe had taken a temporary undercover role while he was still a trooper and led an in-depth investigation into "doctor shopping." (Doctor shopping is the practice of going to several different doctors within days of each other, making the same complaint, and attempting to get narcotics prescriptions from each doctor.) The investigation Bledsoe was involved in had netted dozens of people who, police believed, had obtained prescriptions through such fraudulent means, and then sold the drugs on the street.

But by 2002, Bledsoe had been made a detective and the regular detectives with the Kentucky State Police had too high a profile and too heavy a workload to conduct undercover operations.

Bledsoe's job at the time was to investigate murders, robberies, burglaries, and similar crimes. He said there were detectives at the post assigned to drug investigations, and the duty of making a buy from someone like Blister Cook would probably have fallen to them or to "DESI" or "Special East," both state police slang for the department's Division of Drug Enforcement and Special Investigations.

DESI was divided into two areas—one for eastern Kentucky and one for western Kentucky.

It was the job of those detectives to stay under-cover and conduct drug buys and white-collar crime investigations below the radar.

"Were you aware this young, four-year-old child was living up there where there was regular drug dealing going on?" Butcher asked, edging her voice with incredulity at Bledsoe's answer.

No, Bledsoe said, he was not aware.

Butcher's line of questioning was suddenly cut off when the prosecution objected as Butcher said she "imagined" that members of Cook's family knew about it. Butcher withdrew the question, but the im-plication was already before the jury—that Blister Cook's family was partly responsible for T.J.'s death.

It was a risky ploy by the defense. On one hand, at-tacking the victims might lead a jury to devalue the crime. On the other hand, it might lead the jury to devalue the defense attorney and tune her out. Butcher abandoned the questioning for the moment, bringing the police into her crosshairs again.

She zoomed in on an apparent inconsistency be-tween Bledsoe's testimony and Pratt's. Pratt had tes-tified that he had found a little over $200 on April when he arrested her, but Bledsoe testified that when he picked up the ring to take it to Wal-Mart for identification, there was $150—three $50 bills—in the bag with the ring.

"Anybody know what happened to the rest of the money?" she asked.

Bledsoe answered calmly. The rest of the money was put into evidence at the Kentucky State Police Post. The $150 in the bag and the ring had at first been considered personal property, not evidence, and had not been taken to the post.

Unable to take that questioning any further,

Butcher switched gears again, going back to the
question of who lived at Mountain Breeze Apartments. She asked Bledsoe repeatedly about an affidavit he signed in support of a search warrant for
Jerome Boggs's parents' home, which Bledsoe said
was never used. In the affidavit, Bledsoe said that he
believed some of Jerome Boggs's property was still at
the house.

Butcher discounted Bledsoe's testimony that the
warrant was never used.

"An affidavit for a search warrant is a sworn statement and you would have to have sworn under oath
that Jerome Boggs had not moved all of his belongings from the home. Is that true?"

It was true, but it was not clear why the defense
was so adamant about the line of questioning.
Though it seemed aimed at showing that April had
not planned to take Jerome with her to the apartment at Jenkins, it was a bit perplexing, since
Butcher herself said that the statement said only
some of Jerome's belongings were at his parents'
home.

Butcher tried to get Bledsoe to acknowledge that
police would not have found the murder weapon if
not for April's help. Bledsoe, however, tried not to
say that. Instead, he said police had already planned
to search the area under the bridge and around the
trailer, and probably would have found the gun even
without her statement.

She did, however, garner testimony from Bledsoe
acknowledging that his case file narrative said
searchers were sent to the site where the gun was
found after April made her statement to police.

The detective at first said searchers had been
called out to go to the site while Pratt and Duff were
questioning April; Butcher, however, produced a

copy of the report that Bledsoe had written detailing the case that said otherwise.

That report, a narrative of the case that touched on major developments from beginning to end, and listed the persons whom police interviewed during the course of their investigation, was compiled from periodic progress reports that Bledsoe was required to submit, accounting for the time he spent on the investigation. The condensed report, which was fourteen pages long, was filed when the investigation was completed, but dated the day of the murders. It placed the time of the search for the gun after the interview with April and after she had accompanied Troopers Hall and McCray to look for the holster.

Bledsoe re-read the report as he sat on the witness stand and affirmed to Butcher that he remembered writing the report.

"You're not trying to tell this jury that Mrs. Boggs was not helpful in locating the murder weapon and in locating the holster, are you?" Butcher asked.

"No, she was very helpful in locating the holster," Bledsoe said, noting that April Boggs had gone with the troopers and showed them approximately where it was thrown out of the car. "She was helpful in saying a weapon was thrown in the area. What I was saying is a search was going to be conducted in that area anyway."

But, Butcher noted, no search had been conducted for four days prior to her interview.

"You agree with me, don't you?"

"Yes, I do."

The verbal sparring continued as Butcher turned to grand jury testimony in which Bledsoe said that April Boggs had "confirmed everything" that police had found out, and to the guilty plea by Jerome Boggs. She asked Bledsoe repeatedly if he had participated in the

plea agreement process. Bledsoe said he had, but that
it was mainly between the prosecutor and the family.

Butcher pressed on the issue, saying it was standard practice to involve the investigating officer and
she knew of no prosecutor who would not consult
the police officers before agreeing to a guilty plea.
Bledsoe again said that he had been consulted, but
that the principal decision was made by the family of
the victims.

"All I asked was, did you participate? I didn't ask if
you were the principal decision maker," Butcher
challenged.

Bledsoe repeated that he had participated. In
answer to Butcher's questions, he agreed that Boggs
had initially claimed to have no involvement in the
murders, but changed his plea when the investigation proved his involvement and he had been faced
with the death penalty.

Bledsoe testified that Jerome Boggs had told
police April had nothing to do with the murders
when police interviewed him before his sentencing.

Carnes, seated on the other side of April Boggs
from Butcher, wrote something on a legal pad, un-
derlined it, and reached it across the table in front
of Butcher. She asked only one more question—
again getting Bledsoe to confirm that he could not,
from Jerome Boggs's statement, say that anyone as-
sisted him in the crime.

Butcher asked no more questions of Bledsoe. The
prosecution witnesses so far had set the stage and
raised doubts about exactly how forthcoming April
Boggs had been. The testimony might have raised
doubts with jurors about her honesty and about her
intentions, but it had not been exactly the slam
dunk case that Bartley had foretold in his opening.
Still, it was obvious that April Boggs knew of the
killings after the fact and made no attempt to report

them. That alone might be enough for a jury to convict her, even it didn't meet the letter of the law's definition for facilitation.

The defense had scored points, too. Under cross-examination, Bledsoe had acknowledged that some of what April Boggs had told officers had been helpful. Through Bledsoe's words, the defense had also gotten into the record Jerome Boggs's statement that April was not involved. That alone was a step toward mitigating the damage.

The question now was whether the next few witnesses would add anything new to the case against April Boggs.

Chapter 22

It was already well into the afternoon when Bledsoe finally stepped down from the stand. He was the last police officer to testify. The rest of the prosecution witnesses would be people from whom police had gathered their evidence.

The defense offered no major challenges to the next two witnesses—Gail Cook, the manager of the jewelry department at Wal-Mart, where the engagement ring was purchased, and Katrina Brown, a former clerk at the Family Dollar Store in Whitesburg.

Cook, who was not related to the victims, identified the ring as having been sold by Wal-Mart for a price of either $99 or $199. She also identified a printout of daily sales from the store's jewelry department, with a diamond ring purchase highlighted in yellow.

From the information on the printout, Cook testified that the purchase was made at 7:28 P.M. on February 17, 2002. The ring cost $99, plus tax; the purchaser paid with $110 dollars and received $5.06 in change.

Neither the prosecution nor the defense had many questions for Cook, since her testimony dealt exclusively with the origin of the ring. Carnes asked whether the printout also showed the name of the purchaser. Since it was bought with cash, it did not. Cook said the name would have appeared if the purchase was made with a check.

Carnes also wanted to know how she could be sure the ring was purchased from Wal-Mart and not some other store. Cook said each ring sold by Wal-Mart was marked inside with "10K" or "14K" for ten-karat or fourteen-karat gold, and with a vendor's mark that identified it as a Wal-Mart ring. The ring that Bledsoe had shown her was identified in that way. So, Carnes asked, she could not buy the ring at Kmart and return it to Wal-Mart? That could not be done, Gail Cook testified.

Katrina Brown, the next witness for the prosecution, had been working as an assistant manager at the Family Dollar Store near the murder scene on February 17, 2002.

The store was the second one in the strip of businesses in the Parkway Plaza shopping center. Since it was a Sunday, the supermarket at the other end of the shopping center was the only other store that was open. The store never had more than two employees working at the same time, especially not on Sundays, and February 17, 2002, was no different.

Brown testified that she was in the stockroom preparing merchandise to be put on the sales floor when the lone cashier called for her to come up front. The woman said there was a suspicious customer in the store and she wanted a manager to see him. The customer was Jerome Boggs. He was wandering around the store and acting strangely and Brown said it worried her.

"I told her (the clerk) to go to the back because I thought maybe he was going to shoplift," Brown testified.

Brown said she could see all the way to the back of the building from her vantage point at the cash register and she watched as Jerome Boggs looked around in the hardware section of the store and then picked up a hammer. She said he looked up at her, started "beating it in his hand" and walking toward her.

She testified that she was scared and Boggs was within five feet of her when the front door opened and April Boggs came in and said, "Is my husband in here? I've lost my husband." Brown said it was odd because she was no more than ten feet from Jerome Boggs when she asked the question and had to have seen him.

She said Jerome walked back around the back of the store, put the hammer on a shelf, and left with April.

Brown said she watched the two cross the nearly empty parking lot toward a green car parked in front of a closed insurance office on the opposite side of the parking lot, near the entrance to the shopping center. It was about an hour later, Brown said, when she heard sirens passing by the store. She heard later still that there had been a double murder a short distance from the shopping center.

Under questioning by Bartley, Brown said that April Boggs had been inside the store with her husband earlier. Brown said she had seen the two of them there before she went into the stockroom, but when the cashier called her to come up front, April had left the store.

Brown said as far as she knew, the two had not returned any merchandise.

While there was no sure evidence that the couple had not returned any items, the fact that Brown testified that to her knowledge they had not was significant for the prosecution. The investigation showed that the couple had told other people that they had returned wedding presents to the store on the day of the murders. If prosecutors could raise doubt about that part of the story, it might lead jurors to believe that the trip to the Family Dollar Store was planned not to return gifts, but to rob the store.

Though Brown said she had been very scared about the incident and thought about calling the police, she didn't, until after she saw Jerome and April Boggs on television after their arrests. Until then, she hadn't connected the murders to the incident at the store.

Brown testified on cross-examination that after her initial fear, she thought little about the incident, until she saw the video of Jerome and April Boggs. It was then, after talking to a coworker who was somehow related to the Cooks, that she decided to call police.

"So you didn't call police until after you talked to a member of the Cook family?" Butcher asked.

Brown said the woman had already known about the incident, and when she learned that the people in the store were the same ones accused in the murder, she encouraged Brown to call police.

"I think she was kin to them, she said something about it," Brown replied.

Though the defense had few questions for Brown, the next two witnesses were more controversial and would not get off as easily.

Chapter 23

Kathy Clark Hall was thirty-seven years old, with wavy black hair and a black T-shirt dress with a tattoo peeking out of the right sleeve. She also had a history with Jerome Boggs.

Clark had lived with Jerome before he went to prison for the robbery of Paschal Fields. She was also to be one of the main witnesses for the commonwealth against April Boggs, because she had been with Jerome and April on the night of the murders.

She testified that her son Chris Duff, who was eighteen at the time of the murders, had asked her to take him to the Super 8 Motel that night because Jerome wanted her to buy beer for him. It was a Sunday night, and most of Kentucky's wet counties had blue laws prohibiting the sale of alcoholic beverages on Sundays. Jerome would have had to drive all the way back to Virginia to buy it himself. Jerome and April didn't have a way to drive there, because they had gotten his parents to drop them off at the motel and given them back the car.

Hall had a car, and she wouldn't even have to drive to Virginia. She told the court that she was a member of the American Legion Club at Neon and could buy beer there, so Jerome had asked her to get it for him.

The testimony raised eyebrows in the courtroom. Though the Legion was widely thought to be bootlegging liquor and beer, and had been raided by police in the past, this was testimony in open court. Under the law, members of private clubs located in dry territories, like Letcher County, may store alcoholic beverages at the club to drink when they were there, but the clubs may not sell.

Yet here was Hall, a nonveteran, testifying that she was a member of the veteran's club and could buy beer there. In fact, she testified not only that she could buy beer there, but she did so for Jerome Boggs. Kentucky also considered it bootlegging to buy alcoholic beverages for another person and deliver them to a dry territory.

Hall told the court that she, her son Chris, and her fifteen-year-old son, Willis, went to the motel to meet Jerome and April and pick up money for the beer. Willis, she said, waited in the car while she and Chris went inside.

She testified that the room was a mess, with pizza boxes everywhere, the bed messed up, and beer cans and bottles sitting around. Jerome sat in the middle of the couch rolling a joint. April was there, too, but she left to get Jerome some coffee while Hall and her son were there.

Bartley asked Hall how April had acted when Jerome asked her to get his coffee.

"She just leaned over and hugged him and gave him a kiss and said, 'Yes, honey, I'll get it for you.'"

Hall testified that April had acted as she normally did that night, and at Jerome's urging, she showed Hall the engagement ring Jerome had bought her that day. Hall said the ring was "real pretty" and Jerome told her it had cost "four or five hundred dollars."

Hall testified that Jerome gave her $100 so she could buy gas and cigarettes for herself and beer for him; then she and Willis drove to Neon to get the beer. She said she spent $8 to fill up the tank on her truck and bought chips and a soft drink for her son before she went to the Legion to pick up the beer.

When she returned, she said, she sat on the side of the Jacuzzi and watched the late news as reporters talked about the murders.

Prompted by Bartley, Hall said she had seen Jerome smoke marijuana and then pass the joint to April, who also smoked it and then passed it to her son. She testified she saw no marks on April to indicate she had been hit and that April did not ask her for help and did not appear frightened.

When the bailiff passed her the engagement ring in its plastic evidence bag, Hall said it appeared to be the same one that April showed her on the night of the murders.

The defense could not let Kathy Clark Hall's testimony pass. Hall had already testified to buying bootleg beer and watching her eighteen-year-old son smoke pot. This was a prosecution witness that Butcher could tear apart without fear of alienating the jury.

Under questioning from Butcher, Hall said she had lived with Jerome for about three months, seven or eight years before, but the living arrangement was broken up when he was sent to jail for the robbery of Paschal Fields. Her son Chris had met Jerome then, and she would take him to visit Jerome even after Jerome and April were married. Chris was not Jerome's son, and Butcher pounced on the testimony, pointing out his age again.

"Seventeen or eighteen, and you drove him down there to smoke pot with Jerome Boggs in a motel room?" Butcher asked.

"No, I took him down there to get beer," Hall returned. Besides, she said, he was eighteen years old.

"I can't do nothing with him," she said.

She acknowledged that she had taken her fifteen-year-old son, too, but said she had left him in the car while she went inside the motel. She denied smoking pot herself or drinking beer, but said that she "did snort a pill with Jerome."

Hall denied that she bought the pills with the money Jerome Boggs had given her. She said the pill was a 7.5-milligram Lorcet pain pill for which she had a prescription because of a back injury she had suffered in a car accident, Hall said.

"The doctor who gave you these pills, did he prescribe or state for you to snort them?"

"No," Hall answered.

Butcher also pounced on apparent inconsistencies in Hall's story. She had told Bledsoe when he interviewed her that Jerome had given her only $50, but she testified in court that he had given her $100. Hall said he had given her $50 first, then took it back and gave her $100.

Butcher asked if that didn't strike Hall as strange that Jerome would have $100 to hand over to her, but Hall said it didn't.

"He told me a week before that, maybe a week and a half, that he got his check back," she said.

However, she said, when she got to the motel room and asked him about his check, he said he hadn't gotten it. April said the same thing. Why then, Butcher asked, did it not seem strange that Jerome had money to burn?

"I thought he got his check back," she insisted. "I thought he might have thought I wanted to borrow some and just said that."

The defense also tried to paint Hall as a jealous

former lover of Jerome's. Butcher had objected during the prosecution questioning when Hall tried to testify that Jerome had told her April was jealous of her, but Butcher tried to turn the question around now.

She noted early on in her questioning that even though Kathy Clark Hall and Jerome Boggs had lived together when he was sent to prison the first time, he did not move back to her house when he got out in 2001. Instead, he started seeing April and asked her to marry him.

"Jerome never bought you a ring, did he?" the attorney asked.

Yes, Hall replied, he had given her a ring when they lived together. Had she kept it? Butcher wanted to know.

"I gave them back to that cop," Hall said. "I had two rings and I gave him both of them. I said he probably stole those, too."

Butcher also questioned if Hall had maintained her relationship with Jerome by visiting him in prison. Hall said she visited him in jail after he was arrested in the Paschal Fields case, but had not visited him again after he was sentenced and sent to prison. She said she had called him only once when he was in prison.

She and April were not friends then, were they?

"She was nice to me; I was nice to her," Hall said.

Butcher said that was not what she had asked.

"You were not April's friend, were you? You were Jerome's friend."

"I didn't know her that well," Hall replied.

In other words, Butcher said, there was no reason for April to ask her for help or ask her to take her with her when she left the motel room.

Hall agreed that there was not.

Her son fared no better than she had, when he

was called to testify after she left the stand. It had been Christopher Brandon Duff who identified the holster that police had found in the grass near Jenkins, and it was he who had told police that Jerome had loaned him a .22 revolver to target shoot.

Chris Duff had just taken the oath to tell the truth and taken a seat on the witness stand when Deputy Bert Slone laid the murder weapon and holster on the oak rail in front of him.

Chris testified that it looked like the same gun Bledsoe had shown him soon after Jerome and April Boggs were arrested, but that was not the first time he had seen it. He testified that he had seen the gun two or three months before the murders when he and Jerome had used it to target shoot. Bartley, the prosecutor, asked him whether the holster was the same one he used then, but Chris picked it up and looked at the back before answering. It was the same, he said.

Bartley wanted to know why he picked it up and looked at the back.

"Because of the belt buckle," Chris answered.

He said the holster he had used had a loop on the back and he had to unfasten his belt and slip it through that loop to wear the pistol on his side.

Jerome had not worn the pistol that day, Chris testified. Instead, he had carried a .22 rifle to target shoot.

Chris Duff testified to the things the prosecutor needed him for—he linked the gun to Jerome Boggs, he said he was present at the motel the night of the murders, and he described a party at Jerome and April Boggs's apartment at Jenkins a couple of days later.

But while Chris Duff's testimony confirmed many of the things Bartley wanted to get before the jury, it also went off in entirely new directions. Rather than testifying that Jerome had called him and asked him to get some beer for him, as he said in his statement to police, Duff testified that April had called him and asked him to sell Jerome some drugs. He also testified, over the objection of the defense, that April was "sketching" on the telephone book when he went to the motel.

Bartley asked the question about the telephone book after first getting Chris Duff to describe what he saw in the motel room, and asking if he had ever seen April use the telephone while he was in the room.

According to Chris's account, the motel room was fairly large and open. Jerome was sitting on the couch rolling up marijuana, and April was somewhere near the bed when he came into the room. He said April later took another bag of pot out of a drawer.

No one else was there when Chris Duff and his mother arrived. Later, his mother left and his friend Amanda Burton arrived to give him a ride home. A pizza deliveryman also came to the door once.

Barley wanted to know if he had seen April use the telephone, and when Chris said that he had, Bartley asked if he had seen the phone book. When Duff said the book was next to April, Bartley asked if there was anything unusual about the phone book. Before Chris Duff could answer, the defense objected to the question.

The prosecution had intended that testimony to help them introduce the writing on the telephone book, which the judge had earlier excluded from the trial unless the author could be established.

However, the defense sought to head off the testimony. While Carnes cited the judge's pretrial ruling, Butcher drew attention to his other testimony.

She said she had a copy of the statement he gave to

Bledsoe—a statement Chris Duff signed—and said his testimony already was inconsistent with that statement.

"His testimony is already—before we go any further—contradictory in many direct and important ways," Butcher whispered at the bench. She said allowing him to go even further afield by testifying about the telephone book would cause irreparable harm to the defense case.

Wright disagreed, overruling the objection. While Bartley earned the right to ask the question again, it only seemed to perplex Chris Duff when the prosecutor asked him if there was anything unusual about the phone book.

"What do you mean by unusual?" Chris asked.

"I don't know. I wasn't there," Bartley replied. But, he said, Chris Duff had already testified he saw April and saw the telephone book.

"Was there anything unusual about it?" Bartley asked.

"She was sketching on it, if that would be unusual," Chris said.

Chris, however, said he could not see what she was sketching on the telephone book. Unable to draw a conclusion about the writing on the telephone book from Chris Duff, Bartley moved on.

Chris testified to seeing April take more marijuana from a drawer in the room, and testified that he had told his mother to leave and he would find a ride home later.

Bartley wanted to know why he had done that.

"I'm not going to lie. I smoke marijuana," Chris testified. "He (Jerome) had marijuana there and I was going to stay and smoke it."

Chris testified to partying with Jerome and April again later that week at their apartment in Jenkins. He said he did not know a lot of the people at that party, but he said some of his friends were there.

He also testified that he had helped the couple move furniture into the apartment. He had helped out some on the morning that Jerome and April Boggs were arrested, but Jerome had not. He said Jerome was just driving into the parking lot in a white Yugo when state police drove into the parking lot behind him, pulled him over, and arrested him.

Again, as with the other witnesses, Bartley questioned Chris carefully about his time with the Boggses after the murders, asking in each situation if April Boggs had asked him to help her get away from Jerome.

"She's never shown any symptoms of trying to get out," he answered.

Chris Duff was intended to be a star witness, putting the murder weapon in Jerome Boggs's hands and showing that April Boggs was so captivated with her husband that she doodled her love for him on the phone book the very night he told her he had killed a four-year-old child. His testimony was meant to show that April Boggs had been fully invested in her marriage and that the murders had made no change in her feelings toward her husband.

Though the testimony headed in that direction, while Bartley did the questioning, when it came time for cross-examination, Chris Duff's testimony seemed a disaster.

Butcher asked only four preliminary questions before getting to the red meat of the cross-examination: she asked Chris's age, if he had a job, if he was attending school, and if he had any source of income.

He testified that he was nineteen, had no job, was not going to school, and had no income.

"Do you sell drugs now?" Butcher asked casually.

The prosecution sprang up to object, but before the judge could call the attorneys to the bench, Chris

Duff, his eyes blinking rapidly below his messy hi-lo haircut, apparently felt compelled to say something.

"That's irrelevant to this trial. This is not my trial," he blurted.

"When we have an objection, you wait until I rule," Wright snapped.

At the bench, Bartley tried to rescue his witness.

"As the witness said, I think it's irrelevant," Bartley said. "It's certainly prejudicial and trying to impeach his character with specific bad acts, which is improper."

Butcher, however, noted that Chris Duff himself had testified that Jerome had wanted Chris to sell him drugs. Wright agreed that he had, but the judge asked, since that was already established, why had Butcher asked the question?

"I guess I just want to know if that's still his source of income—if he's moved up in the world or if he's still a drug dealer," she said.

The judge still didn't buy the legitimacy of the question, however. Butcher said the situation "always goes to a person's credibility," but said she would withdraw the question.

"I have other things to ask," she said.

Butcher left that line of questioning for a moment, but only for a moment. She elicited testimony that Chris Duff lived with a female cousin in Fleming-Neon, not his mother, and that he had not had contact with Jerome Boggs since Boggs's arrest. She also questioned him about whether he had met Jerome Boggs while Jerome was living with Chris's mother several years before. She then returned to the drug question quickly, asking him what kind of drugs he had been selling. Chris answered the question, but Butcher claimed not to have heard his answer.

"They was wanting alcoholic beverages and narcotics," he said loudly.

Butcher wanted to know what kind of narcotics Boggs had wanted.

"Medication."

"Was there a particular name of the pill you specialized in?"

"Hydrocodone," he answered.

Butcher also asked if he was sure that it was April and not Jerome who called him. Chris said he was positive that it was April and that she called him twice. Chris said he did not remember the time of the calls, but said April had told him they had "big money" and asked if he could "get anything."

"I said, 'Yes, what were you looking for?' and they told me," Chris said.

"April told you or they told you?"

"April told me, but Jerome was in the background."

Butcher questioned him closely on whether he had told the truth when he gave his statement to Bledsoe and on whether he had read the statement. Butcher gave a copy of Chris's statement to him to review on the stand, but he declined to read it to the jury, and became hostile when Butcher asked if he had a chance to review it.

"I just did, didn't I?" he asked.

Butcher read part of the statement back that said Jerome had called him and said he was at the Super 8 Motel and wanted to know if there was any way he could get to the beer store.

Chris replied that April had actually called him, instead of Jerome.

"So this statement that you gave to the detective within a few days of when this occurred is a complete and total lie. Is that what you're saying?"

The prosecution objected to Butcher characterizing the statement that way, noting that Chris never said his statement was "a complete and total lie."

Judge Wright agreed, but the question had already been asked in front of the jury.

When Butcher rephrased her question to point out that the statement did not mention April calling him, Chris said he was intoxicated when the statement was taken.

"You were intoxicated. Did you tell that to Detective Bledsoe?"

"No."

"And he is a trained police officer, is that right?"

"I'm pretty sure he is," Chris said.

Butcher questioned whether Chris Duff knew what he was doing when he signed the statement.

"My signature is on there isn't it?"

Butcher asked for copies of the statement to be given to the jury and the court took a fifteen-minute recess to allow that. Chris, however, would have to return to the stand when the recess was over.

When he did, Butcher attacked his credibility again, noting that he had said in his statement that Jerome showed him the bags of marijuana, but that he had testified that April had gotten them out. Chris said April had taken then out when Jerome asked for them, but Jerome had shown them to him.

"You didn't say that," Butcher said.

"I didn't write that; it's not my problem," he said.

"You signed it, though?"

"So? And your point is?"

The judge stopped the exchange, ordering Chris to answer the question. He acknowledged that he had signed the statement.

Rebuttal from Bartley and a recross from Butcher showed that Bledsoe had written out the statement as Chris talked, and that Chris had signed it. In answer to her last question, Duff testified that he did not intend to say that Bledsoe had made up the statement.

But Butcher had raised credibility questions about

Chris Duff that were bound to make at least some in the courtroom question whether he had made it up. Two of the prosecution's main witnesses had testified to illegal activities themselves. The defense was banking on the hope that the jury would discount their testimony entirely. If so, there would be no proof that April Boggs had written love notes on the telephone book, no proof she had been out of Jerome Boggs's sight, and no proof that she had been unaffected by the revelation that her husband had killed two people.

After Kathy Clark Hall's and Chris Duff's testimony, it was beginning to look as though April Boggs had a chance of beating the charges against her.

Chapter 24

The court recessed for forty minutes after Duff's testimony, giving the prosecution time to regroup. It had only four more witnesses—Bartley estimated about thirty minutes of testimony—and it would be done with the case against April Boggs. A case that had taken more than a year to build would be over in less than a day. Then it would be Butcher and Carnes's turn to try and convince the jury that their client was innocent.

So far, the prosecution case had been a roller-coaster ride. From the riveting taped statement by April Boggs, to the descriptions of Jerome and April's activities after the murders, the case had seemed to be picking up steam against April Boggs. But the defense had done some damage, too, able to point out that April Boggs had cooperated with police, and calling into question the testimony of two of the prosecution's key witnesses.

Lawyers know that what jurors hear about at the end of the day gives them something to ponder through the night, and to stop after Chris Duff's testimony would not be good for the commonwealth. The prosecution had only four more witnesses to present to swing the case back in its favor, and Bartley and Banks wanted to do that before closing for the day.

Those four witnesses, while not blockbusters with shocking statements, were nonetheless solid witnesses that were difficult for the defense attorneys to attack without damaging their own client. Butcher could argue and belittle Chris Duff without much fear that the jury would perceive her as a shrew. But the prosecution's final four witnesses had no discernible bias against April Boggs. In fact, the first prosecution witness after the break was a friend of April's, and the other three didn't even know her.

It was 4:42 P.M. when court resumed, almost the end of the day in this blue-collar community where supper was early, timed to coincide with the end of a hard shift. The jury would be getting hungry and tired, and the lawyers had to be mindful of that irritable state. The faster it could get its case over with, the better it would be.

Amanda Burton was a pretty twenty-one-year-old brunette, a soft-spoken friend of April Boggs's. She had transferred into Letcher High School when she was a junior and had made friends with April, a classmate who was thoroughly at home at the school.

Burton was also a friend of Chris Duff's, and at the time of the murders, she was living at Mountain Breeze Apartments with Duff's cousin, the same one he was living with at the time of the trial. She remembered the murders well because they had been committed the day after her birthday, and because Chris had called her that night and asked her to come to the Super 8 Motel and pick him up.

It was 11:45 P.M. when he called, and Burton said she was out of cigarettes. She had to go to her mother's house to borrow money for cigarettes, but before she could leave, Chris called her again. This time he

promised that Jerome would give her money for cigarettes and gas if she would come and pick Chris up.

When she arrived, Jerome and April Boggs and
Chris Duff were the only ones in the room. They
talked some about the murders that occurred, but
Burton said there was no indication that the Boggses
were involved. Jerome, however, wasn't acting normal.

"Jerome was just really messed up. He was on
something, and April wasn't talking that much. We
talked a little about friends from school and stuff,
but . . . ," she said.

April did show her the engagement ring, and
Burton testified that April told her she had gotten it
the day before in Tennessee. She also testified that
Jerome had "a large amount of money," possibly in
a rubber band. She saw the roll when Jerome got it
out to pay her for picking Chris up.

Jerome also showed her marijuana in what Burton
described as "a big freezer bag. It was not half full,
but it was almost half full." Burton was in the motel
room about thirty minutes—long enough to talk for
a little while and smoke a joint with Jerome, April,
and Chris, before she and Chris Duff left for the
night. She testified later that April left the room
once for about ten minutes alone. She said Jerome
was "really worried about her" and kept wondering
aloud where she was, but she did not remember
whether Jerome had gone to get her or if she came
back on her own.

The day after the murders, the Boggses moved to
Mountain Breeze, and became Burton's neighbors.
Burton said she went to their apartment on the
Tuesday and Wednesday after the murders. Once
again, Jerome and April were entertaining friends
on Tuesday, but on Wednesday, Jerome was alone on
the couch and April was apparently in bed.

"There was all kinds of people there Tuesday.

They was just partying and stuff. They had liquor, more pot, beer—just partying."

Near the end of Burton's testimony, Bartley asked again: did April ask Amanda to help her get away? Burton's answer was the same as Kathy Clark Hall's and Chris Duff's: April had not asked her to help her get away from Jerome Boggs.

Butcher again did the cross-examination, but tread more lightly with Burton. She wanted to know when she met April, when she met Jerome, and if Burton had ever been Jerome's girlfriend. Burton said she had met him the summer before and had gone riding around with him once, but had considered him a friend, not a boyfriend. She had known April since she was seventeen.

Burton said Jerome had pulled the marijuana out from under the couch cushion at the motel room, and yes, she had smoked some with him that day and on the following Wednesday when she visited at the Boggses' apartment at Mountain Breeze.

She left the witness stand without any of the hostile exchanges that had marked the two witnesses before her.

The only thing the defense seemed to gain from her testimony was that April had not been the one to get the marijuana out to show it to her.

The prosecution, however, had shown that a four-year friend of April's had been with her the night of the murders and had noticed nothing really unusual about her behavior. April had also not asked her to help her escape from Jerome. Even better for the prosecution, Burton had not been hostile or evasive toward the defense. With the prosecution's case winding down and the day coming to an end, the testimony had been good for the commonwealth.

The next three witnesses would present little risk to the commonwealth's case, either. The first was the desk clerk who had checked April and Jerome into the Super 8.

Lisa Reed didn't really know either Jerome or April, but had dealt with them briefly at the motel. She identified the room receipt, and testified that she remembered when they checked in because there was a problem with renting the room.

"I told them I need an ID. She showed me hers, but where[as] she was under twenty-one, I couldn't rent her a room," Reed remembered.

Jerome claimed not to have any identification, telling the clerk he had just gotten out of prison. At that time, he had been out of prison for eight months, however, and April pointed out that he had been out awhile and had rented a room at the motel before.

Reed checked his past record at the motel, and after finding that he had paid his bill and caused no damages, she rented a room to him using the information already on file. He asked for a particular room—the Jacuzzi room that overlooked the river.

Using the receipt for reference, Reed said they checked into the room at 3:13 P.M., but she didn't need a reference to remember that police were still across the river at the Cook residence at the time. Jerome called the desk shortly after they arrived and complained that the heat in the room wasn't working. Reed said when she and a maintenance person went to the room to check the heat, Jerome and April were sitting on the couch, eating pizza, and watching the police investigate the murders across the river.

"He asked me what happened and I said apparently someone murdered that man and his baby," Reed recalled. "He said, 'Blister?' I hadn't mentioned any name, but he said, 'Blister,' and she said, 'And his baby.'"

Reed said later that evening she had left the lobby

again, and when she returned, April was sitting on
the sofa near the desk. When Reed asked if she
needed anything, she replied that she was waiting
for more pizza.

Reed also saw Jerome in the lobby that evening—
once to get change, and once "just pacing."

The defense let Reed leave the stand with only a
couple of questions to stress the fact that it was
Jerome—not April—who had asked for the Jacuzzi
room facing the crime scene.

Kathy Brown, a housekeeper at the motel in February 2002, testified that she had seen the Boggses
the next morning. She was assigned to clean the
room in which they had stayed the night before and
said it was obvious from the condition of the room
that someone had been partying.

She said there were liquor bottles, beer cans, food
boxes, marijuana seeds, and papers all over the
room. Jerome and April had not left the motel yet,
and she also noted their behavior.

"They looked anxious. They were going up and
down the hallway looking out the doors," Brown
said.

The defense let her pass with only one inconse-
quential question.

The final prosecution witness drew an objection
from the defense because they claimed they had not
been notified she would be a witness. Banks, however, said he had notified them that she might be a
witness.

As it turned out, it mattered little. Tammy Whitaker
was an employee of the Leslie Knott Letcher Perry
Community Action Agency (LKLP), an antipoverty
social services agency. The agency handled applica-
tions for food for the local Food Pantry, a nonprofit
Christian organization that provided emergency food
to the poor.

The Food Pantry, run out of an old house near downtown Whitesburg, would give emergency food to anyone who needed it, once every three months.

Whitaker's only reason for testifying was to identify a Food Pantry application that Jerome Boggs and April Boggs had filled out on January 23, less than a month before the murders, saying they had no money and no food.

The prosecution intended to use the application to show that the two said they had no means of support less than a month earlier, but that Jerome was flashing a roll of money to everyone the night of the murders.

The defense had no questions at all for Whitaker. The prosecution's case was over. It ended not with high drama, but with the mundane identification of a document with no direct bearing at all on the case at hand. All that the document showed was that Jerome and April Boggs had no money a month before the murders—a fact that seemed painfully obvious given that neither of them had a regular job.

The prosecution's case had been mainly intended to show that April Boggs had ample opportunity to leave her husband and call police when she learned he had committed the murders, but she did nothing to report the crimes or get away from her husband. Much of the testimony was aimed at proving to the jury that Jerome Boggs had committed the crimes, and at gaining sympathy for T.J. Cook. Nothing was presented showing that April knew of the plot beforehand, though prosecutors hinted that she did, when they introduced testimony about Jerome Boggs's behavior at Family Dollar.

The testimony of Katrina Brown, the store's assistant manager, had been meant to raise questions in the jurors' minds. If April Boggs had not known her husband planned to rob someone, why had she parked on the other side of the empty shopping center rather than in front of the door? Also, why would she burst in as he approached the clerk with a hammer and ask where he was, even though he was in plain sight? If they were going to the store to return wedding gifts, why didn't they return them?

There was no evidence to prove she knew of the alleged attempt to rob the store, but the hints fit in well with the prosecution's theory that she had told Jerome they had to have money, and that he had gotten them money by killing Blister and T.J. Cook and stealing $1,500. Perhaps Jerome failed to get money at the first place he tried, became frustrated, and took more extreme measures at the second place—Blister Cook's trailer. The evidence was circumstantial, but as prosecutors were fond of telling juries, circumstantial evidence meant only that common sense would tell anyone that the circumstances presented added up to a crime.

Police and the commonwealth's attorney believed it was possible that April had known Jerome planned to rob the Family Dollar, but got scared at the last minute and stopped him. They also believed she dropped him off at the Sugar Shack knowing he planned to rob Blister Cook, but didn't go to the trailer with him because she couldn't stomach it. The problem was getting jurors to believe it.

While the jurors turned the testimony over in their minds that night, the attorneys on both sides turned the pages of law books. By the next morning, the defense had formulated a new line of attack, this time aimed at the prosecution's entire case.

The defense had stressed to the jury that the only bad acts that could be proven were committed by Jerome—not by April. But to the judge, they claimed the prosecution's case did not fit the elements of the crime as set out in Kentucky law, and asked for a directed verdict of acquittal.

The state statute on facilitation said that an accused must have been "acting with knowledge that another person is committing or intends to commit a crime, he engages in conduct which knowingly provides such person with means or opportunity for the commission of the crime, and which in fact aids such person to commit the crime."

Butcher and Carnes argued—many would say accurately—that the prosecution had not proved beyond a reasonable doubt that April Boggs had known her husband was going to commit the murders.

But Commonwealth's Attorney Banks presented case law that said proof of prior knowledge was not required to convict a person of facilitation to a crime. Banks contended that the defendant had only to provide the means for someone else to commit a crime, and that a reasonable person could infer from the course of conduct that a crime was going to be committed.

He argued that the prosecution showed beyond any doubt that April Boggs had provided her husband with the means to commit the crime by driving him to the Sugar Shack, dropping him off, then returning within the specified time to pick him up. His conduct prior to the crime, particularly in the Family Dollar Store, had been such that April Boggs should have been able to infer that he planned to commit a crime, Banks argued.

Carnes, however, continued to argue that the law required prior knowledge of the crime, and at the earliest, April Boggs's knowledge of the crime began when her husband got back in the car and told her he had killed two people.

The judge agreed with Banks, overruling the defense motion to order April Boggs's acquittal. The defense would have to put on a case before the jury.

If the prosecution truly had not made its case, then the defense had little to worry about. As long as their witnesses were not impeachable, and as long as they didn't trip up, April Boggs would have it made. The prosecution had had two witnesses that may have really hurt their case against April Boggs. If they really had had that effect on the jury, then as long as the defense could avoid the same kind of mishap with its witnesses, they would be all right.

But few believed that the prosecution had failed to make its case. They showed that Jerome Boggs had committed the crimes, that April Boggs had learned of them as soon as she picked him up, and that she didn't report her husband to police, even when she had the opportunity to do so. Perhaps the most damaging testimony had come not from the police officers or from the friends of the Boggses', but from the motel clerk who had seen April Boggs sitting on the couch with her husband and eating pizza as the two of them watched police investigate the murders.

That, coupled with the knowledge that April Boggs had omitted from her statement any mention of the engagement ring purchased on the night of the murders, would most likely push the jury over the edge to a guilty verdict.

The problem was, that no attorney knew what was going on in the mind of a juror. Even the defense attorneys' own actions might have turned jurors against April Boggs. Not only had the defense attorneys gone after the mother and son who had visited the motel, and had done drugs with Jerome and April Boggs, they had also gone after the lead investigator—a long-time state police officer with no black marks on his record. In addition to that, one of the victims was a child and the defense had not yet made any acknowledgment of that tragedy. The jury might also be put off by the tone of the defense case. Sarcasm dripped from Butcher's words as she tried to impeach Bledsoe and the other witnesses' testimony.

The defense would have to proceed as though they were losing the battle.

Chapter 25

Day three of the trial would determine whether
April Boggs would go to prison or go free. Though
the defense had argued that her actions were not illegal, the truth was that the jury would convict her,
unless the defense could put on a much stronger
case than most people expected.

And there was one huge question mark in the defense's case. Its witness list included Jerome Boggs:
would they dare call him?

Boggs pleaded guilty six months earlier, but the
defense had asked that he be made available to testify for his wife's defense. He had told police she had
nothing to do with the crimes he had committed,
but calling him to the witness stand would represent
a huge risk.

On the one hand, he could testify that he had
acted alone—that April Boggs had known nothing
of what he intended to do. On the other hand, who
would believe him? He was a convicted felon—
worse, he was an admitted baby killer. The jurors, at
best, would be disgusted by him. At worst, they
would be reminded of the fact that April Boggs was
married to him, and might believe that they were
still in love if he testified on her behalf.

How could anyone love a man who had murdered a four-year-old child? The jury might end up loathing April Boggs as much as they loathed Jerome.

Also, the defense had already ridiculed two of the prosecution's witnesses for drug use. What would the prosecution do to Jerome, considering the amount of testimony that already had been given about his drug use—not to mention his other crimes.

An even greater risk than the jury's perception of Jerome Boggs was the risk that Jerome would testify that he had lied when he gave his statement to police. He was unpredictable, and since April Boggs was suing him for divorce, he could choose to be vindictive and testify against her rather than for her. He could testify that April, in fact, had known about or even helped plan the murders. If the defense then brought up the fact that he had already said she wasn't involved, he could say merely that he was not under oath when police took his statement before his guilty plea. And if the defense called him, it would be difficult for them to impeach their own witness. It would look ridiculous to call him as a witness and then call him a liar.

Calling Jerome Boggs as a witness was a tremendous risk, but the defense had to consider it. If all else failed, there was a bare chance that his testimony could exonerate his wife.

The arguments the defense had made to dismiss the case took up an hour of that morning, and the jury again waited until just after 10:00 A.M. before being allowed to file out of the back room and into the jury box.

When they did, the first witness was not a psychologist who could explain away April's failure to notify police by saying she had Stockholm syndrome, or that she was suffering from paranoia. It wasn't a friend who could counter the testimony of her other high-school friend, Amanda Burton, by saying April had asked for help getting away from Jerome. It was not Jerome Boggs, the convicted murderer and robber.

The first witness was April Boggs's father.

Darrell Banks was a forty-nine-year-old lifelong resident of Little Cowan, the same community where Jerome had lived. Quiet and easygoing, with a mane of curly gray-and-black hair and a thick, droopy mustache, Banks spent his workdays handing out orders to clean up dumps and yards, and writing tickets to people caught littering. He was the litter control officer, or "garbage warden," for the county. He had also been designated as special deputy sheriff in order to give him authority to serve warrants and summonses to litterbugs.

Banks was divorced from April's mother in 1986 and April lived most of her life with her mother. She moved in with her dad after high school, he testified, and held several short-term jobs, including working as a clerk at a gas station and a supermarket.

In 2001, April was living with him on Little Cowan. Banks testified that he didn't remember exactly when April and Jerome met, only that Jerome's brother had brought him around one day when he came to watch a ball game. From then on, Jerome's visits with his brother became commonplace. Jerome and April would sit at the table and play cards, while his brother and her father watched sports on television.

"He paid a lot of attention to her and I guess she needed someone," Banks testified. "There wasn't much excitement in what we were doing."

April had a few friends, but not many, and her relationship with Jerome Boggs seemed "more like a friendship than a romance," Banks testified.

He was surprised and concerned when April came to him and told him she was getting married.

"I told her she really needed to make sure this was what she wanted, but she seemed to be happy. She'd made her mind up," Banks said.

The couple were married at Banks's house in December 2001, and went to live with Jerome's parents. Banks testified that he had never heard her complain about living there, and to the best of his knowledge, she loved Jerome's parents and they loved her.

Contrary to the theory presented by the prosecution, Banks testified, April didn't seem worried about money and never asked to borrow money from him.

"Jerome always had money. I guess he was drawing a check," he testified.

Banks said he was at home the afternoon before the murders when Jerome and April came to visit. Jerome was flush with money and was flashing it, bragging about how much he had. Banks said he didn't ask how much it was and tried to ignore it.

"Anybody wanting to show off their money, I don't go for that. I went back to watching TV," he said.

The couple left and came back around 8:00 P.M. That time, Banks said, Jerome was acting "real strange—like he was on something," but April was acting normal.

Prompted by the defense, Banks said he had never seen Jerome take any pills, but said he had seen other people who were on drugs. He testified that that was his impression of Jerome, because his son-in-law was "talking about things that didn't make any sense." Banks could not recount the conversation, because he said it was so outlandish he didn't understand it.

He didn't see them again until a day or so after the murders. He said he asked April then if they were going to the funeral, and she replied that Jerome might go.

Asked by the defense, Banks said he discouraged his daughter from marrying Jerome, because of his criminal background, but "he had convinced me he'd changed."

The prosecution took little time with Banks and asked few questions about the account he had already given. Bartley asked if he was afraid of Jerome Boggs, to which Banks answered no. He said he would have gone to get April if she had told him she wanted to leave her husband.

He also confirmed for the prosecution that his daughter was not mentally impaired, though he said she was "a little backward."

The only thing new that came out of the cross-examination was the fact that a purse with money in it had been missing from Banks's home the day before the murders.

Banks said some friends had been over, and one woman's purse was gone when she started to leave the house. Jerome and April had been there during that time, and Banks said he suspected Jerome had taken it. The prosecution asked again if he would have protected his daughter if she had told him she was afraid of Jerome, and again Banks answered that he would have. With no more questions, Banks left the witness stand.

While he had painted a sympathetic picture of his daughter, he had offered no insight into the events surrounding the murders. The defense would have to find some other way to sway the jury. And though the jury did not know it, the question still remained of whether they would hear Jerome Boggs testify in his wife's defense.

The defense called April's mother.

Bonita Collins was a short, nervous woman, with short sandy hair. She answered many of the same questions as her ex-husband, telling of April's jobs, her friends, and where she had lived.

And like Banks, she said she had heard little from her daughter about Jerome Boggs until April said she was marrying him. Bonita Collins lived in Knott County, but she had grown up in Letcher County and had family there. She knew who Jerome Boggs was, and she knew what he had done to Paschal Fields. She was horrified by the thought that her daughter was about to marry someone who would beat an old man with a hammer.

"I asked her not to marry him, and she said, 'Mom, I'm twenty years old. You can't stop me. I'm going to marry him,'" Collins testified.

But unlike her ex-husband, Collins said, she did hear her daughter say she wanted to have a place of her own, and she knew that April was having money trouble. Jerome Boggs didn't work at all, she testified, and April only worked as a babysitter and housekeeper.

April often asked to borrow money, but Bonita said she didn't lend it to her. Despite that, she testified that she did not hear Jerome and April argue about money, and on the day before the murders, Jerome had money.

Bonita testified that she had taken them to Jenkins to a discount store, and she had watched Jerome's brother pay April $50 for cleaning his house before they left. She said April was acting "normal" that day, but that Jerome had seemed paranoid. All the way to Jenkins, she said, he kept asking over and over where they were going.

Once they got there, he hung around the counter so long that Bonita felt he was scaring the clerk and she made them leave without buying anything. They stopped again at the Dollar General Store at Mayking, just outside Whitesburg; then she took April and Jerome home and "put him out."

She said his behavior had embarrassed her and irritated her and she told him she wouldn't take him anywhere else that day.

Bonita said after April and Jerome married, she rarely got to see her daughter alone, but she talked to her on the phone. She said she told April about the problems she saw with Jerome "every day." Bonita said she was especially upset when she went to the house one day and found Jerome lying on the couch, asleep, while April carried in wood for heating.

It bothered her, she said, that Jerome would let his wife go in and out in the cold, carrying heavy loads of wood while he lay on the couch—especially since it was a job that his father had told him to do.

Butcher asked if she had noticed any change in her daughter after her marriage to Jerome Boggs.

"Yes. She didn't bath, she didn't shower; she wore the same clothes day after day," she said.

Bonita said she saw her daughter about 1:00 P.M. on the day of the murders, when April stopped by Parkway Restaurant, where Bonita Collins worked as a cook. Collins said her face had a red mark around her nose and mouth, where Jerome had hit her.

Bonita had gone to the car to have a talk with Jerome. The couple left and she didn't see them again that night, but she talked to April on the phone just before Bonita left home for Sunday-night church services.

She didn't see her daughter again until Tuesday, two days after the murders, when April called her to ask for help moving into her new apartment at Jenkins.

Bonita said that day April hadn't bathed and her hair was greasy. "She looked dirty," Bonita recalled. She said that's the day she tried to get April alone so she could talk to her.

"That's when I asked her to go with me, and she said, 'I can't. My husband won't let me ride with nobody but him.'"

Bartley began his cross-examination by asking directions. Where was Parkway Restaurant? Where was Little Cowan? Did April's father have family there?

After a series of questions, Bartley showed the jurors, who were more familiar with the geography of Letcher County than he was, that Parkway Inn and Restaurant was just north of Whitesburg, and that Little Cowan was located between the motel/restaurant and town. Until 3:00 P.M., when the restaurant closed on Sundays, April could have driven five or ten minutes from the Super 8 Motel and been with her mother or her father. After three, she could still have been with her father, uncles, or aunts, testimony showed.

Bartley also led Bonita Collins through the conversation with her daughter on the night of the murders. When Bonita talked to April that night, it was April who had placed the phone call. She told her mother she was staying the night at the Super 8 Motel, Bonita told Bartley. No, she didn't ask for Bonita to pick her up.

On that Tuesday, she helped move April's bed and some things that her father had given her out of his trailer. On Thursday, the next day that they moved items, the belongings again came from Jerome's parents' home, and Jerome went with them to the new apartment both times.

"Was he going to move in with her?" Bartley asked.

"I don't know," she replied.

Bonita testified that April did not show her the diamond ring during the trips to move furniture. She also didn't tell her mother that she knew anything about the murders, which Collins heard about the same night, before she went to church.

"If she had told you, Jerome had done that, would you have gone and gotten her?" Bartley asked.

Bonita confirmed that she would have.

"No matter what stood in your way?"

Again Bonita answered affirmatively.

Butcher asked only two questions on redirect: whether April had any transportation (she did not), and if she had relied on Jerome's family or Jerome to go anywhere (she did).

In a surprise move, the defense rested after Bonita Collins's testimony. Butcher and Carnes had called only two witnesses—the father and mother of the accused. They offered no evidence from experts, no evidence from other witnesses, no alternative theory about what had happened. And they had not called Jerome Boggs, the riskiest witness on their list. Incredibly, there had been no testimony, no questions at all, about April's divorce petition.

The jury was left with the perception that April and Jerome Boggs were still happily married, or at least as happily married as a couple serving time in two different lockups could be.

April Boggs's case stood solely on the testimony of the two people who loved her the most.

In contrast, the prosecution had called eleven witnesses, ranging from friends of April's to Jerome's ex-girlfriend to people who had seen them only in passing. Police officers had talked about the crime scene, the coroner had talked about the wounds that had killed Timothy and T.J. Cook, and April herself, on tape, had talked about when she had learned of the murders.

The defense witnesses had talked about her childhood, and the conditions of her marriage. The die was cast and the spectators could believe nothing other than a guilty verdict was in the making.

It was 11:08 A.M. when the prosecution declared they had nothing more to offer in rebuttal. The defense renewed its motion for a directed verdict of acquittal, a motion the judge overruled summarily.

Juries are unpredictable. While instructions specifically say that jurors "shall" find a person guilty "if and only if" they believe beyond a reasonable doubt that certain facts are true, juries routinely bend those rules. They often negotiate and craft compromises in order to reach a unanimous decision.

With that in mind, defense attorneys who believe their clients are about to be found guilty often ask that "lesser included" charges be added to the jury instructions. The common belief among lawyers is that jurors who feel they have to convict on something will vote for the lesser charge if they have any doubts at all about the greater charge.

In April Boggs's case, the defense tried to have a charge of receiving stolen property added to the jury instructions, reasoning that it should be considered a "lesser included," since April had money in her possession legitimately, and there was no way to prove how much of the money that police confiscated was stolen.

Bartley, however, said the reasoning was faulty. He said it would be "sort of true" if April had been charged with theft, but she was not.

"Receiving stolen property would not be a lesser to facilitation to first-degree robbery," he said.

The defense lost that battle. The jury would have only an up-or-down choice: she was either guilty of the individual charges against her, or she was innocent. There would be little room for compromise in the jury room.

The jury would consider five charges against her:

- *Two counts of criminal facilitation to murder:* The jurors would find April Boggs guilty if they believed that she dropped her husband off at

the Sugar Shack and agreed to pick him up;
if they believed she knew he intended to go
to the Cook home to kill Timothy Louis "Blister" Cook and T.J. Cook; and if they believed
Jerome Boggs did kill Blister and T.J.

- *Criminal Facilitation to first-degree robbery:* The
  jurors would find April Boggs guilty if they
  believed she dropped off and picked up
  Jerome Boggs to steal money or other items;
  if they believed Jerome Boggs threatened or
  used force to steal; if he was armed with a
  pistol; and if they believed April knew he intended to commit robbery.

- *Criminal facilitation to first-degree burglary:* The
  jurors would find April Boggs guilty if they
  believed she dropped off and picked up
  Jerome Boggs so he could commit burglary;
  if he entered and remained in the house
  without permission; if he knew he didn't have
  permission; if he intended to commit a
  crime; if he was armed with a pistol; and if
  April Boggs knew his intentions.

- *Complicity to trafficking in less than eight ounces
  of marijuana:* The jurors would find her
  guilty if they believed Jerome had marijuana; if he gave or sold it to another person;
  if he had it in his possession for that purpose; if April conspired, aided, or consulted
  with Jerome to take those actions or attempted to do so; and if she intended that
  Jerome traffic in marijuana.

In a way, the conditions for a guilty verdict had
gone full circle. While Commonwealth's Attorney

Banks had argued earlier that he needed only to prove that April could infer that a crime had been committed, the instructions imposed the much stricter standard advocated by the defense. Though the judge had ruled against a directed verdict based on those grounds, the jury instructions imposed just such limits on the jurors' considerations.

Whether the argument would resonate any more with the jury than with the judge remained to be seen.

The two sides still had to present closing arguments. The jury would not hear those arguments or see the instructions until after lunch. Then the hardest part of the case for both sides would begin—the wait for a verdict.

Chapter 26

It was 1:15 P.M. when court began again. The break had lasted an hour and a half, but participants still had to rush back to attend the daily security ritual.

After Wright read the instructions to the jury, Carnes stood and walked to a podium in front of the jury box. There was, she said, no doubt that April Boggs did not rob or kill Blister and T.J. Cook. There was no doubt that Jerome Boggs was the person who did, and he was already locked in a prison cell.

Carnes said April Boggs had no knowledge beforehand of what was going to happen, and the prosecution had failed to prove that she did.

Though the defense had decided not to call Jerome Boggs as a witness, Carnes conjured his unsworn statement to police as though he had testified on the witness stand.

"He took sole responsibility," Carnes said. "If he's the kind of guy that would slap his wife around, do you think he wouldn't sell her out in half a minute?"

Then Carnes took another risk. She pulled out the love letter she had so desperately tried to exclude from evidence and began to read it to the jury. The letter, from April to Jerome, talked about how happy she was that she was Mrs. Jerome Boggs, and how nice it was that he was providing things for her.

"Nobody ever wanted to buy me anything before," the letter read. "If I wanted something like that, I had to get it myself."

Carnes shook her head at the letter, and called her client "dumber than dumb.

"If she was indicted for being dumb and making terrible choices in men, I'd plead her guilty," Carnes said.

But April Boggs was charged with facilitation to murder—not being dumb. Carnes said the prosecution failed to prove its opening statement, saying she never heard any testimony that Jerome had told April he would get them some money. She also called the testimony from the Family Dollar Store clerk "the most curious thing" about the trial, and suggested that the story had more to do with the woman working with a relative of the Cooks than with the facts.

She also belittled what she called the prosecution's "alcohol-drinkin', pot-smokin', pill-snortin' witnesses.

"They interviewed half the pot smokers in Letcher County and half of them were at Blister's the day he was killed," Carnes said.

She showed the engagement ring to the jury and acknowledged that it was bought within hours of the murder with stolen money, but she noted that it was also money Blister Cook had received in exchange for drugs. If it had not been stolen, "most likely it would have been used to buy another shipment of marijuana," she said.

Finally she told the jury that they should not judge April too harshly for not reporting Jerome Boggs to police immediately.

"It's not so easy to get out of any abusive relationship," she said. "It's not so easy to be brave when some guy tells you he just killed two people and you find out he really did."

During the entire statement, Carnes had tried to ignore T.J. Cook's death and instead focused a laser light of scorn on his father and on the prosecution's witnesses. Few people in the community expressed sympathy for Blister Cook, but they were universally livid over the murder of a four-year-old child.

If the jury could be made to blame T.J.'s father for his fate, perhaps April Boggs would get off without being convicted.

The prosecution knew the attitude of the community as well, and they weren't about to let the jury's focus change.

"The pitiful thing is exhibit number one—a picture of a four-year-old dead baby," Bartley began, waving the picture at the jury. "If you want to talk about something pitiful in this case, that's pitiful."

Then Bartley, a father himself, tried to put the tale in more personal terms.

"I left here yesterday evening. I got out at five-thirty [and] my son was supposed to start playing baseball at five-thirty. I watched little girls and little boys the age of this little boy running and playing, their dogs there, and I sat there and cried," he said.

Then he questioned again why April Boggs had not driven on the hill the day of the murders, when she always had before. It didn't make sense, he said, that April didn't park outside the trailer, leave the motor running, and wait for Jerome to "run in and get his little bag of pot."

He also defended his own witnesses, telling the jury that he didn't choose the witnesses. "They were her (April's) friends."

Bartley also showed them the holster, again

showed how it had to be worn, and questioned how April could have kept from seeing Jerome wearing it.

He also wondered aloud again why she didn't go to Little Cowan or the Parkway Restaurant and ask her parents for help if she really intended to leave Jerome. She dropped him off at the Sugar Shack. She was alone. She knew her parents would take care of her, Bartley argued.

Finally he told the jury to look at the proof of what April did after Jerome told her he had gotten them some money, and that he had killed two people.

"What did she do for four days? She partied it up."

He also dismissed the defense's argument that April Boggs couldn't get away from her husband. She took Jerome to Kentucky River Community Care and waited outside for "two or three hours," but didn't go to police, Bartley said. He told the jury to "put two and two together.

"She wanted money; they got money. She helped him go up there and get the money. She wasn't upset about how they got the money."

Katrina Brown, the Family Dollar Store clerk, was "one lucky woman," Bartley said. She had known what Jerome Boggs had planned to do to her, and it was only by luck that she had avoided being a victim herself, Bartley told the jury.

It was, he said, hard to believe that someone so callous that she put more value on money than human life could be in the same courtroom with them.

"Right there sits one," he said, pointing at April Boggs.

"What kind of person would sit there, knowing a four-year-old baby had been killed for a bag of pot and a thousand dollars?"

Bartley's closing statement had lasted less than twenty minutes, but it had pulled the jurors' focus back to T.J. Cook and away from the drug deals of his father. The last argument the jury heard before being sent away was not a stinging invective aimed at "pot-smokin', pill-snortin'" prosecution witnesses, but a reminder that one of Jerome Boggs's victims was a four-year-old child—an innocent killed purely for profit—and that April Boggs had shared in that profit.

The clerk pulled the badge numbers of twelve jurors, releasing the two alternates. The rest—six men and six women—filed through the back door of the courtroom to begin their deliberations at 2:14 P.M.

April Boggs would have a long wait ahead.

Chapter 27

No conventional wisdom exists about juries. No matter what a lawyer or a spectator expects, the jury's true actions always seem to confound them. Some would say that a jury leaving in the early afternoon on a fairly short case would be back by dinnertime to give their verdict and go home. But as dinnertime approached, then passed, this jury remained behind closed doors.

During the trial, April Dawn Boggs had sat between her two lawyers, often taking notes on a legal pad as witnesses testified, sometimes staring down at the table. What would a jury make of her behavior? Was she cold and heartless, unmoved by the testimony about the murders and her actions in the days that followed? Or was she scared of what the jury might read into tears? Would the six men and six women see them as tears of fear? Of guilt? Or would they see them as tears of remorse? And how would jurors make any of those hypotheses about her behavior? How would they react—with sympathy or with scorn?

The jury had heard her cry on the taped statement she had given to police, but could the jury make any of the same assumptions about those tears? She was, after all, in a tiny interrogation room faced by police officers, a two-way mirror filling one wall. Perhaps her tears were caused by the fear of what was going to happen to her, rather than sadness over the death of T.J. Cook.

The jury had not heard the family of the victims cry, but they had seen them in the courtroom. Some wiped their eyes. Others glared at April with undisguised hatred. Even though the jurors had professed not to know much about the case, at least some surely remembered the attack the Cook family had made on Jerome Boggs during his arraignment fifteen months earlier. It had been replayed, time after time, on the local television station.

They had also heard from police officers who spoke about the grisly evidence of murder, and they had heard April and Jerome's friends talk about going to the motel and smoking pot with them on the night of the murders. Had any of the jurors smoked pot before? Would they discount the drug use as unimportant? And what of the allegations that Blister Cook dealt in marijuana? Would jurors believe, as the defense hoped, that he should have expected to be killed and that he brought his son's killer into the house by his own actions? Or did one or two of the jurors have their own secret garden of hemp in the backyard or in a sheltered hollow in the woods?

How much weight would jurors give to the testimony of April Boggs's mother and father? They were her parents. They were supposed to love her unconditionally. Would it matter to the jury that they spoke in April's defense? No one else did. Even her lawyers had called her "dumber than dumb." That loneliness might speak to some of the jurors and make them feel for this girl looking desperately for someone to love her. Or they might feel that she deserved to be alone in a prison cell for a long, long time.

There were clues about what jurors felt was important. They had been out of the room for less than forty-five minutes when the bailiff passed the first note to Judge Wright. The jury wanted a written transcript of April Boggs's taped statement. It had been too difficult to understand the words on the hissing magnetic tape and the jury wanted to be able to read along to keep up.

The judge and members of both legal teams convened in the conference room of the judge's chambers. All agreed that parts of the tape were difficult to understand, and it was not transcribed for that reason—the prosecution did not want to get it wrong. The judge's final decision was to tell the jury simply that no transcript existed.

It was more than three hours later when the jury's second note came to the judge: jurors wanted clarification of their instructions on first-degree burglary.

The jury did not include an explanation of its question, but the confusion was most likely caused by the inclusion of both robbery and burglary charges.

To most people, burglary means theft. But burglary, as defined by the law, can be committed without stealing anything. It is more akin to what television police dramas commonly call breaking and entering. To be guilty of burglary, one only has to enter or remain inside a building without the owner's permission, and they must reasonably know that they did not have permission. Even if a person was invited into a home, they can be convicted of burglary if they commit another crime while there, or if the owner asks them to leave and they refuse. First-degree burglary, one of the charges to which Jerome Boggs pleaded guilty, deals with an occupied home.

To be guilty of facilitation to burglary, a person

must have provided the means for someone else to commit burglary. Prosecutors argued that April Boggs had done so, by dropping her husband off at the foot of the hill below the murder scene, and then picking him up again, as he had told her to do.

Again the two teams of lawyers met in the judge's conference room, and again agreed that there was nothing they felt comfortable sending into the jury room.

The judge wrote a second note to the jury telling them that instructions were written to conform to state law, and that no further clarification or alteration could be made.

For 2½ more hours, attorneys, spectators, police officers, and April Boggs waited for the jury to announce its decision.

Shortly before nine o'clock, the bailiff returned to the judge's chambers with a third message. The jury had no more questions. It was ready to report.

It had taken 6½ hours for the jury to reach a verdict. Long deliberations usually bode well for the defendant. It means the jury was torn over some aspect of the case. It could mean that there were holdouts who felt April Boggs was innocent and refused to find her guilty. It could mean that the majority thought she was innocent, but that some jurors believed she had to be found guilty of something to satisfy the family of the victims. Either way, there would have been negotiations—give-and-take between the jurors as they tried to reach the unanimous decision required by law.

It could also mean that the jurors felt they were hopelessly deadlocked and wanted the judge to declare a mistrial and send them home. That would not necessarily be good news for April Boggs. If that were the case after only 6½ hours, the judge would surely send the jury back into the room with instructions to work out their differences. Even if the jury did eventually hang, it would mean April Boggs would be stuck in jail for months more, waiting for a new trial.

Whatever it meant, there was little chance that the jury was of one mind about the charges against April Boggs. The question was, what had given them cause to doubt? Had the defense's description of the prosecution's witnesses as "pot-smokin', pill-snortin' witnesses" hold sway over the jury? Had the emotion of April's parents made jurors think of what would happen to their own daughters if they hooked up with the wrong men?

It was two minutes before nine o'clock when Judge Sam Wright popped out of the door, where he habitually stood hidden until the bailiff announced him, and allowed spectators to be seated.

The jury was in the box, and during the break, police officers from all over the county had congregated in the courtroom. Deputies in their brown pants and khaki shirts, city police in various shades of blue, gray, and black, and state troopers in their trademark steely gray uniforms and Smokey-the-Bear hats guarded the door, the benches, and the opening that led from the gallery into the front of the courtroom. April Boggs, in a long white blouse and dress pants, with her long sandy hair pulled back from her face, wrung her hands as the court security officer stood over her.

The jury was not hung. When the judge asked if jurors had reached a unanimous decision, the foreperson stood and said they had. The bailiff retrieved the verdict form from her and carried it to the bench, where the judge read it silently to himself before presenting it to open court.

The verdict on the charge of facilitation to the murder of Timothy Louis Cook was first read. It was unexpected and it hit the defense like a hammer.

Guilty.

If the jury had found April Boggs guilty of facilitation in the father's murder, it would most surely have found her guilty of facilitation in the child's murder. The only hope the defense had now was that the jury might have felt that some of the lesser charges amounted to "piling on."

The courtroom was silent as the judge read down the list of verdicts.

Chapter 28

The court security officer hovered over April Boggs as she stood at the defense table awaiting the rest of the verdicts, ready to catch her if she fainted or if she ran. She wavered noticeably as the verdicts were read, one by one.

Count one, facilitation to the murder of Timothy Louis Cook.

Guilty.

Count two, facilitation to the murder of Timothy James (T.J.) Cook.

Guilty.

Count three, facilitation to first-degree robbery.

Guilty.

Count four, facilitation to first-degree burglary.

Not guilty.

Count five, complicity to trafficking in less than eight ounces of marijuana.

Guilty.

Of the five charges against April Boggs, the jury had found her guilty of four. The long deliberation had meant nothing, after all. There was no telling what the jury had discussed for more than six hours, but one thing was clear: the defense's case had meant little to them.

Defense attorney Jane Butcher asked quietly for the judge to poll the jury—to be sure that the verdict was correct. It was a formality, but it was a formality that a defense attorney who had just lost had no choice but to follow. It was just barely possible that one of the jurors might have misunderstood his or her vote—that they did not realize they were voting guilty. It was a tiny, tiny chance, but it was a chance. If that had happened, a mistrial would have to be declared.

Judge Wright pointed to each juror in turn and asked if the verdicts he had read were the verdicts that each had voted for. One juror after another answered yes. There was no mistake; there would be no mistrial.

After more than six hours of deliberations, the whole thing had taken four minutes.

It was after 9:00 P.M., but the judge wasn't ready to send the jurors home. Instead, he sent them back to the jury room to relax while he and the attorneys discussed the next phase of the trial—the penalty phase. Jurors would have to hear more testimony and make more deliberations before the night was over.

The prosecution planned to call only one witness for the penalty phase, and the defense planned to call none. The jury had already made its decision. The only hope for April Boggs now was that the jury would take pity on her.

Mark Bailey, an officer with the Kentucky Division of Probation and Parole, was the only person jurors would hear from. He would have nothing to say about April Boggs at all, instead explaining the state's parole system. Under that system, she would be eligible for parole after serving 20 percent of her sentence.

The maximum April Boggs could receive was fifteen years—five years on each of the three felony counts. The marijuana charge was a misdemeanor punishable by up to a year in the county jail, but by law, the sentence had to run concurrent to the felony sentences, meaning it would not add additional time to her sentence.

Her sentence would also be reduced by the amount of time she had already spent in jail. Bartley attempted to elicit more specific testimony about that provision of the sentencing law, but the defense objected.

Carnes, in her final statement to the jury, said that she could not stand up before them and tell them that she was pleased with the verdict.

"I'd be lying."

But, she said, she respected the jury process and would not argue anymore that her client should have been found innocent. Instead, she argued that the jury should consider the lower range of punishments available because of April Boggs's lack of a criminal history. The law offered any sentence from one to five years on each of the counts because "the punishment should fit the particular defendant."

Bartley did not argue for the opposite punishment, instead leaving it up to the jury. He said, given the way television shows were written, he understood the problem the jury had with the burglary charge, but "TV's not real."

Bartley said the jury could give April Boggs any punishment from one to five years, and sentences could run concurrently, meaning all at the same time, or consecutively, meaning one after another. Bartley painstakingly explained each term again.

"If you were to give her five years on each one to run concurrently, you might think that's fifteen years, but it's really not."

Instead, such a sentence would amount to only five years. In order for the sentence to be fifteen years, all three 5-year terms would have to run consecutively.

Within four minutes of leaving the courtroom, the

jury sent a note to the judge requesting a copy of the
state's Certification of Parole Eligibility, a chart used
to determine the number of years a person would
have to serve for any sentence.

Both teams of lawyers again agreed not to send
the chart back, because it included different sentences listed by their legal class, rather than by their
offense. In Kentucky, felonies are listed as Class A, B,
C, or D crimes. The charges with which April Boggs
were charged were all Class D crimes, and attorneys
on both sides said they feared the additional information in the chart would only serve to confuse
jurors.

Without the chart, it took the jury thirty-eight
minutes to return to the courtroom. Jurors had sentenced April Boggs to the maximum of five years in
prison on each of the facilitation-to-murder charges,
four years on the facilitation-to-robbery charge, and
twelve months on the marijuana charge.

The jury recommended that the charges run con-
secutive to each other for a total of fourteen years in
prison.

Police handcuffed April Boggs's hands in front
of her and led her back to jail. The trial was over.
Though the jury had made its recommendations,
the judge would conduct formal sentencing later. If
the jury's recommendation was upheld, she would
be eligible for parole in thirty months.

Though it had not come up at trial, April Boggs had
another conviction already on her record that could
have affected her sentencing. Court records showed
she pleaded guilty to shoplifting, in November 2000,
and was assessed court costs of $92.35. She was sen-
tenced to two years' probation on the condition that
she obey the law and stay out of Wal-Mart. That two-
year period had not expired when the murders were

committed, but the record was never brought up during the court proceedings.

The jury also never heard some evidence that may have been to her advantage. Though April Boggs had filed for divorce in October of the previous year, the jury never heard any testimony that she was divorcing Jerome Boggs. As far as the jury was concerned, she was still Mrs. Jerome Boggs and had made no effort to change that. There was no way of knowing whether either case would have made a difference in the outcome of the criminal trial.

Her lawyer mailed a proposed order of dissolution to the domestic-relations commissioner on June 4. The judge signed it on July 15, more than two months after she was convicted. The order granted her divorce and restored her maiden name. The next day, he signed her final sentencing order confirming the penalty recommended by the jury. The court order signed by the judge specified that she was to serve a maximum of fourteen years in prison, but records of the Department of Corrections set her sentence at nine years. Though it was never clear why, the projected serve-out date set by the state was December 29, 2011. She would be eligible for parole not in thirty months, but in nineteen.

April Banks Boggs was in the Pike County Jail when the order setting her sentence became final. It included a provision that she be placed in the first available prison cell. On September 29, 2003, she was transferred to the Kentucky Correctional Institute for Women in Peewee Valley, near Louisville.

Built in 1937, the Correctional Institute for Women was the oldest women's prison in the state, and the only one run by state government.

The prison included about fifty buildings in its 270-acre compound and housed women serving from one year to life. It also included a death row for the one woman in Kentucky who had been sentenced to die for murder. April Banks would be one of about seven hundred women serving their sentences at Peewee Valley.

Chapter 29

April Banks had been through two court proceedings already in 2003—a divorce and a criminal trial. She had prevailed in her attempt to dissolve her marriage, but she had failed terribly in her attempt to stay out of prison.

Despite the jury decision and the judge's order, she continued to fight to cut her sentence short. She moved into prison on September 29, and by the end of October, she had already completed another losing battle.

April Boggs had filed for shock probation. Intended to let first-time offenders convicted of minor crimes go free soon after experiencing the shock of going to prison, Boggs argued that she should qualify.

She had been in one jail or another since she was arrested twenty months before, and she was determined to get out. Wright denied her motion on October 30, 2003, but that didn't derail her efforts.

She filed another motion for shock probation less than three weeks later, begging Wright to let her out of prison. Though the motion was filed pro se, or without an attorney, it referred to April Banks in the third person.

"Movant persuades this Court to believe that she

would succeed on probation because she has now been to prison and experienced the hardship and by having been separated from her family and those who support her, she has learned a valuable lesson," a memorandum in support of the motion said.

The memo said her mother "will provide a safe, reliable home," and said she had a supportive family that would help her. She also promised to find a job.

She followed the motion with a letter directly to Commonwealth's Attorney Edison Banks, asking him not to oppose her bid for shock probation. Commonwealth's Attorney Banks filed the letter with the court, since he was prohibited by court rules from speaking directly with the accused.

In the letter, she was asking Edison Banks not to oppose shock probation, "not because I am tired of prison life, and I want out, but because I think I deserve a chance."

She told the commonwealth's attorney that her twenty-one months in prison had been very hard and she had seen things she wished she had not.

"It's a very tough place," she wrote. "No one wants to associate with you unless you are gay or bisexual. I am neither."

She also told Banks she was employed as a medical aide in the prison, and that she had enrolled in college classes. She said she was attending Alcoholic Anonymous meetings every Saturday night, and church and Bible-study classes three times a week.

She also said she had written then-governor Paul Patton, the Kentucky Bar Association, "legal advocacy," and other groups, and she claimed to be writing a book about her situation.

"I just want to say I understand to a point, and respect your decision if you object to my making shock. But I will not give up on getting out of here," she wrote.

April went on to say that she understood how serious the crime was, and knew that there were consequences to her action.

"But when I do get out, I plan on having a job, and somehow talking to teens about what drugs can do and being around them can get you into," April said in her letter.

Edison Banks did oppose shock probation, as he had when she filed her first motion. The judge was also unmoved by her story.

Wright ruled on December 31, 2003, that she had already filed for shock probation, had already had an evidentiary hearing, and that he had already ruled she was not eligible. State law did not allow for review of an order denying shock probation, except on the issue of whether the court where the motion was filed had jurisdiction, Wright ruled.

However, April Banks still had a right to appeal and she still had the possibility of parole, though parole eligibility was still a year away.

For her appeal, her family hired Whitesburg attorney James Wiley Craft III. Craft was a young lawyer who had seen some success in the local courts. He was the son of a brilliant former commonwealth's attorney who had lost his license after pleading guilty to federal perjury charges. The younger Craft had no such stain on his own record. He was seen as the attorney to get—if you were facing serious charges in Letcher County.

Craft filed the appeal based on Wright's denial of Butcher and Carnes's two motions for a directed verdict. The lawyers had made the motions at the conclusion of the prosecution's case and at the end of the trial, claiming that the commonwealth had failed to prove that April Boggs knew about the crimes in advance. They argued that a charge of facilitation of a crime required prior knowledge that a crime was going to be committed.

A three-judge panel denied the appeal, noting that Kentucky law required that in denying or granting a motion for directed verdict, the trial judge must look at the evidence in a way that was most favorable to the prosecution.

If there was any way that the jury could interpret the evidence and believe that April Boggs had known about the murders in advance, Wright was required to deny the motion, the court of appeals ruled.

Writing for the unanimous panel, Judge David A. Barber stepped through the evidence, beginning with the application for food Jerome and April Boggs had filed with the Food Pantry a few weeks before the murders, to their return of wedding gifts in exchange for cash.

He then noted that they paid $110 for a wedding ring the night of the murders and checked into the Super 8 Motel.

Barber also noted that April Boggs said she normally drove Jerome to the Cook residence, but that on the day of the murders, she dropped him off at the Sugar Shack, the convenience store/station at the foot of the hill.

Barber also commented on evidence that the gun used to kill Blister and T.J. Cook was too large for April not to have seen it with Jerome when he was riding in the car. Finally, Barber wrote, Jerome Boggs and April were apart several times after the murders, but that she "never made any attempt to leave him.

"A person who provides a means of transportation to a killer, knowing that the transportation will be used to assist in the commission of a crime is guilty of facilitation," Barber wrote.

Whether the evidence was sufficient to prove that

was up to the trial judge to decide, Barber wrote. April Banks's lawyer did not prove Wright had made any reversible errors in that decision.

The order was filed and became final on October 7, 2004, a year and five months after April Banks Boggs's conviction. By that time, she had been in jail or the women's prison for nearly three years.

She had only two months to go before she would be eligible for parole. The denial, though discouraging, would not necessarily mean another seven years in prison.

She went before the parole board as scheduled, on December 8, 2004. But when the board met, April Banks did not get what she expected.

A panel of the parole board did not approve her application. Instead, it deferred her parole for the maximum amount of time that it could.

It would be another five years before April Banks would be eligible to apply for release from prison. If approved then, it would take six years off the prison sentence set out in her court records.

In the meantime, the loss of a contract by a private prison company led Kentucky prison officials to begin transferring women to a private correctional facility in Floyd County, in July 2005, and April Banks was among the inmates moved.

Floyd County is separated from Letcher by barely a sliver of land along the Knott and Pike County border, making it an easy drive for family members of eastern Kentucky prisoners. Though it was a step closer to home for April, it was also a step into a much wider world.

Located at Wheelwright, a historic coal camp in the southern tip of Floyd County, Otter Creek Correctional Center was a world away from Peewee Valley. Though with 656 beds it was slightly smaller than the Correctional Institute for Women at

Peewee Valley, Otter Creek drew its inmates from a much broader population.

Until 2005, the prison population was made up exclusively of inmates from the Indiana prison system. That state had contracted with the company that then owned Otter Creek to house prisoners as a money-saving measure. But the move was controversial because of the distance family members had to travel to visit prisoners. By 2005, it became even more controversial, not because of the issue of visitation, but because of the issue of money.

The plan to house Indiana prisoners in private prisons had originally been intended to save the state money, but by 2005, Indiana had shipped out so many prisoners that it had two thousand empty prison beds in its own facilities. The Indiana Legislature declined to renew its contract with Corrections Corporation of America (CCA) and transferred all of the Otter Creek inmates back into state-owned prisons.

With the loss of all of its prisoners, Otter Creek was facing the very real possibility of closing, if it could not get another contract. Since Wheelwright had a population of only 1,048, the prospect of losing 150 prison jobs at Otter Creek was not an attractive proposition for Kentucky officials. The state stepped in to help CCA by transferring some of its own prisoners to the private lockup.

April Banks was one of four hundred women transferred to the prison from Peewee Valley.

Being a private prison, Otter Creek was not limited to taking prisoners from Kentucky, and CCA also began courting other states.

Instead of being in contact only with inmates from Kentucky, April Banks would now be in a prison population made up of women from as far away as Hawaii.

Chapter 30

By the time April Banks came up for parole, nearly three years had passed since the murders. The community was back to normal, though the families involved never would be.

Jerome Boggs still sat in the Green River Correctional Complex, where he was sentenced to remain for the rest of his life. Under the sentence imposed by the court, there would be no "good time" to reduce his stay in prison. Sentenced to two life sentences, plus 111 years, all to run concurrently, parole was out of the question. Because his crimes were violent, and he was a persistent felony offender, he was not eligible for shock probation.

With the sentence he had received, the only way anyone could foresee him leaving prison was in a coffin.

Instead of a quick, officially painless death afforded by lethal injection, Jerome Boggs would grow old in prison, dying a little each day for the next thirty, forty, or fifty years.

It was as it should be, the community had decided. Many of the people who advocated the death penalty now said they were much more pleased with the prospects of Boggs rotting away in a prison cell.

Another year came and went, and most people had gone on with their lives, giving little thought to Jerome Boggs. Christmas came again, then New Year's, then a letter.

On January 9, 2006, the Letcher Commonwealth's Attorney's Office and the Letcher County Circuit Clerk's Office opened thick envelopes from inmate Jerome Boggs at the Green River Correctional Complex. It was nothing unusual for the commonwealth's attorney or the clerk to receive letters from inmates— together they had received several letters from April Banks asking for various copies of documents in her file or asking for help getting out of prison.

But there was an important difference. April Banks had been convicted by a jury. She had maintained her innocence to the last. She had sought shock probation; she had appealed.

Those were options not available to Jerome Boggs.

He had admitted before a judge and a courtroom full of police and spectators that he went to the home of Blister and T.J. Cook, he pointed a gun at them, and he shot them.

He had admitted that he stole money and marijuana, and he agreed to spend the rest of his life in prison if the prosecution would only allow him to die naturally.

He told the world that he had not been coerced or threatened in order to force a confession, he agreed with his attorneys that he was mentally capable to make the decision, and he told the judge that he fully understood the consequences of pleading guilty.

He had given up his right to appeal; he had no hope of shock probation.

For more than three years since his sentencing, Jerome Boggs had sat quietly in his cell at Green River Correctional Complex, and had been nearly forgotten by the community he had wronged.

But three years was a long time to dwell on the prospect of spending the rest of one's life in a tiny prison cell, of being told when to eat and when to sleep and when to wash. Jerome Boggs, who had sworn to accept his fate quietly in order to avoid the medical gurney and a fatal IV, had come to believe he had been railroaded.

The letter to Edison Banks contained more than fifty pages of motions and memorandums, rife with misspellings and in tortured legal jargon.

Jerome Boggs, the career thief, liar, and murderer, had done what he signed a contract not to do.

Jerome Boggs had filed an appeal.

The criminal with a seventh-grade education had filed a motion to overturn his conviction and sentence based on the only grounds he could possibly file on, given his signature was on the form waiving his right to appeal. He had filed under Rule 11.42 of the Kentucky Rules of Criminal Procedure, claiming that his attorneys had not adequately represented him.

The "motion to vacate" was not the only document enclosed. Among the plethora of filings was a motion for Judge Sam Wright to step down from the case, and for the appointment of a special judge.

Boggs homed in on Wright's own comments during his sentencing hearing, and on the string of witnesses Wright allowed to verbally lash Boggs during that hearing.

The victims' family had agreed to allow Boggs to plead guilty as a way to avoid lengthy appeals and hurtful testimony. More than three years later, they were facing exactly the scenario they had tried to avoid.

Jerome Boggs had appealed and was seeking an evidentiary hearing and a new trial. The man the community had tried to forget was trying to worm his way back into its collective consciousness.

Chapter 31

Criminal cases would be so much simpler for prosecutors if the defendants would just admit to the crimes they were accused of and then went quietly to prison. There would be no need for strong evidence, no need for a trial, no need to worry about whether a jury would convict. There would also be no appeals and no drawn-out legal proceedings for victims to suffer through.

It would be so easy, in fact, that the law must protect defendants from the possibility that some prosecutors would inevitably succumb to the temptation of tricking or coercing confessions and guilty pleas. The law assumes that everyone is innocent until proven guilty, and prosecutors are forbidden from taking shortcuts to make the process move more quickly and easily.

When an accused person pleads guilty to a crime, he or she must certify that he or she was not coerced into making the decision; that he understood the consequences of his plea; that he was not under the influence of drugs or alcohol when he made the decision; and that he was not mentally incapacitated.

Jerome Boggs signed the form making all of those certifications, and on November 7, 2002, he reiterated those answers to the judge, during the hearing on his motion to enter a plea.

He stood before the bench, his hands cuffed behind him and his legs in shackles, and answered, "Yes, Your Honor" and "No, Your Honor" to each of the questions as Judge Wright asked them. The only question he didn't answer was the question of mental incapacity. His attorney answered that question for him, telling the judge that the psychiatrist provided by the court had certified him as mentally fit.

Now it was January 2006 and he was trying to take back all of the things he had said in court. It was as though Jerome Boggs, while his hands were cuffed behind his back, had crossed his fingers when he admitted to killing Timothy and T.J. Cook.

Though he had waived his right to appeal, Kentucky law still allowed defendants the right to appeal under Rule 11.42. That rule, which deals with motions to set aside, vacate, or correct sentences, is the only exception to the waiver of appeal, and it was the avenue that Jerome Boggs had chosen to follow.

Rule 11.42 actions were common enough, and were often filed under the claim that the original defense attorney was ineffective or incompetent. Lawyers had even been known to file motions claiming ineffective assistance of counsel when they themselves handled the original case.

The rule was basically the same as that used by so-called "Mafia Cop" Louis J. Eppolito to challenge his conviction on federal racketeering charges in New York in 2006. The judge threw that argument out before testimony was even complete.

It was also a difficult argument to swallow in Boggs's case, because his attorneys were not inexperienced young lawyers who had never tried a murder case. Bette Niemi was the director of the Capital Trials Branch of the Department of Public Advocacy, and

George Sornberger, whom Boggs referred to in his appeal as "John Sandburg," was the manager of the Trial Division.

Still, Jerome Boggs was arguing that the lawyers did so little to advise him that their inaction resulted in "an involuntary, unintelligent, and unknowing guilty plea."

He claimed the attorneys should have sought a change of venue, that they failed to investigate the charges against him or make any preparations for trial, and that they failed to determine that he was mentally unfit to stand trial.

Boggs claimed that the media coverage "saturated the county," and cited the large presence of police in the courtroom as proof that the trial should have been moved to protect him from members of the Cook family.

"The Defendant needed a change of venue for trial to seperate [*sic*] this case from the saturation of publicity and protect the Defendant and his family and witnesses from the treats [*sic*] and intimidation," the motion said.

He claimed that he had asked his attorneys to file a motion for change of venue, but that they had not.

The memorandum cited the crowd of members of the victims' family and the large police presence to support the argument that Boggs's attorneys should have sought a change of venue.

"The anger and hatred of the community was brought home to Boggs every day. He was held in isolation at the Letcher County jail to protect him from the wrath of other inmates," the memorandum stated. "The only day in day out contact he had in isolation was talking with a person lodged close to him who Boggs knew was a jailhouse snitch."

Boggs's memorandum also cited the parade of witnesses at his sentencing hearing, and pointed out

PRECIOUS BLOOD

the threats made against him by some of those witnesses. He also cited the fact that police had to restrain Donald Keith Cook during the hearing.

The memorandum noted that Letcher County, with a population of about twenty-five thousand people, was small and the newspapers covered every aspect of the case.

"The media coverage was so extensive that early on in the case, Boggs' attorney, Betty Neimi, [*sic*] investigation consisted primarily of reading the news reports about the case," the memorandum said.

Still, the appeal was not based solely on press coverage. Instead, Boggs cited case law, saying that a defendant had a right to a trial in a location where he and his witnesses would not suffer from intimidation. Boggs claimed that was not possible in Letcher County.

The memorandum said there was "a very hostile element which posed a threat" to him. He said there were threats made toward anyone who helped him, and that his attorneys and local officials were aware of those threats.

Boggs said in his memorandum that he discussed the matter with his attorneys and they agreed that a change of venue was necessary, but they never pursued it.

"Had his attorney's [*sic*] sought a change of venue and been denied, Boggs would at least have had the opportunity to raise the issue for appellate review," the memo said. "As it was, Boggs felt he had no choice but to enter a guilty plea."

As proof there had been no investigation by his attorneys, Boggs claimed that during the nine months between his arraignment and his guilty plea, the only thing Niemi and Sornberger discussed with him was that he would be convicted and sentenced to death.

In a memorandum submitted with his motion to

vacate, Boggs claimed that his attorneys never discussed any alternative theory that could be used as his defense, and never told him about the evidence against him.

The memorandum said Boggs was "coming off a drunk wherein he had passed out and had been using alcohol and drugs the entire day of the event. He wanted his attorney's [*sic*] to make some investigation into his diminished capacity due to intoxication."

Boggs claimed that he told the lawyers he was "almost comatose, having indulged himself the night before to the point he passed out having consumed alot [*sic*] of drugs and alcohol the day of the event."

The memo stated the lawyers "never discussed this in any detail." Instead, it said the only thing ever discussed at any length was the belief that he was going to be sentenced to death.

Boggs also claimed the lawyers were ineffective for "failing to establish the Defendant's mental capasity [*sic*] or an adequate I.Q. score."

Court records showed that the judge issued an order on July 23, 2002, to have Boggs transferred to the Oldham County Jail, where he would be held until a psychological evaluation could be conducted at the Kentucky Correctional Psychiatric Center (KCPC).

KCPC was the state's forensic hospital. Located at LaGrange, the center performed all psychological or criminal-responsibility tests ordered by Kentucky courts.

The memorandum filed by Boggs claimed that he had suffered from various mental illnesses, including schizophrenia and anxiety disorders "combined with a limited education and long history of drug and alcohol abuse." He acknowledged in the memo that his attorneys had taken him to a psychologist for evaluation, but after four days of testing, the psychologist thought he was "malingering."

Though the court questioned Boggs about his mental state and his attorneys indicated that he was not taking any prescription drugs that would impair his ability to understand or make a decision, Boggs tried to pursue that defense anyway in his 11.42 appeal.

Boggs maintained that the doctor at the state psychiatric center was unable to determine an IQ score for him, and given his life history, "it is reasonably foreseeable that Boggs was suffering from mental retardation and mental illness."

He claimed that if that determination had been made by a psychologist, it would have precluded any consideration of the death penalty for him.

"Unfortunately, counsel did not take this step. Counsel choose [*sic*] instead to have Boggs, an arguably mentally ill, retarded, incompetent defendant, enter a guilty plea."

Essentially, Boggs's entire argument was that his attorneys were incompetent because they did not get the death penalty removed as an option, did not get the trial moved to another county, and did not let him proceed to trial rather than plead guilty.

Since the psychiatric center could not determine an IQ, however, it was unlikely the court would have eliminated the death penalty. Even if it were eliminated, and Boggs had been given a trial, it might not have turned out to be as desirable as he imagined in his appeal.

Not only would he have faced the same evidence as before, he might have faced an even more hostile crowd. Several police officers have said privately that they would be perfectly happy to have Boggs return to the court for another trial, intimating that they might be too busy this time to come to court to protect him.

The second part of Boggs's appeal seemed to be based more in fact, and attacked an aspect of the hearing about which some police officers had privately expressed discomfort.

Boggs was asking in his appeal that Judge Sam Wright be removed from the case and another judge be appointed. For his reasons, he cited the hostility and threats by members of the Cook family and a family friend during the sentencing hearing.

Officers speaking anonymously, because they did not want to make the judge angry, said they were shocked that some witnesses were allowed to make death threats toward Boggs and his family without being called to account by the judge. They said they had at the time felt something should be done, but believed that the courtroom was the jurisdiction of the judge.

Boggs's motion for Wright to step down from hearing the appeal noted Wright's comments during sentencing. During that hearing, Wright said, "Jerome Watson Boggs, you disgust me. If anybody ever deserved the death penalty for the crimes they have committed, you do." The judge went on to say that Boggs was not fit for the company of decent people.

Boggs's motion maintained that in light of the judge's comments, it would be impossible for him to be impartial in hearing the appeal. Court rules required judges to step down if there was even an appearance of impropriety.

At press time, Wright had not ruled on the motion for recusal or the motion to vacate, however, Commonwealth's Attorney Banks had asked that the court dismiss the motion to vacate "with prejudice," meaning it could not be filed again.

Edison Banks argued that appeals such as Boggs's must be filed within three years of the sentence becoming final. Since Boggs did not file a direct appeal, the sentence became final on December 3,

2002. His appeal was not mailed from the prison until January 4, 2006, even though the documents inside were all dated September 14, 2004. The mailing date was past the deadline for filing the appeal. Commonwealth's Attorney Banks said that if the date on the documents was accurate, it showed that Boggs was ready to file on time, but waited until after the deadline to send the appeal.

Edison Banks also wrote in his response that the mental capacity issue could not be raised in an appeal filed under the ineffective assistance rule, and that the question of whether his IQ would have precluded him from being sentenced to death was moot. Boggs was not sentenced to death; he was sentenced to life in prison.

The four-page motion to dismiss was only an abbreviated response to Boggs's nearly fifty pages of filings. Edison Banks also filed a motion on February 8, 2006, asking for additional time to fully respond to Boggs, citing a need to wait until the judge ruled on the motion to dismiss before spending time on a response.

Wright must also rule on the motion to recuse. If he does choose to step down from the case, the chief circuit judge of the Mountain Region will choose a replacement from among the other sitting judges in the twenty-two-county area, or from among a pool of retired judges.

As we go to press, Banks has made no response to the motion for Wright to be recused, but state law says 11.42 motions must be heard by the trial court. It is not clear how that requirement would affect Boggs's effort to remove Wright.

In the meantime, the case is in limbo. Jerome Boggs is still in prison, but the possibility remains that he could be granted an evidentiary hearing on his 11.42 motion. Edison Banks will not file a formal answer to the motion until after Wright decides whether to step down from the case. No timetable has been set for that decision.

Whatever happens could trigger a whole new round of appeals. If Wright does not step down, Boggs is expected to appeal that decision. Whether or not he steps down, if the ruling on the motion goes against Boggs, he could conceivably allege that the proceedings violated his civil rights and seek a writ of habeas corpus, prompting a review from the federal courts. Even if he does not succeed, the case will undoubtedly continue to be debated for months, if not years.

Even if Boggs ultimately loses his battle and remains in prison, the Cook family will have had to face the endless appeals that were supposedly preempted by allowing Boggs to plead guilty and avoid the death penalty.

Commonwealth's Attorney Banks filed a motion in June 2006 asking for a conference on the status of the case. Banks said that while some people might argue that he should let Boggs rot in prison while his appeal lies untouched, he prefers to get it done and off the docket.

"I don't see any chance that he'll get a new trial, but I don't want to take a chance that he could get a new trial and I might lose some of my witnesses or evidence," Edison Banks said.

Some witnesses have already moved away, and at least one has been sent to prison. The evidence, however, was still locked in a steel cage in the basement of city hall and in a locker on the second floor of the Letcher County Courthouse, waiting for the day it might have to be pulled back out of storage and used again.

Epilogue

The grass has grown lush and green over the single grave where Timothy "Blister" Cook and his baby T.J. are buried.

Their grave site, on a windswept hillside overlooking the Kentucky River, is the epitome of the age-old epitaph: "Gone but not forgotten." Toy cars adorn the tombstone alongside flowers and an angel statuette. An archway stands over the foot of the grave as an American flag flutters beside the veteran's stone that recognizes Timothy Cook's service in the army.

The black granite headstone bears an almost photo-quality likeness of Timothy Cook, holding his son in overalls in his arm. In the background are engravings of a black Ford Mustang and a weed trimmer lying in the freshly cut grass.

It is summertime in the engraving; the trees are covered with leaves. It recalls a happier time—not the cold, breezy day in February 2002 when death strolled into their home.

It is summertime, too, in Letcher County as the prosecutor awaits word of whether Judge Sam Wright will step down from hearing the murderer's appeal, or whether he will smack down Jerome

Boggs's attempt to subvert the agreement he made to accept a life behind bars.

Timothy and T.J. Cook are gone, but they are not forgotten.

At Mountain Montessori School, the fire department certificate recognizing T.J. still hangs in the vestibule, and bags of his Hot Wheels cars still sit in a cabinet in the director's office. Come October 5, students who never knew him will celebrate T.J.'s birthday, as students there do every year.

The mobile home where the murders were committed is just a memory, too. It was pulled away before April Banks Boggs ever came to trial and was replaced with another. A family member still lives there.

Evidence of the crimes still sits locked up in a steel cabinet in the Letcher Circuit Clerk's Office and in the basement of Whitesburg City Hall. Family members had requested that some of the items that were confiscated be returned early in 2006, but Commonwealth's Attorney Edison Banks denied the request after Jerome Boggs filed his appeal.

As unlikely as a new trial is, it is still a possibility. Until Boggs exhausts the appeals that he promised he would not file, the evidence will remain locked in bankers' boxes inside a steel cage. The paperwork related to the case could remain there forever, since state law excludes anything in the possession of commonwealth's attorneys from its definition of open records.

As far as the Kentucky State Police are concerned, the case is closed for good. Records have been transferred from Post 13 to the archives in Frankfort to make room for the steadily increasing case load in the southeastern mountains. The evidence left over, which was not used in the trial, was handed over to the commonwealth's attorney's office.

Banks worried that dragging the case on could

lead to a loss of evidence and witnesses, and his fears are partially founded in fact. While the evidence is locked away and safe in the stone basement of city hall, and in the steel cabinets of the circuit clerk's office, witnesses and memories gradually fade away.

Most of the police officers involved in the investigation have been transferred to other parts of the state or have retired. Bledsoe still lives in the area, but is no longer assigned to Post 13. Detective John Pratt has been transferred to the governor's mansion in Frankfort as part of the executive security detail. Detective Ken Duff was promoted and transferred to Western Kentucky. Whitesburg Police Chief Paul Miles has given up his position as chief to take a job investigating "doctor shoppers" at the same regional drug task force to which Sergeant Sean Blair is attached.

Donnie Baker, the man who first told police that Jerome Boggs had been in the trailer just before the murders, is in prison himself. He is serving a five-year sentence for a reckless homicide charge from Perry County involving a fatal automobile accident. He is also serving five years for facilitation to robbery in Letcher County.

As the years go by, the chance of witnesses dying or moving away becomes even greater, and the appeal filed by Jerome Boggs seemed designed to drag out the appeals process. It would take time for Wright to determine whether he should step down. If he did, the chief regional judge would have to appoint a replacement who would then have to familiarize himself with the case and make a decision.

As the months and years pass, memories could become less sure. Important details could be forgotten.

While Timothy and T.J., Jerome and April, are not yet forgotten, the case is in some ways like that of Floyd Frazier's, the only man ever legally hanged in

Letcher County. Some descendants of Frazier's are still touchy about the subject, nearly one hundred years after the trapdoor dropped and Frazier was hanged by the neck until dead.

Everyone knows about the case, but few are willing to talk about it. It is a situation that family members of those involved would as soon not bring up.

The same is true of the Cook murders. Community members won't talk about the case for fear of offending the Cook family. The Cooks say they are not emotionally able to talk about it themselves.

For now, neighbors will remember Blister and T.J. Cook through the certificate in the Mountain Montessori School, the annual birthday parties held there for T.J., and the advertisements still placed by their family in the local newspaper.

February 17, 2002, was a painful day in Whitesburg. The town lost two of its own that day, one of them a four-year-old as friendly as the welcome sign at the edge of town. But January 9, 2006, was a painful day as well. It was the day that Jerome Boggs filed the appeal that was never supposed to be.

That thick file folder in the circuit clerk's office is what the community has to remember Jerome Boggs by.

Most would have preferred a thick hemp rope, tied in a noose and preserved under glass.

MORE MUST-READ TRUE CRIME FROM
M. William Phelps

HORRIFYING TRUE CRIME
FROM PINNACLE BOOKS

Body Count
by Burl Barer   0-7860-1405-9 $6.50US/$8.50CAN

The Babyface Killer
by Jon Bellini   0-7860-1202-1 $6.50US/$8.50CAN

Love Me to Death
by Steve Jackson   0-7860-1458-X $6.50US/$8.50CAN

The Boston Stranglers
by Susan Kelly   0-7860-1466-0 $6.50US/$8.50CAN

Body Double
by Don Lasseter   0-7860-1474-1 $6.50US/$8.50CAN

The Killers Next Door
by Joel Norris   0-7860-1502-0 $6.50US/$8.50CAN

Available Wherever Books Are Sold!

Visit our website at **www.kensingtonbooks.com**.